THE EXTENSION MOVEMENT in THEOLOGICAL EDUCATION

by f. ross kinsler

a call to the renewal of the ministry

207.
K62

THE EXTENSION MOVEMENT IN THEOLOGICAL EDUCATION

by f. ross kinsler

a call to the
renewal of
the ministry

Library of Congress Cataloging in Publication Data
Kinsler, F   Ross..
    The extension movement in theological education.

    Bibliography: p.
    1. Seminary extension--Collected works. I. Title.
BV4164.K56   207'.11   78-5992
ISBN 0-87808-734-6

Published by the William Carey Library
533 Hermosa Street
South Pasadena, California 91030
Telephone (213) 798-0819

In accord with some of the most recent thinking in the academic
press, the William Carey Library is present this
scholarly book which has been prepared from an author-edited
and author-prepared camera ready copy.

PRINTED IN THE UNITED STATES OF AMERICA

Contents

Foreword   vii
Preface   ix
Introduction   xi

PART I: FUNDAMENTAL CONCEPTS AND VISION
         OF THE EXTENSION MOVEMENT

CHAPTER 1. BASES FOR CHANGE IN THEOLOGICAL EDUCATION   3

            Theological Bases: What is the Ministry?   4
            Historical Bases: Can the People Participate
               Fully in Theological Study and Ministry?   8
            Sociological Bases: Who Are the Leaders?   12
            Educational Bases: How Can the Leaders Be
               Trained?   15
            Economic Bases: What Kind of Theological
               Education Can We Afford?   19
            Missiological Bases: What Are the Goals of
               Our Training Programs?   21

CHAPTER 2. WHAT IS EXTENSION?   25

CHAPTER 3. A WORKING DEFINITION OF THEOLOGICAL EDUCATION
               BY EXTENSION   30

            The Purpose of Theological Education by
               Extension   31

Various Dimensions of Theological Education
   by Extension   32
Three Essential Elements in Theological
   Education by Extension   34
Extension and Other Types of Theological
   Education   35
Some Examples of Theological Education by
   Extension   37

CHAPTER 4. EXTENSION: AN ALTERNATIVE MODEL FOR
            THEOLOGICAL EDUCATION   41

The Structures of Theological Education--
   Contextualization   42
The Methodology of Theological Education--
   Conscientization   47
The Content of Theological Education--
   Liberation   51

CHAPTER 5. OPEN THEOLOGICAL EDUCATION   61

Structures and Methods   62
Motivation and Curriculum Design   67
The Role of the Student and the Role of
   the Teacher   72
Evaluation and Validation   77
Conclusions   83

CHAPTER 6. THEOLOGICAL EDUCATION BY EXTENSION:
            SERVICE OR SUBVERSION?   89

How Should We Conceive of Theological
   Education?   91
What Is Our Understanding of the Nature
   of the Ministry?   93
What Constitutes the Church?   95
How Is the Church to Carry Out Its Mission?   97
Conclusion   100

PART II: REGIONAL ISSUES AND ADAPTATIONS OF
          THE EXTENSION MOVEMENT

CHAPTER 7. DIALOGUE ON ALTERNATIVES IN THEOLOGICAL
            EDUCATION--LATIN AMERICA   105

Traditional Patterns of Leadership
   Formation   106
The Need For Alternative Approaches to
   Theological Education   114
The Extension Movement   123
Continuing Concerns   141

CHAPTER 8. DIALOGUE ON ALTERNATIVES IN THEOLOGICAL
EDUCATION--INDIA   148

     Prelude: New York, Amsterdam, Geneva   149
     India: Bombay, Nagercoil, Trivandrum,
       Madurai, Madras, Bangalore, Hyderabad,
       Yeotmal, Calcutta   152
     Postlude: Singapore, Manila, Hong Kong,
       Seoul, Tokyo, Los Angeles, Guatemala   166

CHAPTER 9. DIALOGUE ON ALTERNATIVES IN THEOLOGICAL
EDUCATION--SOUTHERN AFRICA   170

     Challenging Experiences   171
     General Impressions and Basic Concerns   177
     Tentative Recommendations   182

CHAPTER 10. DIALOGUE ON ALTERNATIVES IN THEOLOGICAL
EDUCATION--U.S.A.   188

     Crises in the Ministry and in Theological
       Education   189
     Fundamental Issues   193
     Areas for Exploration and Innovation   198
     The Future Shape of Theological Education
       and Ministry   202

     PART III: TOOLS FOR CHANGE AND DEVELOPMENT IN
       THE EXTENSION MOVEMENT

CHAPTER 11. MATERIALS FOR WORKSHOPS ON THEOLOGICAL
EDUCATION BY EXTENSION   209

     Bases for Change in Theological Education   211
     A Working Definition of Theological
       Education by Extension   214
     The Logistics of Theological Education by
       Extension   219
     Demonstration of an Extension Center Meeting   228
     Self-Study Materials for Extension Students   239

CHAPTER 12. THE SPANISH INTERTEXT PROJECT   253

     The History of CATA   254
     Major Problems CATA Faced   256
     Aids For Authors   262

CHAPTER 13. THE ALISTE PROJECT FOR TRAINING EXTENSION
SPECIALISTS 265

Objectives 265
Program 267
Candidates 270

CHAPTER 14. CENTERS FOR STUDIES IN THEOLOGICAL EDUCATION
AND MINISTRY 273

Specific Reasons for the Proposal 274
The Central Concepts of the Proposal 276
Possible Tasks for the Centers 277
How to Operate a Center 278
Conclusions 279

APPENDIX A. EXTENSION SEMINARY QUARTERLY BULLETIN--
LIST OF ARTICLES 283

APPENDIX B. GUATEMALA CENTER FOR STUDIES IN THEOLOGICAL
EDUCATION AND MINISTRY--OCCASIONAL PAPERS 287

Foreword

In 1963 the Evangelical Presbyterian Seminary of Guatemala
began its experiment in what was called "extension theological
education," a program to meet the needs of a vital, expanding
church. This church had come into being by the work of a group
of very capable missionaries, who walked the mountain passes
and jungle trails, living as the people, meeting them at their
level, and in their languages. From the beginning most of the
ministry was carried on by the laymen, and in the rural areas,
the few pastors had generally received their preparation "on
the trail" beside the missionary, in the exercise of the work,
with little class work and few term papers. A seminary had
grown up to prepare a more elite ministry that filled the pul-
pits of the few city churches, but proved singularly inept at
supplying the sort of leader needed in the much larger number
of rural and village congregations. Probably 90% of the preaching, teaching, and evangelism in the rural churches was carried
on by the laymen and women, and the few ordained men were
rapidly approaching retirement age.

Dr. Ross Kinsler arrived in Guatemala the second year of the
extension program, while it was in its formative stage, expanding rapidly, but with a precarious future due to the opposition
of denomination. Since that time, Ross Kinsler has been completely involved in all phases of the extension seminary, and
the growing movement world-wide. He has been one of the most
productive authors of the specialized materials required for
students who have to learn to study, and to do most of it on
their own. He has been one of the most inspiring teachers, and
wherever he has gone to open centers, large numbers of students

have accepted the challenge and dedicated the time and effort
to continue extension studies.

As other extension programs began, he traveled, first to
Mexico and Central America, then to South America, Africa,
Southeast Asia, and the Far East to hold workshops, participate
in conferences, and consult with theological educators. At the
same time he has not only continued actively as a seminary professor, but also as a popular preacher and teacher in the local
churches in Guatemala. He did not follow the tradition of the
earlier workers and make the rounds on foot, but with the extensive road system today, he has worked with the most remote
as well as the urban congregations. Where occasion demanded in
the areas without roads, the horse or dugout canoe served to
reach remote Indian congregations.

From this rich experience at all levels has come this series
of articles that delineate the mature reflection on theological
education and its relation to the life of the Christian community. Christian leaders today need to pay attention to those
with experience at the humbler levels of society. The churches
in the West as well as in many growing traditions have adopted
the patterns, life style and symbols of the secular world where
power, prestige, and wealth are the criteria of the successful
church and clergy. However, one person said, "You know that
those who are supposed to rule over the Gentiles lord it over
them, and their great men exercise authority over them. But it
shall not be so among you; but whoever would be great among you
must be your servant, and whoever would be first among you must
be the slave of all. For the Son of Man also came not to be
served, but to serve and to give his life as a ransom for many."
Extension theological education is directed toward working out
this value system in the church. It is hoped that these articles will serve to provoke Christians to focus on their true
ministry, and to get on with it.

                              James H. Emery
                              B.D., Ph.D.

Preface

It is a perplexing puzzle to me how the original concept of the
Theological Education by Extension movement could have been so
generally misunderstood and yet in fifteen years gained such
worldwide momentum.

Those of us who were involved in its early development may not
have clearly understood all the reasons why we ourselves were doing what we did.   Then, pleased at the results and eager to share
the idea, we listed off for people all the reasons we could re-
call.   We told people it cost less per student.   We told people
it allowed a smaller faculty to deal with a larger number of
students.   We said that it stressed independent study and reflection, that it attracted more candidates to the ministry, that it
allowed teaching on several levels more easily, that it allowed
students to stay closer to the people of their own kind rather
than be uprooted and sent off to a capital city, etc., etc.

And we even predicted that people would gravely misunderstand
the whole idea if they thought of it primarily as a new method
of teaching rather than a new method of selection.   It would now
appear that many have in fact chosen the approach for some of
the lesser reasons and are still missing the main point.

Well, it is a new method -- extension by my definition is
simply "that form of education which yields to the life cycle of
the student, does not destroy or prevent his productive relation
to society, and does not make the student fit into the needs of
a 'residential' school."

But the underlying *purpose* for working by extension is in
fact much more important than any of the kaleidoscopic varieties
of extension as a method -- it is the simple goal of enlisting
and equipping for ministry precisely those who are best suited
to it. We had told people it would "extend" to almost any person wherever he lived or whatever his schedule. Perhaps we
failed to stress why this one trait, this one unusual character-
istic, overshadows all others in importance.

Thus, in fifteen-year hindsight, the immense, truly immense
significance of extension is the fact that few church movements
in the world today operate in such a way as to assimilate to
pastoral leadership those members among them most gifted for
such ministry. Rather, the churches of the world, especially in
the Western world where roots are deep, and where the example to
the rest of the world is unfortunately influential, have almost
all tended to go over to a professional system that makes pastoral ministry a profession you train for, like medicine or law,
rather than a leadership role like that of a mayor or a senator,
for which you are elected.

Extension is capable of supplying professional training to
"elected" or at least "selected" leaders, thus combining the
values of training with the importance of gifts. That is its
chief value.

As I move around, however, I see vast and widespread diver-
gence from this precious achievement. I see extension used not
for theological education but for lay training, thus preventing
key leaders from ordained ministry when it was designed and first
used to do the opposite. I see it as a second class auxiliary
when surprisingly, in God's sight, its students may outweigh the
young men in any residential program.

I cannot go on further here. This is what this book is all
about. Kinsler is the most persistent and voluminous commentator
on the subject of Theological Education by Extension. What a
challenge for these valuable writings now to be available in
book form!

Ralph D. Winter
Director,
U.S. Center for World Mission

Introduction

When we moved to Guatemala and joined the faculty of the
Seminario Evangélico Presbiteriano in 1964, the extension program was in its second year, and it was struggling to survive.
We had no lofty ideas about the reform of theological education
or the renewal of the ministry. No one realized that we would
soon be caught up in a worldwide movement. We were simply trying to find a way to provide adequate, appropriate training for
the leaders of the congregations. This concern became--for me
and for many others--a personal pilgrimage.

James Emery and Ralph Winter gave birth to the extension concept and transformed it into a functioning program. José
Carrera, Charles Ainley, and Baudilio Recinos have provided outstanding pastoral leadership at the Seminary in Guatemala over
the years. Benjamín and Nelly Jacobs have taken increasing
responsibility for running and expanding the program. I count
it a unique opportunity to have been a part of that fellowship,
a member of that team. I could not begin to enumerate the
lessons I have learned, the experiences we have shared, the
debts I could never repay.

Ultimately, the vision that has bound us together and
inspired all our efforts comes from the people, the members of
the churches who sincerely want to prepare themselves for service even as they lead their congregations and carry all their
other responsibilities. For 13 years it was my great privilege
to meet each week with men and women of all walks of life--young

and old, Indian and Ladino, elders and deacons and pastors and
church workers, mature Christians and new believers, some highly
trained in their professions and many more with little or no
schooling--in extension centers all across Guatemala. From
these brothers and sisters in Christ I have come to see what
theological education should and can be, what the ministry
really is.

The fellowship of those who share this vision and have joined
this pilgrimage now extends throughout Latin America and on
across the world--from Alaska to Australia, the urban jungle
of Sao Paulo through the vast interior of Brazil, the high
Andean plateau of South America to the islands of the Pacific;
in India and Indonesia, East, West, and Southern Africa, Taiwan
and Thailand, Mexico and Central America, the Philippines and
Pakistan; at Tempe and Pasadena, Hong Kong and Singapore,
Bromley and Geneva. I have no doubt that the learning and
sharing in which we are engaged will bear much fruit in the
years to come.

THE EXTENSION MOVEMENT

The rapid expansion of the extension movement is in itself
extraordinary and challenging. The Guatemala experiment began
less than 15 years ago, and the first extension workshop was
held just ten years ago. But there are already about 300 programs with 30,000 to 40,000 extension students in 75 countries
around the globe. These statistics are very general because
hard data are hard to come by. But there is no question that an
enormous amount of innovation is taking place and that the
extension movement is an important vehicle for change.

Theological education by extension is now clearly established as the most vigorous alternative creative form of
preparation for the ministry. It may soon outdistance
residential patterns of training as the dominant form of
training for the ministry. (Theological Education Fund
Report for 1976, p. 11.)

The changes taking place through the extension movement are
not just institutional or programmatic. They concern the nature
of the ministry, the vitality and renewal of the church, and the
mission of the church in the world. The significance of extension lies precisely in the way it relates theological education
to the ministry, the church, and mission.

The extension movement is not without parallels in other
fields of human development that are reshaping the lives and
thinking of our contemporaries. Again and again we have recognized the contribution of Paulo Freire, Ivan Illich, and others

who are unsparingly radical in their critique of traditional approaches to education and development. We have utilized the insights of educational technology, open education, non-formal and decentralized education. We have attempted to take seriously the challenge of liberation theology as set forth by José Míguez Bonino and other Latin American colleagues. We are most interested in new approaches to education, health care, community development, legal aid, and political action that, like theological education by extension, encourage and enable people everywhere to be responsible for their own lives, to meet their own needs, and to build a more just, more human social order.

Finally, the extension movement challenges and humbles because it brings down the high altars of academic prestige, professional privilege, clerical status, and institutional presumption. It goes against the elitist tendencies of our societies and against the selfish bent of natural man. It calls in question our own position and self image in the light of Jesus' example and his commandment to his disciples: "It shall not be so among you . . . whoever would be great among you must be your servant" (Mk. 10:43).

THE CONTENTS OF THIS BOOK

The papers in this book come out of the extension movement. They do not form a systematic treatise, having been written over the past eight years, but they do fit together and find their continuity in a growing understanding of the nature of theological education and the ministry. They are all based on our experience in Guatemala.

Part I contains six different expositions of the fundamental concepts and vision of the extension movement, focussing on various dimensions of ministerial formation and drawing on sociological and educational as well as biblical and theological sources. These papers were written to raise questions, provoke discussion, and suggest areas for experimentation, not to provide pat answers or easy solutions. *Part II* presents four papers that address regional issues in the current dialogue on alternatives in theological education and describe how theological education by extension is being--or can be--adapted to meet those concerns. The one on Latin America draws on many years of work and travel and consultation in this region; the other three are based on much more limited exposure to India, Southern Africa, and the U.S.A. *Part III* brings together four different kinds of tools for change and development in theological education that have been widely used in the extension movement. The collection of materials for workshops provides specific content and guidelines for five exercises dealing with various aspects of theological education by extension; the paper on the Spanish Intertext Project summarizes early attempts to produce a common set of

extension texts in Latin America; the ALISTE Project for Training Extension Specialists is included as originally proposed;
the final paper describes a more recent proposal for Centers for
Studies in Theological Education and Ministry, which is not taking definite forms in several places in Latin America and elsewhere.

All of these papers have appeared in the *Extension Seminary*
Quarterly Bulletin or as Occasional Papers of the Guatemala
Center for Studies in Theological Education and Ministry. Some
have been published in other periodicals and books. They may be
reproduced for use in faculty discussions, seminars and consultations, and wider circulation.

A CALL TO RENEWAL

All who contemplate the extension movement cannot but ask
what is its potential for the renewal of the ministry of the
church for mission. It is always precarious to project graph
statistics into the future, but it appears as if the movement
will continue to grow very rapidly. Certain aspects of the
movement are subject to serious criticisms, but the fundamental
insights of the extension approach have not been seriously
questioned. Thus we have been encouraged to gather these
papers into a book that will present the call of the extension
movement.

The extension concept developed first in a Third World context, and it spread most rapidly through Latin America, Africa,
and Asia, but we can now see that it has tremendous possibilities
in North America and Europe. Although most of the first extension
programs were initiated by evangelical and historic Protestant
churches and seminaries, it now looks as if there is even greater
potential within the Pentecostal, Roman Catholic, and perhaps
also the Orthodox churches. The extension movement is now a
resource of the world Christian movement, and we are all called
to make effective use of it.

In 1961 the New Delhi Assembly of the World Council of
Churches called for an ecumenical study of the training of the
ministry; this was carried out between 1964 and 1968; the final
report was adopted at the Uppsala Assembly. The major documents
are presented and analyzed by Steven Mackie, Executive Secretary
of the study, in his book, *Patterns of Ministry: Theological
Education in a Changing World* (London: Collins, 1969), probably
the most important ecumenical exposition of the subject. Here
are some very significant statements from that study:

This emphasis on the theological education of the whole
people of God is a constant refrain in recent ecumenical
discussion (p. 69).

Without disputing the need for a high standard and for an
academic approach for those that can profit from it, we
may now hold that many Christians can learn to think
theologically in different ways and at a different level
(p. 142).

If the whole people of God is to receive some sort of
theological education, then the structure and institutions
of theological education today must be changed beyond recognition (p. 142).

It must go beyond the selection of an elite and the training of a professional ministry. Hence it cannot normally
involve fulltime study in an institution of higher learning. What is required is rather a center for Christian
further education at the local level, offering parttime,
evening and weekend courses, together with the occasional
longer course. The establishment of such centers should
be considered a priority by the churches.... What is new
in this proposal is the establishment of a network of such
centers on a national or regional basis, sufficient to
cover the total educational needs of the churches. This
process will take time, but if these centers are seen as
the basic institutions of theological education, and therefore as a first priority on the resources of the churches,
existing buildings, funds and personnel can and should be
diverted to them (p. 144).

Particularly striking is Mackie's summary of the state of
theological education: "Theological education is at the point
of change. The general directions of the changes are beginning
to be clear. What is unclear is how the change is to be made."
(P. 91) Those words were published in 1969, the same year that
Ralph Winter published his 600-page book on *Theological Education
by Extension* (South Pasadena: William Carey Library, 1969). The
seeds were already planted, and in less than ten years the extension movement was putting into practice all around the world the
very changes that Mackie and many others were advocating!

Ecclesiastical bodies, ecumenical gatherings, theological
institutions, and study groups have always been far more eloquent
in their words than they are effective in their actions. What
makes the extension movement so promising, its call to the
renewal of the ministry so convincing, is that the changes and
ideals it proposes are actually being worked out in concrete
ways among the people of God--within the churches, at the theological institutions, and in the local congregations.

F. Ross Kinsler
September, 1977

PART
I

Fundamental Concepts and Vision of the Extension Movement

1

Bases for Change in Theological Education

Today few people doubt that changes are needed in theological education. Increasing numbers of Bible institutes and seminaries are rethinking and modifying their structures, methods, curricula, and concepts of ministry. The extension movement is both benefitting from and contributing to this process.

Those of us who are involved in theological education by extension have discovered, at least to some degree, a new perspective from which to view the whole task of ministerial formation. This perspective brings out a number of dimensions of the problem which theological educators have long ignored or underestimated. Our purpose here is to lay out several of these areas for study and debate.

From its inception the extension movement has stirred up controversy. Unfortunately both proponents and critics of the extension concept have frequently missed the basic issues, arguing superficially about residence and extension, posing the ideals and good intentions of one over against the weaknesses and faults of the other, or simply contrasting the visible features of the two systems. It may be that many of those who have embraced the extension alternative, as well as those who reject it, fail to see the real bases for change.

Six areas are to be considered here, and each one will be presented dialectically in order to stimulate discussion. Rather than simply point out the need for change we shall deliberately draw a sharp contrast between the residence and extension approaches to theological education in each area. Our purpose is not to pretend that the extension movement has

solved all the problems but to demonstrate that radical change
is possible. We intend also to bring out the urgency and the
nature of the crisis we face, not only in the Third World but
on all six continents. We hope that this investigation will
stimulate many to work out their own analyses of these issues
and formulate their own philosophy of theological education.

Essential for change in theological education, whether this
leads to extension or some other alternative, are the following:

  I.   THEOLOGICAL BASES: *What Is the Ministry?*
  II.   HISTORICAL BASES: *Can the People Participate Fully
        in Theological Study and Ministry?*
  III. SOCIOLOGICAL BASES: *Who Are the Leaders?*
  IV.   EDUCATIONAL BASES: *How Can the Leaders Be Trained?*
  V.   ECONOMIC BASES: *What Kind of Theological Education
        Can We Afford?*
  VI.   MISSIOLOGICAL BASES: *What Are the Goals of Our
        Training Programs?*

I. THEOLOGICAL BASES:
What Is the Ministry?

There are of course many diverse traditions, and we could
not hope to define the ministry in a few paragraphs or in an
hour's discussion. But we can point out briefly three essential aspects of the ministry which are particularly relevant
for theological education. These concepts stand in judgment
on our traditional Western patterns of training and provide
theological bases for change.

A. First, there continues to be a false dichotomy between
clergy and laity in almost all our ecclesiastical traditions--
Roman Catholic, Protestant, independent, and Pentecostal. The
Medieval Church and its ministry consisted of the clerical
hierarchy and monastic orders; the people were silent, largely
ignorant, superstitious spectators. Since John XXIII there
have been improvements in the Catholic Church; the people can
hear the mass in their own language and participate in the
liturgy; but the essential separation of clergy and laity has
not been changed. This heritage shows up rather ironically in
a major Spanish dictionary; the word *laico* is defined "not
religious" and more specifically "not of the church."

In theory Martin Luther broke this pattern in the 16th Century; one of the major doctrines of the Protestant Reformation
was "the universal priesthood of all believers." One has only
to observe Presbyterian, Lutheran, Anglican, Methodist and
Baptist churches in Europe and North America, however, to see

that this ideal has not become a reality, even in those denominations that grew out of lay movements. When the pastor is
away, a visiting clergyman is required not only to preach but
to lead the entire service of worship. The members, even
though in thousands of congregations they consist of highly
educated people and mature Christians, are never permitted to
baptise or celebrate the Lord's Supper. And if a small congregation cannot support a professional pastor, it must be closed
or yoked to a larger parish.

This dichotomy shows up even in the independent and Pentecostal churches. In some fundamentalist denominations only
ordained clergymen occupy the administrative positions and
form the governing bodies; in almost all cases the clergy run
everything. The Pentecostal churches are noted for their
spontaneous development of leaders; among some groups almost
anyone can become a pastor overnight. On the other hand Pentecostal pastors at times take on greater authority than pastors
of historic, Protestant churches; in some cases only ordained
pastors are allowed to occupy the pulpit or even to ascend to
the platform. Some indigenous movements are completely dominated by overpowering charismatic leaders.

What biblical basis is there for this pervading phenomenon?
Certainly there were religious functionaries, clerical classes,
and theocratic leaders in Old Testament Israel. But the New
Testament does not present any dichotomy between clergy and
laity. This problem requires more than a quick study of the
word *laos*, and it is not solved by simply stating that this
New Testament word means "people of God" and includes all the
members of the body of Christ. We must call in question our
patterns of theological training and concepts of ministry,
even the sacred sentiments of "the call to the ministry," our
well-structured ecclesiastical organizations, the entrenched
interests of our clergy, and the well-schooled dependence of
our members.

B. A most challenging exposition of the ministry is found
in Ephesians 4:11-16. Paul's concept is dynamic and corporate,
a sharp contrast with what we have just described. In v.11 we
note that there are several basic ministries (the list is not
exhaustive) and that they are distributed among several different people. In our congregations one man, the pastor, is
expected to carry out or at least direct all of the ministries.
Instead of a shared, corporate ministry, we have created "a one
man band," a monster among midgets.

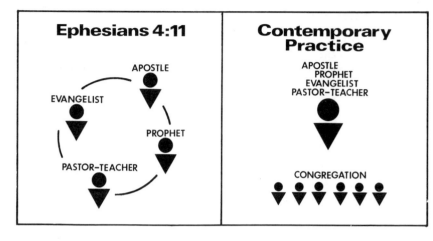

In v.12 it is evident that the aforementioned leaders are called to equip the members for the work of ministry, not to be or to carry out the ministry by themselves. All the members are called to minister, to build up the body of Christ. Quite obviously the leaders themselves are part of the body and in need of upbuilding, not rulers over the others. This relationship is what makes the ministry a dynamic function of all the members and produces growth both within and without. In contrast we who are clergy today find ourselves constantly trying to inject life into our congregations, to keep the committees and programs going, to maintain the attendance and offerings, etc. from a position which gives us little real leverage and produces little spontaneous growth.

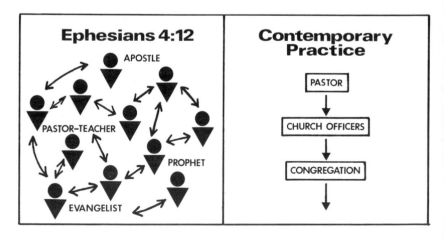

In v.12 and 13 we can see that the ministry requires the active participation of all the members and that all the members can participate effectively in the ministry. The work of the ministry is to build up the body. This includes preaching, evangelism, and missionary work, but it also includes everything that contributes to the mutual edification of the members. Christian education in the home and congregation, participation in corporate worship and fellowship, witness and service in the community, care and exhortation and friendship, all are essential and involve all of the members from the very young to the very old and can never be carried out effectively by a professional staff or even by a select group of leaders.

In v.14 Paul explains what happens when this dynamic, corporate ministry is not functioning properly. The members who are not participating actively in the upbuilding of their congregations are easily carried off by other sects and novel teachings or become embroiled in personal conflicts and controversies, as happens today in so many of our churches. In v.15 Paul again calls us to grow up in Christ, recommending truth and love as two essential ingredients. And in v.16 he closes the paragraph with a resounding reaffirmation that this ministry belongs to "the whole body," "every joint," "each part" and that this corporate ministry is what produces real growth.

C. In the First Century the Gospel was carried quickly around the Roman Empire and even beyond its frontiers; churches sprang up and multiplied; and the leadership of the ministry was immediately placed in the hands of local people. The Apostle Paul apparently had no difficulty discovering and training leaders in each congregation in the space of a few days or weeks or at the most months, and this was a major factor in the rapid expansion of the early church.

Roland Allen and others have pointed out that one of the great errors of the modern missionary movement is that it failed to recognize the legitimacy and the priority of indigenous leadership, i.e. local leaders who could take over readily the responsibilities of all the ministerial functions within their congregations without passing through the lengthy, costly, deculturizing training process imposed by Western tradition. This basic falacy is endemic now throughout the world among the older churches and to a lesser degree among the younger churches. In many denominations it is almost unheard-of for a congregation to develop its own ministry with leaders from among its own members; they all hire trained specialists, seminary graduates, outsiders. Third World churches are striving to emulate the Western pattern of professional ministry, but at this very moment the large denominations of North America and Europe are facing grave financial

crises and declining vitality because of their universal
dependence on professionals.

CONCLUSION: What is the function of theological education
in terms of these three essential aspects of the ministry?
*Traditional training patterns reinforce the dichotomy between
clergy and laity; they debilitate the dynamics of ministry at
the congregational level; and they make the churches dependent
upon highly trained, professional pastors.* Candidates for the
professional ministry are the only serious concern of the
seminaries; upon graduation these young, inexperienced, and
largely unmarried men and women are ordained, set apart, conse-
crated; as pastors or "ministers" they are given a salary,
which in turn means that they are expected to serve fulltime.
The corollary is that the other members are not trained for
ministry; they are not set apart for service in the church;
they receive no salary; and they are not really expected to be
responsible for the work of the ministry.

*Theological education by extension, on the other hand,
breaks down the dichotomy between clergy and laity by encouraging all kinds of leaders to prepare themselves for ministry.
It stimulates the dynamics of ministry at the local level by
training those men and women in the context of their own communities and congregations. It enables the congregations to
develop their own leadership for ministry, so that they do not
need to depend on outside, highly trained professional clergy.*

This brief consideration of certain aspects of the ministry
indicates that change in theological education is urgently
needed. The extension movement demonstrates that change is
possible; it is actually taking place. Noone claims that extension is the only or the ultimate pattern of theological training; on the contrary by breaking with tradition it has opened
the way for other alternatives.

II. HISTORICAL BASES:
*Can the People Participate Fully
in Theological Study and Ministry?*

Most pastors and members would not quarrel with the idea
that the ministry should be corporate and collegiate. Many
preach and teach this concept in their churches. The problem
is not so much the theory (orthodoxy) as it is a matter of
putting it into practice (orthopraxis). And here the question
arises, Can the people in our churches really prepare themselves
theologically and participate fully in the ministry? The natural tendency is to think that the way we do things today is
the way they have always been done--and that this is the only
or the best way. We need to look again at the history of the
church.

H.R. Niebuhr and D.D. Williams (*The Ministry in Historical Perspective*) demonstrated 20 years ago that institutionalized theological education is a very recent phenomenon. Down through history the vast majority of pastors and priests in all ecclesiastical traditions were trained in the field or on the job. Even by 1926, 40 percent of the ministers in the 17 largest denominations in the U.S. had attended neither college nor seminary.

Following are three historical cases, from three different settings, which indicate not only that the common people can participate fully in theological study and ministry but that they are more likely to bring renewal and growth to the churches.

A. John Wesley was to the day he died an Anglican priest, albeit a renegade, and he himself was educated at Oxford. The Methodist movement, however, was forced to depend largely upon unschooled lay preachers, because the clergy were not sympathetic to the movement. Wesley was eminently gifted as an organizer. Not willing to break with the Church of England, he organized his converts into "religious societies," a common device at that time, then further divided them into "classes" of about 12 people. The "class leaders" were charged to collect a penny from each member each week, and the groups developed a kind of spiritual oversight and mutual pastoral care. Out of this process leaders were formed for various lay offices.

The Methodist movement was disciplined, as its name implies, and the lay preachers followed a rigorous program of daily study as they carried out their ministry. They were expected to give 8 hours daily to sleeping and eating, 8 to study, prayer, and meditation, and 8 to preaching, visitation, and social work. Wesley prepared numerous materials, including a 50-volume collection of Christian literature, which the lay preachers were to study and also to sell. John Wesley himself was the greatest example for his followers. During 50 years of intensive ministry he traveled--largely on horseback--an average of 5,000 miles per year, preached 15 sermons a week, directed the many organizations of the growing movement, continued his prodigeous literary output, and maintained his own daily spiritual discipline.

By the time Wesley died the Methodist movement had 71,000 members and 294 preachers in England, 43,000 members and 198 preachers in the U.S. In the New World many Methodists were deprived of the sacraments because there were no Anglican churches in those regions. Unable to obtain Anglican ordination for his preachers, Wesley was finally forced to take the step which caused the final break with the Church of England; in 1784 he and Thomas Coke ordained their first presbyters, and

Wesley appointed Coke and Francis Asbury as Superintendents;
in that same year the Methodist Episcopal Church was organized
in Baltimore.

It would be presumptuous to compare the effectiveness of the
Anglican Church and the Methodist movement in the late 18th
and 19th Centuries, but it certainly is evident in this example
that the people of God (*laos*) are capable of forming their own
leaders, of carrying out serious theological studies far from
any academic institution or special environment, of producing
a vital ministry, and of effecting a world-transforming mission.

B. The second case study takes us to the New World, to the
opening up of the first frontier, when the burgeoning population
of the newly independent United States began to spill over the
Appalachian Mountains in large numbers. Up until this time the
Anglican, Congregational, and Presbyterian Churches were the
most numerous and influential, but they insisted on an educated
clergy. The new situation was primitive; communities were
small and scattered; the people were poor. The established
churches of the East were ill-equipped to respond to the challenge, precisely because of their dependence upon a professional
clergy. Into the vacuum stepped the Methodists and the Baptists.

The Methodists were able to survive and grow in the frontier
situation because they were accustomed to meeting in small
groups for mutual care and edification under lay leaders. The
limited number of Methodist pastors played a crucial role as
circuit riders, visiting the lay leaders and their "classes"
over a broad area.

The Baptists were even more successful because each group
was independent and did not require an educated pastor at all.
Spontaneous preachers, who felt called of God and were selected
from among their peers, led their congregations and developed
their talents through the practice of ministry. Often they
supported themselves, entirely or in part, through farming or
some other employment.

Once again it would be presumptuous to judge the effectiveness of the different ecclesiastical traditions during this
period, but it is clear that the traditional pattern of professional clergy has its limitations and that the common people
can and will produce their own leaders if given a chance to do
so. The Methodist lay leaders and the Baptist preachers led
their churches in ministry during a crucial period in U.S.
history, demonstrating their gifts and achieving remarkable
growth along with the westward march of the people. Due to
them, in large measure, the several Baptist bodies today number
27.7 million and the Methodists 13.2 million, compared with

3.8 million Presbyterians, 2.9 million Anglicans, and perhaps
1.5 million Congregationals in that country.

C. The third case study refers to the Pentecostals in Latin
America today. It might be argued that the churches can survive
and grow under poorly educated leaders in rural, frontier, and
pre-industrial societies but that today they must have a highly
trained clergy. Not so. The story which is being written
right now during the second half of the 20th Century by the
Pentecostals of Latin America is that Christian peoples movements led by their natural leaders can prosper in the modern
world, especially among the urban masses, and not to the exclu-
sion of the middle and even professional classes.

Most of these Pentecostal pastors have little formal schooling and no Bible institute or seminary training. But they are
not uneducated or untrained. Rather their gifts and skills
have been shaped and developed "in the streets" and in the
dynamic life of the churches. New converts are normally incorporated into the active witness of the churches right away,
first by giving their testimony in public, later teaching a
class and leading services of worship, then preaching, taking
charge of a new preaching point, and perhaps becoming a church
worker. Only after long years of experience, testing, and
voluntary service that brings forth fruit in terms of growth in
the church and that meets with the approval of peers and super-
iors does a man become a pastor. This process produces genuine
leadership, men who are capable of leading mother churches that
number, along with their daughter congregations, 10,000, 25,000,
or 40,000 members. The largest Pentecostal denomination in
Latin America, the Assemblies of God in Brazil, is said to have
over 3 million members with about 40,000 workers ranked in
descending order as pastors, evangelists, presbyters, deacons,
and helpers. One of their mother church complexes, spreading
throughout a major city and into the hinterland, numbers
200,000.

So it is that the Pentecostals are now 3 times as numerous as
all the other Protestants in Latin America today, and they continue to grow rapidly. The historic denominations, which initiated work in most of these countries about 100 years ago, remain
for the most part small and weak. Ironic as it may seem, the
Methodists and Baptists, who responded so well to the frontier
challenge in the U.S., have now adopted the traditional pattern
of a professional, educated clergy, and they have now stayed
behind with the Presbyterians and Anglicans.

CONCLUSION: What lessons should we draw from these brief
case studies? *History teaches us that the Western academic-
professional system of clergy tends to be static, incapable of*

*responding to the needs of the masses, preoccupied with position
and privilege at the expense of dynamic, corporate ministry.*
Theological education can in fact be a major obstacle to the
growth of the church and the fulfillment of her ministry.

*On the other hand the extension movement opens up the possi-
bility of preserving the self-evident values of theological
education without destroying the dynamics of leadership formation and church growth. Local leaders can obtain a profound,
integral training while carrying on their ministry in the
streets and in the life of the congregations.* In fact increasing numbers of Pentecostal and other pastors and church workers
are now taking advantage of the new opportunities that extension
programs are opening up to them, especially in Latin America
and also in other places.

III. SOCIOLOGICAL BASES:
Who Are the Leaders?

Biblically, theologically, and historically there are grounds
for insisting that the churches' ministry should be directed
by leaders of the people, not by a professional class of clergy.
This leads us then to our next fundamental question: What is
real leadership? And also we must ask, How are leaders formed?
And, How are they selected, invested with authority, and sustained in positions of leadership? Here we turn to sociology
and anthropology for additional light as we consider bases for
change in existing patterns of theological education.

A. *What is Leadership?*

It would be misleading and erroneous to set up a single
model of leadership; every society and sub-culture has its own
patterns, roles, qualifications. On the other hand it is easy
to point out the fallacy of Western church traditions, precisely
because they ignore or by-pass these social realities. By
imposing certain academic requirements for ministerial candidates and limiting the accessibility of theological education,
these traditions inevitably clash with the existing leadership
patterns in most cultures. This phenomenon goes a long way to
explain why the historic churches are rapidly losing ground to
the Pentecostals in Latin America, the Independent Churches in
Africa, and indigenous churches throughout the Third World. It
raises serious questions about theological education in the
West also.

It should be obvious that leadership is much more than academic credentials. In fact academic credentials may or may not
be important for church leaders, which is not to say that relevant skills and knowledge are unimportant...ever. In every

culture and churches' leaders need, more than schooling, a sense of calling and dedication, gifts (in the traditional and in the charismatic sense), the ability to participate in their group, identification with the group, acceptability to the group, etc. From this point of view any system of theological education is important not so much for what it teaches (quantity and quality) but for how it selects or excludes the real leaders.

Roland Allen (*The Ministry of the Spirit*) developed this essential insight over 50 years ago. He pointed out the significance of Paul's selection of elders and bishops, as described in his Pastoral Epistles. In both 1 Timothy 3:2-7 and Titus 1:6-9 Paul lists 15 qualifications for leadership, and most of them refer to personal and social qualities, i.e. behavior in the home, church, and society. The conclusion of these studies is that leadership implies experience and maturity, and Paul naturally called the leaders he appointed in each church "elders," which included the pastors and/or bishops.

B. *How Are Leaders Formed?*

Leaders are not formed by educational institutions; pastors and elders cannot expect to attain the qualities of genuine church leaders by "going to seminary." Schools can contribute to the intellectual and personal growth of their pupils, but leadership development takes place in society, in the group, in the life of the church. In recent years schools and seminaries have tried to provide more of an environment for integral development, with simulations and field experiences, but these are by and large sporadic and pale immitations of real life. And the socialization process of these institutions can be completely irrelevant or discontinuous or even negative as regards leadership in the churches.

The problem of traditional theological education is not only the fact that the seminaries and Bible institutes are incapable of forming leaders but that they withdraw their students (physically and socially) from the very context and processes where leadership can best be formed. Ideally every pastor should first gain experience in the secular world and serve in a number of lesser leadership roles in the church, just as an ordinary member. Only after demonstrating his personal qualities, gifts, and leadership as a Sunday school teacher, deacon, elder, etc. should he be considered as a possible candidate for "the ministry."

C. *How Are Leaders Selected, Invested with Authority, and Sustained?*

We could not begin to deal with the intricacies and idiosyn-
crasies of the various ways in which our churches select,
install, and support pastors. But, from a sociological perspective, the general pattern of the Western Protestant churches is
all too clear. We select almost exclusively young, single,
inexperienced and unproven men, and we exclude almost entirely
the natural leaders who have gained those essential qualifications for genuine leadership mentioned by Paul, Roland Allen,
and others. We choose these young men on the basis of a highly
subjective sense of call and on the basis of highly theoretical
preparation in schools; we set them apart through the years of
preparation and then in an absolute way through ordination; then
we place them in positions of authority over the churches and
require the members to pay their salaries.

The implications of this process can be devastating, especially in indigenous cultures. Among many Mayan communities
of Guatemala and Southern Mexico, for example, all young men
enter the *cargo* system of civic and religious responsibilities.
Over the years they are obliged to serve as assistants to the
mayor, then as municipal squad leaders, in the lay religious
orders, then as stewards of the saints, and--for those who
fulfill responsibly all these positions--as elders. The very
idea that a young man should declare himself to be called to
the ministry, go off to school, and therewith become a pastor
is utterly incomprehensible, dysfunctional, and very objection-
able.

In modern industrial societies it is argued that the churches
need highly educated pastors, as we have highly educated professional people in other fields. The question here raised is not
the level of training; high level training can be arranged in
several different ways. But the ministry is not fundamentally
a profession; it is a function of the body of believers. Therefore it is as important in these societies as it is among primitive peoples that the churches' leaders be selected and supported by the members.

CONCLUSION: *The Western churches, whatever their concept of
the ministry may be, have developed an academic-professional
model of ministry which is self-defeating in terms of effective
leadership. Within this system theological education serves
to select young, inexperienced men and women, separate them
from the normal processes of leadership formation, and place
them artificially over the other members.*

Theological education by extension recognizes that leaders are best formed and selected among their peers in the on-going life of the church and society and offers to these emerging leaders the resources of ministerial training within that context. This basic difference is pictured in the following diagrams. It provides a sociological basis for change in theological education and the ministry.

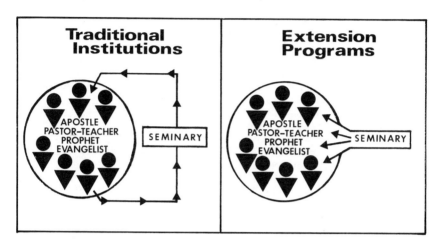

IV. EDUCATIONAL BASES:
How Can the Leaders Be Trained?

This leads us to another dimension of our critique of theological education. If the real leaders necessarily emerge later in life, i.e. when they have left school and taken on the responsibilities of a home, family, and employment, how can they be trained theologically? This question is not merely pragmatic; it opens up the whole educational side of theological education--its structure, its methodology, and its educational philosophy. A brief examination of these issues will give us further bases for change.

A. *Educational Structures*

The legitimization of extension and other non-traditional forms of education has been a long and difficult process, but the evidence is now overwhelming in our favor. Education is not a coefficient of schooling; alternative structures can be as effective or more effective than residential training. Local church leaders *can* obtain a valid theological education without going off to seminary.

There seems to be a peculiar prejudice against new educational structures in the realm of ministerial training,
probably due to its sacred status and emotional attachments.
There are, of course, valid questions to be dealt with, but
the continuing opposition to theological education by extension
has presented few weighty arguments.

In Guatemala several vocal pastors of the old guard continue
to attack our extension system, even though the three largest
universities in Guatemala have in recent years opened up extension centers around the country, belying the old protests that
extension is inferior or for low levels of training only.   In
a remote section of Bolivia the directors of a primary school
level Bible institute declare that they couldn't adopt extension
because of its deficiencies, while in Great Britain the national
government launches its massive Open University program, which
is based primarily on home study. Church leaders in many parts
of the Third World have been slow to consider the possibilities
of theological education by extension in their areas, because
they want only "the best" for their people. On the other hand
the University of South Africa has operated entirely by correspondence since 1946 and now has 6 faculties (including theology)
with about 40,000 students.

Changes in educational structures are necessary not just to
meet the evident needs of society and of the churches but also
for ideological reasons. Ivan Illich, on the basis of extensive
research, reports that the traditional schooling systems in
Latin America are polarizing these societies, forming elites,
and fomenting fascism. They form a very steep pyramid in
which huge amounts are invested in the few (less than 3%) who
rise to the university level. Schools also conceal the tremendous injustices in Latin America, because they continue to
draw in more and more people with the illusion that they are
improving their prospects for the future (or for their children). Each person accepts resignedly his socio-economic slot
in the world according to the level of schooling he has reached.
(Ivan Illich, *En America Latina ¿Para Qué Sirve la Escuela?*)

Similarly seminaries and Bible institutes all around the
world are striving to "up-grade" their entrance requirements
and diplomas. In the U.S. many pastors will shortly have a
doctor's degree. In India the major seminaries have moved up
from the L.Th. to the B.Th. level and are pushing toward the
B.D. In Latin America the ideal is to offer a *Licenciatura* in
theology, which in many countries is an academic level reached
by less than 1% of the population.

The implications of this tendency for the churches are even
more serious than they are for society, for seminary graduates

are not only given a diploma but ordained, which sacralizes
their superior status. The ministerial functions are placed
in the hands of a tiny elite at the top of the steep pyramid,
not only educationally but also economically and socially far
"above" the people.

The extension concept challenges this structure of theological education and offers comparable ministerial training at
every academic level. Since extension students are generally
not young men preparing for an occupation, there is far less
danger that their training will serve as a ladder for personal
advancement. At the same time extension programs are capable
of reaching people at the highest educational levels without
creating a clergy class dependent on the churches for their
relatively high standard of living.

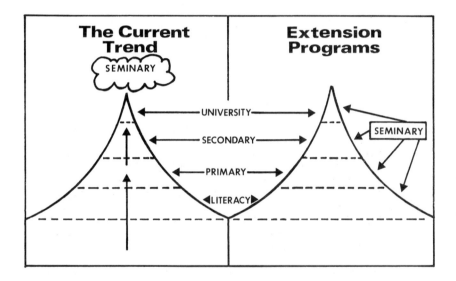

B. *Educational Methodology*

Just as new educational structures have been widely accepted
in recent years, so also we are witnessing unprecedented developments in the field of educational technology. New methods,
equipment, and materials are now available that make the old
classroom procedures an anachronism. Home study, field-based
education, and on-the-job training are now as feasible as
schooling...and far less expensive.

Theological educators have always been "educators" only in
a secondary sense, so it is natural that our seminaries and
Bible institutes should be slow to adopt the new educational
technologies. On the other hand theological extension programs
have been thrust into the ferment of educational technology
because of the demands of their new educational structures.
Although programmed instruction has created more controversy
and frustration than effective instructional tools, it has
given many extension teachers essential insights into the
educational process.

It has, moreover, become evident, from an educational view-
point, that the new relationships brought about by extension
structures provide significant pedagogical advantages for
theological education. Theory and practice can be integrated
as never before. Professors and students can establish a
genuine peer relationship as colleagues in theological reflection and in ministry. The theological institution itself can
now be integrated into the life of the churches it serves.
Instead of preparation *for* ministry we now have training *in*
ministry.

C. *Educational Philosophy*

One of the most essential factors in any educational system,
more basic than structures and methods, is motivation, which
is closely related to meaning. One of the major problems of
traditional schools and seminaries is that the students have a
difficult time relating what they study with their own lives,
needs, concerns, and purposes. In theological education by
extension we have seen that the students have greater interest
in their studies because of their involvement in ministry.
Their studies are meaningful because they relate to present
problems, live questions, immediate needs. Real learning, the
educators tell us, depends on the perceived importance of what
is studied.

Education does not consist of the quantity of information,
books, lectures, and courses that a person can file away in
his brain. And it has little to do with the "level" of schooling he or she can attain. Genuine education has to do with
the understanding and ability to face one's world, deal with
his problems, and meet his own and his group's needs. Theological education is growth in Christian living and ministry, and
it is best achieved through action and reflection in church and
society. Theological education by extension offers the possibility of educational renewal in the ministry in this fundamental sense.

CONCLUSION: The foregoing paragraphs are only suggestive;
they point to large educational issues which provide further
bases for change in theological education. *Traditional semin-*
aries and Bible institutes tend to follow the elitist trends
of our societies, and they perpetuate the image of education
as the accumulation of information.

Theological education by extension has broken with these
traditional structures and concepts in an attempt to define
education in terms of life and ministry. We must confess that
the extension movement still contains much that is inadequate,
useless, or even detrimental. But the door to change has swung
open wide.

<h2 style="text-align:center">V. ECONOMIC BASES:</h2>

What Kind of Theological Education Can We Afford?

We have tried to establish that dynamic ministry requires
shared leadership from within the church, that leaders are
best formed and selected by the normal processes of congregational life, and that they can be trained theologically in
that context. Now we come to a question which is discomforting
and critical today: What kind of theological education can we
afford? There are urgent economic reasons for change.

A. Theological education has always been costly. As seminaries and Bible institutes move up the educational pyramid,
however, the cost factor increases geometrically. Today institutions of higher learning are facing tremendous economic
pressures; in the U.S. many have been forced to cut back on
programs and faculty; the future of small private institutions
is doubtful. Theological institutions are part of that picture.

Ted Ward, an education specialist who knows the international
situation personally, has stated that theological education is
one of the most expensive fields of education, comparable to
the training of psychiatrists and astronauts. And this is
true not only in countries where seminaries are schools of
post-graduate study but also in remote mission fields. This
fact has not been widely known, because the full costs have
been hidden in a number of ways. Often the missionary (and
national) salaries are not reported in the institutional budgets. Student subsidies may or may not be included. The drop-
out rate is rarely considered, certainly not the number who
abandon the ministry after graduation. Capital investment is
taken for granted.

In the U.S. the cost of a basic theological degree (M. Div.
or B.D.) now averages $25,000, including the investment by the
student and by the institution. If we were to estimate that

only half of the graduates stay in the ministry for any length
of time, that figure would rise to $50,000. Ten years ago we
tried to estimate the true cost of ministerial training at a
small institute in Central America which had attained more or
less a secondary school level, and calculated that the investment per graduate in a pastorate was about $30,000. At that
institution and at many others in the Third World the students
paid nothing for their training or for their personal support.

B. Even more critical than the cost of preparing pastors
is the cost of supporting them in the ministry, especially in
the Third World but also in the First World. As theological
education moves up the educational pyramid and the ministry
becomes increasingly professionalized, the students develop,
very naturally, rising expectations as to their own status
and support level. In Guatemala, for example, professional
salaries generally stand at 10 to 20 times the workers' sala-
ries--and the disproportion is increasing. Not a single Protestant church in the whole country now pays a pastor's salary
at that level, and only half a dozen congregations of all the
denominations could hope to do so in the near future.

On the other hand the churches do need, urgently, leaders
who are highly trained, and one of the strategic roles of
theological education by extension is to provide that kind of
leadership. Rather than train young ministerial candidates at
or up to that level, we must design and provide theological
training for more mature leaders who have already established
their economic base in some other profession. If young people
are trained at that level, they will have to be supported more
or less at that level in their future ministry. If older professional people at that level are trained theologically by
extension, they can support themselves and carry out a voluntary,
part-time ministry or enter into a fulltime ministry, if that
is economically possible, and/or serve in the ministry on retirement. In this way the churches could reduce greatly the cost
of high level training and avoid the burden of supporting highly
trained pastors, and they would begin to draw upon their most
capable members for leadership in the ministry.

C. Now that there are options (training in residence, extension, etc.), the churches have to decide how they will invest
their limited resources for theological education. It is not
responsible stewardship to maintain old programs and institutions at any cost. It may no longer be possible to maintain
some institutions at all. Each institution or church must
restudy its needs, evaluate the results of the past, and then
decide what kind(s) of theological education it will support.

The Presbyterian Seminary of Guatemala currently receives $4,000 per year from its parent body. That amount could be used to send one single student to seminary in Puerto Rico, or one married student to the Theological Community of Mexico, or 2 or 3 single students to the Latin American Biblical Seminary in Costa Rica. It could be used to support 10 single students in a 9-month residential program in Guatemala. It is now being used to maintain an extension program with approximately 250 students around the country, all of whom support themselves and pay minimal fees for their books and courses, most of whom have families, and many of whom already occupy leadership positions as pastors, church workers, elders, etc. (The total budget, which depends partly upon donations and sugarcane produced on the Seminary's land, is actually about $17,000.)

Up to now few seminaries and institutes have closed down their residential programs. This means that most extension programs receive only marginal support in funds and personnel and other resources. In spite of this fact the extension movement has grown rapidly around the world. But we have yet to see what might be accomplished in terms of leadership training and renewal of the ministry if the churches should decide to invest a major part of their available resources in theological education by extension and other alternatives.

CONCLUSION: What kind of theological education can we afford? It's a difficult question to answer, and each group will have to make its own decisions. We can simply say that there are economic reasons--along with all the other reasons-- for making radical changes.

Traditional, residential theological schools are extremely expensive, especially if they attempt to reach the more mature leaders of the churches. And they create a heavy financial burden for the churches, for they produce professional pastors at higher and higher support levels.

Theological education by extension is capable of serving large numbers of students, particularly the leaders of the congregations. These students are certain to serve the church, whether they are paid a salary or not, and they generally do not raise their support level expectation by taking extension studies.

VI: MISSIOLOGICAL BASES:
What Are the Goals of Our Theological Training Programs?

Theological education exists not as an end in itself, not to establish the ministry or the church as such, but to enable the church to carry out its mission (God's mission) in the world.

It would be difficult to harmonize the different views of the
mission of the church, but there are some areas of common concern which we can focus upon at this time. It is fitting that
we conclude this paper with a cursory discussion of the goals
of theological education, which will give us missiological
bases for change.

A. *Pastoral Leadership*

Historically the primary goal of theological education has
been to prepare pastors. It has been assumed that every congregation should play the key role in training the other leaders
and in guiding all the members in the Christian life and witness.
His ministry should include preaching, teaching, counseling,
administration, etc. Because the pastor's role is so crucial
and so comprehensive, it is reasoned, he should be highly
trained.

Now we can see that this ideal is unworkable. In Latin
America, for example, we estimate that 4 out of 5 Protestant
congregations are led by men who have had no formal theological
studies--even though there are 400 to 500 Bible institutes and
seminaries in this region. In parts of Africa pastors of the
historic denominations commonly supervise 5, 10, 20, or as many
as 30 congregations. In India many congregations have not had
a "pastoral" visit and received the Lord's Supper for one to
five years, and the seminaries confess that their graduates
have no time to use their theological skills. Even in the U.S.
the historic churches find that more than half of their congregations have less than 200 members and may no longer be able
to support professional pastors.

Faced with this critical situation, we affirm that every
congregation can have its own pastor(s) and that these pastors
can receive adequate theological training by extension (or by
other alternative means.) The churches need only to encourage
and to recognize the leadership gifts among their own members;
the seminaries and Bible institutes need only to design programs
and materials to allow these local leaders to prepare themselves
and carry out their various ministries where they are. Existing
resources could do the job.

Vested interests (prestige, salaries, ecclesiastical structures, institutions, power) make it unlikely that the clergy
will accept any radical changes in the present ways of doing
theological education and ministry. The changes suggested in
this paper require not only new approaches to theological
education and new patterns of ministry but a new self-image
among pastors and "laymen" alike. Such changes will be possible
if the churches capture a new vision of and make a new commitment to God's mission in the world.

B. *Facing Today's World*

Any definition of the mission of the church must deal with
the growing world crises, and any statement of goals for theological education must show how the churches' leaders can lead
the churches in their response to human needs that are reaching
unbelievable proportions. The training of pastors to care for
flocks of believers is not enough! The task of theological
education is far greater, far more complex, much more comprehensive.

First, we must recognize that our traditional concepts of
pastors and lay leaders are hopelessly inadequate. The churches
urgently need to engage their most capable leaders--most of
whom are not pastors and therefore have never taken seriously
God's call to them--in theological reflection about the burning
issues of our time. These leaders, who are deeply involved in
the economic, social and political structures and who represent
every profession and field of knowledge, must be challenged to
work out the meaning of the Gospel in today's world and to lead
the church in mission. The clergy, despite valiant, isolated
efforts, are utterly incapable of doing this job.

Furthermore, the churches cannot depend on any one group of
leaders, whether they be professional pastors or laymen. Our
burgeoning, suffering world demands the mobilization and revit-
alization of all sectors of the church--young people and women
as well as men, deacons and elders as well as pastors, the
poor and minority groups as well as middle class Christians.
Believers can now be found in every society and sub-culture and
they are all essential for the church's missionary encounter
with the world. Therefore theological education must be extended to every sector of the church.

C. *Building Up the Body of Christ*

Finally, we return to our starting point, the church, a
body which grows as its members minister to each other and to
those around them in truth and love. The church needs its
pastors and teachers, evangelists, prophets, and apostles. But
these are called not to stand out as individuals or as "ministers" but to enable others to develop these very ministries.
It is, after all, the church which is called to carry out God's
mission in the world.

How can the church, the whole church, be awakened, renewed,
and challenged for mission? This is the ultimate goal of theological education, and theological education holds one of the
most important keys to renewal and mission. The seminaries
have traditionally narrowed down the selection of those who

can be trained and accredited for "the ministry"; they have
chosen the young and the inexperienced and excluded the mature
and the proven; they have imposed "standards" which further
limit leadership to the highly educated; and they have created
a profession of the ministry. So the church has remained as
a sleeping giant. Now theological education by extension
throws out a new challenge to the whole church to involve itself
in ministry and mission and to prepare itself through reflection
on that ministry and mission. This could be a new day dawning.
The world awaits desperately our response.

CONCLUSION: We have considered theological, historical,
sociological, educational, and economic bases for change in
theological education, but our ultimate concern is the mission
of the church. Theological education exists to train those
who will lead the whole people of God in the fulfilment of His
missionary task in the world. *Traditional theological institutions are far too limited in their outreach, and they have
inherent fallacies. New alternatives are urgently needed, and
theological education by extension has opened the way to fundamental changes in training and ministry for mission.*

This is not to say that traditional programs are entirely
bad; some are excellent--within the limitations of any residential system. But why should we continue to invest so many of
our resources in this kind of system when we could achieve so
much more? Nor can we say that extension programs are all
good; some have failed or fallen short of their stated goals.
But theological education by extension has enormous potential
because it responds in new ways to the basic factors outlined
in this paper.

There are several profound bases for change in theological
education. The changes we have considered could well bring
new life to the churches, new dynamics to the ministry, a new
vision of and a new commitment to mission. Neither theological
education by extension nor any other model is a magic formula.
Its effectiveness will be determined by its ability to handle
critically and creatively the basic factors set forth above.
And it will be determined by the willingness of the churches to
respond to the challenge, to make fundamental changes, and to
invest the necessary resources.

2
What is Extension?

To me, extension has to do primarily with people.

Much has been written about theological education by extension, and a great deal more will be said. The movement is still relatively small, it is growing rapidly, and it continues to take on new dimensions and new forms. There are many different ways of talking about extension--in terms of the biblical concept of the church and its ministry, the socio-economic context, the problem of leadership and indigenization, educational principles and structures and materials, church growth, etc. Ralph Winter's book, *Theological Education by Extension*, runs over 600 pages, discussing extension in these different ways.

But theoretical analyses and even detailed, practical explanations of extension fall short of the real thing, I fear. You really have to look at the people who can be and are now being reached by extension programs; people who are largely beyond the reach of traditional residential seminaries and Bible institutes.

The word extension itself indicates that our concern in this movement is to extend (stretch, expand, spread, adapt) the resources of theological education in order to reach the people who are the natural leaders of our churches. Most of these people are mature men and women, married and with families, settled in their communities and professions. So we must extend our seminaries and institutes to where they live, i.e. to the whole area of our churches. We have to adjust our

schedules to fit theirs, our thinking to communicate within
the varied sub-cultures which they represent, our teaching to
match their different academic levels, our materials to carry
a greater proportion of the cognitive input. We need to extend
our concept of theological education to include, besides candidates for the ministry, lay workers, elders, youth leaders,
ordained pastors, i.e. those who carry the primary responsibilities in our churches and congregations, especially in those
areas where there is scarce hope in this generation or the next
for an established, fulltime, salaried ministry.

Forgive me if I talk about the Presbyterian Seminary of
Guatemala, but these are the people I know. The history of our
extension program has been told elsewhere, and it isn't necessary here anyway. I just want to introduce some of our students.

These are the people who are studying by extension in two
very different geographical areas, which correspond to two of
our presbyteries, under the direction of one fulltime professor
with the parttime help of two pastors. The students attend
weekly sessions in 6 regional centers and study at home in
their "free" time, usually in the evenings and on weekends.
They represent about one third of our seminary's extension
program, which altogether covers 6 presbyteries, includes 16
regional centers with almost 200 students, and has its headquarters in the other end of the country.

1. *North Presbytery* is composed of 8 churches, 6 organized
congregations, and a number of preaching points. The area is
depressed, apparently with little life in the small rural communities or in the churches, and only one church pays an "adequate" pastor's salary. This year we have 3 wide-awake centers
operating in the North with a total of 24 students, mostly
studying at the post-elementary-school level. They include the
only 2 active pastors of the presbytery, the only 2 paid, unordained church workers, the other 3 long-standing candidates
for the ministry (mature men), the president, secretary, and
treasurer of the presbytery plus another member of the executive
committee, the president, secretary, and treasurer of the regional youth organization, 7 ruling elders representing 5 different
congregations, and 3 Sunday school superintendents.

Even this information doesn't tell the extension story very
well. Take a closer look at a smaller sampling of these same
students. Mardoqueo Munoz is the 25-year-old pastor of the
church in El Progreso, secretary of the presbytery, involved in
a number of local, regional, and national programs. He was
graduated from the seminary 4 years ago with a Diploma in Theology, having studied partly by extension, some in residence.

Since then he has gone on in his secular studies, completing 3
years of secondary by correspondence, and this year he has come
back into the seminary program so as to complement his previous
work and earn the next higher theological degree, the "Bachil-
lerato" in Theology. He has obviously learned how to carry a
rigorous study program and a fulltime job at the same time. The
church of which he is pastor is in the final stages of a new,
impressive construction. In his 15 months in El Progreso, a
county seat, Mardoqueo has set a number of important precedents
in pastoral work and initiated several new programs--new for
the church, the presbytery, and some perhaps for the whole
denomination. And the church is responding.

Samuel Mejia, 39 years of age, is an experienced teacher,
professor of the Vocational Institute of El Progreso. An
elder and Sunday school teacher, he has held numerous positions
and carried much responsibility in the El Progreso church for
years, including some of the preaching. At present he serves
also as treasurer for the North Presbytery and member of the
executive committee. Perhaps his most significant contribution
has been his role in the early experimentation, recent establishment, and present direction of a new intermediate youth
program in Guatemala called "Icthus," which now has chapters
in a dozen churches and is growing rapidly.

Salvador Rodas, 47, a farmer, lives in the small village of
La Estancia. His industriousness is evident in the fact that
he owns one of the few tractors in the area, and his leadership
ability is evident in the fact that he is mayor of the large
nearby town of San Cristobal. For years he has been an elder
of his church, a position which implies preaching and pastoral
responsibilities because the church has no pastor. Recently
Salvador was elected president of the North Presbytery for a
one-year term.

2. *Central Presbytery* covers the capital city and several
surrounding towns, has 12 churches plus 4 organized congregations and some preaching points. Although there are 16 pastors
on the rolls, only 4 are fully supported and fully occupied in
the ministry, another 4 parttime, and the rest incidentally.
So even in this urban situation, largely for economic reasons,
much of the work depends on lay leadership. The seminary has
at the moment 3 centers in the city, a total of 60 students
fairly evenly divided between the post-elementary, secondary,
and university levels. They include 7 pastors (not just Presbyterians), 9 ruling elders, the director of a mission (denomination), the director of a national Protestant social service
agency (a woman), the secretary of the Alliance of Protestant
Churches in Guatemala, and the president of the regional women's organization.

Twenty-four of these students are studying theological
courses at the university level, and several of these already
have professional university degrees. This is a fact of some
significance because at present no pastor of our denomination
has a university degree (although two will shortly graduate),
and, in fact, less than 1% of the population of Guatemala has
any university training at all. As an indication of the leadership ability of these students in society as well as in the
church, we may note that several are teachers, other account-
ants, one a former member of congress, another a judge, and
still another head of the economics department of a local
university.

Samuel Andrade, 42, is an electrician who works parttime for
a company and parttime on his own. His family has long been a
mainstay at the Central Presbyterian Church in Guatemala City,
the largest of our denomination with a regular Sunday morning
attendance, including Sunday school, of 600 to 700. His wife
and 4 of his 5 children are active in the Sunday school and
women's and youth activities. Samuel is an elder, and, although
the church has an outstanding fulltime pastor plus some colla-
boration from two "associate" pastors, he might be considered
a pastor too. As superintendent of the Intermediate Department
of the Sunday shcool he presides over a two and a half hour
program for 75 lively young people each Sunday morning, including six classes and a worship service separate from the congregational service of worship.

Julio Paz, 38, is a brother-in-law of Samuel Andrade, holds
a responsible position as accountant for INCAP, an international
nutrition research organization. His family, which includes
7 children, is also outstanding in its contribution to the life
of Central Church. Julio is an elder, organist, choir director,
and Director of Christian Education. He has served in the past
as a leader of the national youth organization and treasurer of
the Synod. Not only he but also his wife and 2 of his sons are
students of the seminary this year.

Augusto Marroquin, 19, is in his first year at the national
university, studying engineering, and he works in a printing
shop during the day. Converted just a few months ago, he feels
called to the ministry and is able to carry two seminary courses
as well as his other studies and work.

Raul Echeverria, 64, is the pastor of a large independent
church in Guatemala City and oversees the work of a Protestant
primary school and an adult primary education correspondence
program. An indefatigable worker, he was for years a parttime
professor at our seminary and at the large Central American
Bible Institute, has edited a magazine and published several

books and numerous pamphlets, and is at present the Secretary of
the Alliance of Protestant Churches of Guatemala. He travels
widely as a preacher and lecturer. As a recognition of his
contribution to Guatemala, the government recently awarded him
the Order of the Quetzal, the nation's highest honor. As a
young man Raul was graduated from a national secondary school
with a teaching certificate, went on to graduate from Moody
Bible Institute in the U.S., later completed two years of university studies in the national university of Guatemala. He
is now finishing his requirements for the Licenciatura in
Theology (roughly equivalent to the M.Th.) in our seminary.

These and many others like them are the people that make
extension a challenging and exciting experiment in theological
education even in our small institution. They are the reason
why churches and missions throughout Latin America are changing
radically the structures of their institutions. They, the
extension students, call us to a new understanding of the ministry, a new vision of the church, and a new hope for growth in
witness, maturity, community, and service.

Let's be quite clear about one thing. Not one in ten of
these people who make up our extension family could ever study
in a traditional residence seminary, even with full scholarships. And if they could, they wouldn't be able to take the
same courses in the same classrooms. And if they were by some
stretch of the imagination to be trained in a residence seminary for three years, it is doubtful that they would be able to
return in large numbers to their communities and churches to
take up their old leadership positions either on the basis of
self-support or as professional ministers.

Or, to direct some questions in the other direction, are
traditional seminaries in Guatemala, Latin America, or elsewhere, reaching as many students with such diversity and this
quality of leadership? What kinds of students attend residence
institutions? Who are the *people* we should be reaching with
our programs of theological education?

3

A Working Definition
of Theological Education
by Extension

People who are new to the extension concept continue to ask,
What is theological education by extension? Those who are
involved in the extension movement are constantly rethinking
the bases and the nature of their programs. This paper is an
expression of that process of definition, intended especially
for group discussion by seminary faculties, in theological
consultations, and at extension workshops.

At a recent ASIT consultation in Chile it became evident
that there is no simple, exact definition of theological education by extension or even a clear distinction between extension
and residence programs in Latin America today. There are now
many varied adaptations of extension; residence and extension
have been combined in several different ways; many residence
programs have broken out of the traditional stereotypes. All
across the board there is a growing sensitivity to the concerns
of contextualization and an increasing openness to new alternatives.

It is useful to look at theological education by extension
as a movement and a vision rather than a specific technique or
system. From the beginning one of the dangers has been that
extension might become a fixed formula, another confining tradition to replace or complement the residential pattern that had
dominated for so long. Definitions are often limiting; their
function is normally to enclose and exclude. Our intention
here is to develop a working definition of extension that will
be challenging and liberating rather than polarizing and confining.

I. THE PURPOSE OF THEOLOGICAL EDUCATION BY EXTENSION

Throughout the brief history of the extension movement there has been a common, overriding purpose: to extend the resources of theological education to the functioning and developing leaders of the congregations. Within this general goal many different reasons have been set forth, and these arguments merit more discussion than is possible here. But whatever the specific reasons for each extension program, the shared vision has been *to encourage and enable local leaders to develop their gifts and ministries without leaving their homes, jobs, communities, and local congregations.*

A. This purpose has been expressed *pragmatically and numerically*. We must take our training programs to the local church leaders because they cannot come to our seminaries and institutes. Or, we can reach many more students, and we are more likely to get the leaders, if we go to the congregations. This argument is very important, especially when it is linked to the other arguments that follow, but it can give the impression that extension is a stop-gap, second-rate approach to theological education.

B. Others have asserted the legitimacy or even the superiority of extension as *an alternative system of theological education*. Using widely accepted arguments from specialists in education, they affirm that real learning must integrate theory and practice creatively, that teachers and students must relate to each other as persons and as complementary equals, that learning takes place in all of life and is often more effective outside of our academic institutions. These insights do not in themselves make extension programs effective, but they do suggest that the extension approach has tremendous potential because these insights can be applied far more naturally in extension than traditional programs.

C. One of the basic concerns of extension advocates has been *the nature of the ministry*. The Western pattern of theological education has projected a professional model of the ministry, which encourages the non-trained to take a very secondary role. In Latin America this tendency is aggravated by the dominant Roman Catholic tradition, which still maintains a great divorce between clergy and laity. And throughout the Third World education, including theological education, plays an increasing role in the formation of elite classes. Extension can reverse these trends because it opens the door to theological education and the ministry to all, not just high-level candidates for the professional clergy.

D. There is a similar *ideological argument* for extension.
Throughout the world we find hierarchical social and economic
structures of power and privilege, based on race, wealth, class,
technology, and education. In our churches this situation is
repeated and exacerbated through traditional patterns of theological education, ordination, and the unique authority of the
clergy—among Roman Catholics, Protestants, independent churches
and Pentecostals. Most members of most denominations are overwhelmingly proletarian, but the clergy-dominated power structures are usually identified with the ruling classes. If
extension opens the door to theological education to the natural
leaders of all our congregations, then the ministry should more
nearly reflect the concerns and serve the needs of the masses.

E. The extension movement now stretches across many ecclesiastical and ideological positions, and it includes many
different concerns, but it shares a common vision for *the renewal of the ministry of the whole church for mission.* Its
purpose is not primarily bound up with theological institutions
as such or even with the church as an end in itself but rather
with the mobilization of the church for mission in the world.
To the extent that this vision prevails, the concepts and
patterns of the extension movement must themselves fall under
constant criticism and be subject to change. We have barely
begun to reach and incorporate the leaders of all our local
congregations in theological education...for ministry...in the
church's mission.

II. VARIOUS DIMENSIONS OF THEOLOGICAL EDUCATION BY EXTENSION

In working out the purpose of theological education by extension several different dimensions should be kept in mind.
The most obvious is geographical, but this is not the only dimension nor the most important. Each extension program should
analyze and respond to the leadership needs of its churches in
all of the following dimensions. Our purpose is to extend our
resources for theological education in all these ways.

A. *Geographically.* Obviously if we intend to reach the
leaders of all our congregations without extracting them from
their local situations, we have to decentralize our training
programs. Extension centers must be located within reasonable
travel time of all the congregations.

B. *Chronologically.* Not only must extension centers be
located close to the students; extension meetings or classes
must be scheduled at times when they can attend. Most of them
hold jobs or are housewives or attend school. Some are church
workers and pastors and are especially busy on weekends. Rural
people are often self-employed and can meet during weekdays;
city people are more likely to meet in the evenings.

C. *Culturally.* Often an extension program is expected to serve urban and rural churches, and the students may represent several different sub-cultures. The course materials may be the same, but the center meetings must adapt the content to the needs, customs, language, and thought patterns of each group. The teachers must fit into each local environment and encourage full discussion by the students so that their studies will be integrated into their understanding and applied in their ministry effectively.

D. *Academically.* Ideally, extension programs should offer theological courses at all the academic levels represented in the churches they serve. This often means that higher as well as lower levels must be added to that which has traditionally been the norm. Two problems emerge at once: How to provide materials and personnel for such a wide range and how to avoid pretense and prejudice between students and graduates of the different levels. An essential principle of the extension philosophy has been the functional parity of different academic levels; students at all levels must be given equal recognition for ministry. Course materials can be adjusted or produced separately for the different levels. As the purpose of renewal and mission becomes clear to the students, they should become proud of their diversity and committed to a common ministry.

E. *Socially.* As a corollary to the previous points, extension reaches people of all different social classes and economic levels. It is important to note, however, that extension programs are not normally the means of social or economic advancement. On the contrary these programs serve people who have already made their place in life through a non-religious profession, who support themselves while they study theology, and who are not expecting to find a better paid job in the professional ministry. Extension programs are thus able to train theologically professional people who rarely enter a traditional seminary and also to avoid the support problem of graduates from high level theological seminaries, especailly in Third World countries, where pastors' salaries at this level are almost non-existent.

F. *Ecclesiastically.* Traditionally, theological institutions have accepted only candidates for "fulltime" ministries, primarily because of their high cost and limited space, and only such candidates could afford to attend those institutions. In extension this all changes; elders and deacons and ordinary members can "enter" just as easily as ministerial candidates. Some extension programs have been set up primarily or exclusively for church workers, pastors, and candidates; others are described as lay training. If our purpose is to broaden the concept of ministry and renew the ministry of the whole church, however,

it is important to encourage non-clergy to participate along-
side the clergy.

G. *Numerically, ideologically, and theologically.* Using
the same resources, extension programs readily train far more
students than traditional institutions. And they include a
far wider spread of the churches' leadership: older as well
as young people, women as well as men, non-clergy as well as
candidates for the ministry and church workers, people from
all academic levels, sub-cultures, and social-economic groups.
This is not merely a quantitative concern but ideological and
theological also. The ministry should involve the whole body
of Christ and serve all sectors of human society. Theological
education by extension facilitates the formation of ministry
of the people, by the people, and for the people.

III. THREE ESSENTIAL ELEMENTS
IN THEOLOGICAL EDUCATION BY EXTENSION

Although there is no magic formula for theological education
by extension, every program should include and integrate these
three elements: self-study materials for individual study,
practical work in the congregations, and regular class encounters or seminars. All three of these elements are essential
to the effectiveness of extension as a learning system, especially as they relate to each other.

A. *Self-study materials* are essential for extension students
because they must get the basic content of their courses on
their own. Extension classes are normally held just once a
week or even less frequently and the limited time available (one
to three hours) cannot be squandered passing out information.
Extension professors have gone to great pains to prepare and
place in the hands of their students not only textbooks but
also workbooks that will guide them effectively through the
important points toward their objectives. On the one hand
recent educational technology has been helpful in defining objectives, identifying student capabilities, setting up learning
sequences, and evaluating these materials. On the other hand
there is an increasing awareness of the significance of non-
printed and non-formal educational processes, especially among
people whose reading ability is limited. The search for more
effective self-study materials and procedures continues.

B. In many places extension has been successful primarily
because the students are so involved in *practical work* in their
own congregations. This was not planned so much as assumed,
because the students are the leaders, often the functioning
pastors of their churches. Much more thought needs to be given,
however, to the effective use of practical work in the formation

of extension students and in the development of extension
curricula. Although extension students naturally raise pertinent questions and make direct application of their courses
as they study, some extension programs make very poor use of
this invaluable relationship between theory and practice.

C. The third essential ingredient in extension learning
systems is the *regular encounters or seminars* at each extension
center. One important function of the center meetings is to
provide fellowship and inspiration for the extension students
and professors. Another is to provide motivation and clarification and confirmation of their studies. Another is to integrate through discussion the course content and the practical
problems and work in the congregations. This expression and
exchange of ideas and experiences is itself an important addition to the students' formation which cannot be reduced to the
printed page nor left to the student on his own. The center
meetings are really the heart of the program; the effectiveness
of the other two elements, self-study materials and practical
work, is to a great extent determined by what goes on in the
brief but vital meetings of students and professors at each
center. Most extension programs have found that the optimum
frequency for center meetings is once a week, which allows for
working students to cover a reasonable amount of study material
and also provides them with a regular stimulus for daily study
on top of all their other responsibilities. Needless to say it
is essential that extension students maintain a steady discipline of home study in order to be able to participate meaningfully in the center meetings and to progress effectively toward
their learning objectives.

IV. EXTENSION AND OTHER TYPES OF THEOLOGICAL EDUCATION

In defining theological education by extension it can be
helpful to compare and distinguish several other types. Although residential seminaries and Bible institutes have become
the norm or standard of full theological training, other systems of leadership training continue to be used widely in the
Third World: correspondence courses, brief institutes, and
evening classes. The following contrasts only bring out the
broad differences and are not meant to be prejudicial. In
widely different situations each type may at times be the only
or the best way to do theological education. In the future we
shall probably see more combining and exchange between these
and other forms.

A. *Residential programs* generally take their students from
their normal, diverse contexts and provide intensive, long-term
studies at some central location. The training itself is usually the primary concern of the students for 2, 3, or more years,
and most of them are young, single men preparing for fulltime

church work. *Extension programs* do not take their students
away from their communities, congregations, jobs, and families.
The training is fitted into their life-style and added to all
their other responsibilities and may take 5 to 15 years to
complete. The students normally work fulltime at some secular
job or in their congregations, and many of them are older,
mature leaders. They may or may not be candidates for ordination as pastors, fulltime or otherwise.

B. *Correspondence courses* are usually offered to all kinds
of people, pastors and workers as well as ordinary members and
non-members, sometimes in great numbers. They do not take the
students out of their normal settings, nor do they provide any
personal contact other than the printed page, or in some cases
cassettes. Therefore there is little opportunity to clarify,
adapt, expand, or debate the course content for individual or
group understanding. Often, but not always, these courses are
very elementary, and the level of drop-outs is usually very
high. *Extension programs* usually depend heavily upon printed
materials, but they also provide regular personal contact
between each group of students and their professors. This
allows for greater depth and adaptation of the courses, provides
motivation and clarification for the students, facilitates
integration of theory and practice, and adds the vital inter-
personal dimension to the learning experience.

C. *Brief institutes* vary greatly as to length, content, and
methodology. They bring students together at some central
location, but they do not normally cut them off from their
families, jobs, communities, and congregations. They may be
theoretical or practical or both, but they usually do not provide for or sustain on-going study or application of what is
learned. They may reach a wide selection of local church
leaders, but they usually do not give them sufficient training
or accreditation to become recognized as pastors. *Extension
programs* bring together their students at local centers regularly and provide daily home-study materials to assure on-going
study throughout most or all of the year. Many of these programs offer full ministerial training, and those who are candidates may be ordained as pastors upon graduation.

D. *Night Bible schools* are prevalent in many countries,
especially in urban areas, and reach large numbers of students,
many of whom are older, married, and employed, and some of whom
are the leaders of their congregations. Classes are held two
to five evenings a week, for 2 or 3 hours. Because so much of
the students' limited free time is spent getting to and attending classes, little time is left for independent study. The
students usually listen to the professors' lectures, take
notes, and memorize them for examination purposes. *Extension
programs* provide the basic course content in the form of self-

study materials. The weekly class sessions are not intended
to pass out information but to discuss the concerns and problems of the students as they work through these materials and
try to relate them to their own lives and ministry.

V. SOME EXAMPLES OF THEOLOGICAL EDUCATION BY EXTENSION

No doubt there are many, many different possible adaptations
and combinations of theological education by extension. At the
ASIT consultation in Chile the group that worked on a definition of extension suggested several different models and recommended certain guidelines to evaluate these models. Perhaps
future consultations and workshops will carry forward this
task. There is much to be learned from the great diversity of
extension programs that are already operating. Following are
samples selected from among at least 250 extension programs in
60 countries around the world, most of which were initiated
during the past 5 to 10 years.

A. The most commented extension program is the Presbyterian
Seminary of Guatemala which is based at a central campus with
a core faculty, administration, and publishing operation all
committed to extension work. The fulltime faculty members,
some of whom do not live at the seminary, visit all the centers
once a week for 2 to 3-hour sessions, and larger 2 or 3-day
gatherings are held at the central campus 2 or 3 times per year.
This type of extension is not uncommon, but few institutions
have been willing to phase out their residential programs in
favor of extension.

B. Many seminaries and Bible institutes have added extension programs to their regular residential programs. In Colombia, for example, the United Biblical Seminary at Medellin, the
Christian and Missionary Alliance Institute at Armenia, and
the Caribbean Bible Center at Sincelejo have parallel programs
of residence and extension. In some places extension serves
a lower academic level; in others it reaches above and below
the residence program. In most cases it causes additional
burdens for the same staff and additional strain on limited
budgets. For these and other reasons it may become the second-
best training program.

C. Extension and residence have been combined in several
different ways. The Evangelical United Seminary in Mexico, for
example, offers basic ministerial training by extension at the
secondary level; outstanding students are encouraged to take
advanced training on campus at the university level. Other
extension programs find that their students become interested
in further studies and go on to residential schools. Some
have pointed out that the extension program may well give new
life to the residential institutions, increasing the number of

applicants and attracting more mature and more committed students. There is a danger, however, that this relationship will reinforce the idea that extension is only a step toward further, more accredited training.

D. Some extension programs have had to adapt the Guatemala model to serve vast geographical areas. The Eduardo Lane Bible Institute, for example, covers 120,000 square miles in Central Brazil. The central staff is unable to visit the extension centers weekly even with the help of small planes, so pastors and other qualified people tutor local groups, and faculty members supervise them through monthly visits and by correspondence.

E. The George Allan Extension Theological Seminary in Bolivia also serves an enormous region and has further complications with cultural, linguistic, and geographic differences. The work is divided into districts, and staff teams have developed in several places which participate in the preparation of materials as well as the teaching in the centers.

F. The Peruvian Evangelical Church has for some time had a number of Bible institutes with long or short-term residence programs in different parts of the country. Now the national Christian education committee hopes to utilize these bases to build up their incipient extension program throughout the presbyteries with the help of a national coordinator.

G. The TAFTEE program in India has been able to build up local, largely voluntary extension faculties for their 25 widely separated centers, each with a locally named dean or coordinator. Another promising development is the use of upper level extension students to teach lower level extension classes as part of their required work. If each of the present 350 university-level students were to teach 10 more, they could begin to meet the vast needs for training in the thousands of local congregations.

H. The Conservative Baptist extension program in Northern Honduras emphasizes the significance of teaching or discipleship in the formation of their students. Each student is required to teach at least one other student from the very beginning and to train him to teach others. This chain effect is focussed on the formation of new congregations, which is the chief task of every student.

I. The Apostolic Church of Mexico is launching a series of extension programs under its department of education and a national extension coordinator. These programs are planned to meet specific needs, such as the formation of Sunday school teachers and deacons, the continuing education of pastors, and

the preparation of candidates for the ministry. They even plan
to train extension teachers through an extension program.

J. The Latin American Biblical Seminary of Costa Rica is
one of the largest, most influencial, and most competent theological institutions in Latin America, and it has become involved in the extension movement in several creative ways. An
extension committee of faculty and advanced students provides
advice, materials, training, and supervision for extension
programs in Costa Rica. A specialization in theological education by extension is offered for regular degree-level students.
And a new program, now in its experimental stage, will enable
individuals and groups scattered throughout Latin America to
design and carry out high-level theological studies pertinent
to their interests and needs, based in their local situations,
utilizing local resources, with the advice and accreditation
of the Latin American Biblical Seminary.

K. The South African Council of Churches' Department of
Theological Education is now planning a vast extension program
that will bring together the resources of many of the major
denominations and offer fully recognized ministerial training
for local leaders throughout the country. Participating churches will contribute funds and personnel, some of whom will
give fulltime to teaching and the preparation of self-instructional materials. At first three academic levels will be
offered, and centers will be set up in ten major cities. Once
initiated (in 1977) the program will probably expand rapidly
to 25 or more centers, and many of these centers will probably
have to reach out into the rural areas and form sub-centers.
It will be interesting to see the effect of such a massive
thrust in theological education by extension upon largely traditional churches in a tense, racist society.

We have considered the purpose of theological education by
extension, including several reasons or arguments for extension,
various dimensions of theological education by extension,
three essential elements in extension as an educational system,
a broad comparison of extension and other types of theological
education, and some examples or models of theological education
by extension. Each of these topics calls for considerable
discussion in theoretical and in practical terms. These notes
are presented not as a set formula but as a working definition
of theological education by extension. Each church and institution should work through the issues and possibilities suggested here in terms of its available resources and objectives
or needs.

This paper may be used by faculties, consultations, and work-shops in several different ways. Participants may be given copies for individual study and then come together for discussion section by section. Or each section could be presented orally and then discussed in groups. Questions for discussion over each section can be prepared ahead of time or the groups themselves can identify the issues and questions to be discussed. Many issues and practical questions arise readily from the material presented. Every effort should be made to focus directly on the needs and possibilities of the churches and programs represented. If some of the participants are already working in extension programs, their experiences, problems, and insights should be invaluable.

Any study of the extension concept and movement should include critical evaluation. It is not enough to ask what is the purpose of theological education by extension; we must also ask whether this purpose is being fulfilled. It is not enough to look at the different dimensions and elements in extension; we must also ask ourselves to what extent we are responding to these dimensions and providing for the effective integration of these elements. It is not enough to review the many possibilities of theological education by extension; we must ask whether our vision is in fact being incarnated in effective training, in the renewal of the ministry, in the mobilization of the whole church for mission.

4

Extension:
An Alternative Model
for Theological Education

We have bungled badly in education. Not merely in the
ways noted by most school critics: too little money for
education, outdated curricula, poorly trained teachers.
But in more fundamental ways. It isn't just that our
schools fail to achieve their stated purposes, that they
are not the exalted places their proponents claim.
Rather, many are not even decent places for our children
to be. They damage, they thwart, they stifle children's
natural capacity to learn and grow healthily. To use
Jonathan Kozol's frightening but necessary metaphor:
they destroy the minds and hearts of our children(1).

This is what radical critics are saying about the most
heavily supported, highly developed school system the world has
ever known. Some of us have suspected that a similar radical
criticism should be made of our theological schools. The
majority of our theological educators are still concerned
basically with internal problems: budget, curricula, personnel.
Many are sincerely dedicated to the upgrading of their programs
so that they will be exalted communities of theological reflexion and spiritual formation. But a few have suggested that our
seminaries and Bible institutes are not even appropriate places
in which to carry out theological education. They may in fact
damage, thwart, and stifle the churches' natural capacity to
grow and develop their own leaders and carry out a dynamic
ministry to their own members and to society.

The movement called theological education by extension has
come on the horizon at this particular moment of history as an

alternative model to the traditional schools of the past 150
years. It demands attention because of its phenomenal growth.
The most recent survey indicates that there are now approximately
80 programs with 11,000 students in Latin America alone(2).   The
concept has been accepted and applied among historic denomina-
tions (Presbyterians, Lutherans, Episcopalians, Baptists,
Methodists, Mennonites, Quakers), even moreso among independent
and conservative groups (Latin America Mission, Christian and
Missionary Alliance, TEAM, Inter-American Mission, Andies
Evangelical Mission, West Indies Mission, Gospel Missionary
Union), and increasingly among pentecostal groups (Assemblies of
God, Apostolic Church of the Faith in Jesus Christ, Church of
God). And this movement began with a small experiment in
Guatemala just ten years ago; the concept was first presented
at an international workshop just over five years ago(3).

The real challenge of the extension movement is not its
extraordinary growth and size, however, but its response to the
radical critique of traditional schooling, theological and otherwise. The very fact that so many churches and institutions have
embraced the extension concept so rapidly implies a widespread
dissatisfaction with the old patterns. Those of us who have
been involved in extension have realized that we did not have to
"sell" the idea; most of the early "converts" were already more
than 50% convinced before they even heard of the Guatemala
experiment. Moreover, as we began to consider the implications
of the extension concept and look for theoretical underpinnings,
we discovered that similar things were happening in other fields
of education and training. Theological education by extension
is merely one example of the worldwide interest today in new
patterns of formal and non-formal education.

Our concern here will be to consider the extension model as a
response to the radical critique of theological education today,
with special reference to the Third World. We shall look at
three basic concerns of theological education which are parallel
to the basic concerns of development and education in general.
We shall consider the structures of theological education, the
methodology of theological education, and the content of theological education. And we shall draw upon three concepts of
great importance today, especially in Latin America: contextualization, conscientization, and liberation. Our main reference
point will be the Presbyterian Seminary of Guatemala, because
this is where the movement began and because this is where our
experience is based.

I.   THE STRUCTURES OF THEOLOGICAL EDUCATION--
CONTEXTUALIZATION

One of the most important issues in theological education
today is the matter of structures. It is in this area of

structural change that the extension model has already made very significant strides forward.

Radical analyses of development, general education, and theological institutions run along very similar lines. They focus on the structural relationships between people, classes, and nations and come to the conclusion that existing institutions and programs are imperialistic, consciously or unconsciously, for they maintain the privileges and power of an elite and foment an attitude of dependence. The radical critics propose a break with the status quo, a reversal of the system, and a return to the people and local values of each region and nation, culture and sub-culture. This has been called contextualization.

In Latin America it has been pointed out that even the most idealistic development programs have failed miserably because they depend upon and reinforce existing structures(4). Development is usually defined in terms of economic growth, technological advancement, industrialization, and increased participation in world trade. But everyone knows that the U.S., Europe, and Japan have such a concentration of capital, technology, industry, and commerce that Third World countries have no chance of catching up. So they are tied in to a process not of development but of underdevelopment, i.e. perpetual dependence. This makes them vulnerable to exploitation, identifies them as second-class nations, and downgrades their culture and values(5).

Public and private schooling is likewise structured so that the elite maintain their status and the masses struggle after an unattainable goal. The few poor and middle class students who do reach the top, even the revolutionary university students, are effectively silenced by graduation into a world of privilege and comfort. The rest are drop-outs or rejects sentenced to the lower levels of economic advantage and social status. And the entire system is adamantly defended and covered over by the myth of universal, free, compulsory, public schooling(6).

The churches maintain a similar elitism in the ministry, largely through a pattern of theological education developed over the last 150 years. Western missionaries concerned with the formation of well-trained leaders naturally established the kinds of institutions they were accustomed to and inculcated a concern for ever "higher" standards. Today there is a perennial struggle to "upgrade" the seminaries and Bible institutes in the Third World, producing an increasingly select group of pastors and leaders to serve a progressively smaller circle of churches and church institutions. Meanwhile, in Latin America at least, thousands of congregations continue to grow and multiply and

develop indigenous leaders with gifts and dedication but with
little or no training. It is doubtful whether traditional
institutions could ever train enough pastors for these churches.
Certainly the majority of the churches will be unable to support
university or secondary graduates in the forseeable future. But
the more fundamental question is whether the elitist pattern of
theological training for a professional ministry is at all
appropriate in the Latin American context(7).

The formation of the ministry at the local level is a
structural problem, and theological education plays a crucial
role. It is traditionally believed that God calls young men to
the ministry, and traditional theological institutions are
equipped primarily for young men and almost exclusively for
candidates to the ministry. Because these men are young, they
have little experience as responsible members of society or as
leaders in their congregations, and once they become candidates
for the ministry, they are excluded from the normal processes
of leadership selection and experience. They are drawn out of
their homes, communities, and churches, set in an esoteric
religious-academic environment, and after several years are
sent out into local congregations as the top leaders. Placed
over mature men and women who have struggled with the problems
of daily life, have demonstrated their gifts and Christian
character over the years, have perhaps preached and taught and
pastored, and have earned the right to lead, these young
graduates come with only artificial credentials, a diploma and
ordination, and as professionals who demand a salary, generally
above the level of the average church member. This pattern
discourages serious participation by local leaders, dampens the
natural dynamics of corporate ministry, and often produces
mediocre leadership. It forms in the mind of the pastor
complexes which are difficult to surmount: a sense of trying
to be something that he is not, of having to justify his role,
of attempting to carry out all the functions of the ministry,
of being the one who is called and trained and paid to do the
job. And it forms in the minds of the members the inverse
complexes which are so prevalent: a sense of being less
capable than they really are, of not having any essential role,
of not possessing the gifts of the ministry, of not being
really called--because they are not trained or paid or ordained.
Thus the minister (servant) actually becomes the ruler; the
concept of the ministry (service) is inverted to mean privilege;
and the members maintain their dependence upon an "imported"
clergy to direct the life of the churches.

The extension approach to theological education can and does
break these patterns of ecclesiastical and theological dependence. It reverses the elitist tendency of the ministry. It
recognizes and values and elevates local leadership in a process
of contextualization(8).

The Presbyterian Seminary of Guatemala followed the traditional residencial pattern in the capital city for 25 years. Through this program some of the key leaders of the church were formed and accredited. As time went on, however, it became evident that this program was limited in its effectiveness and that the majority of the local congregations received no benefit. The extension plan was born out of a simple recognition of fact and a simple decision. The fact: We were training the wrong people. We were preparing more and more young, unproven men for a middle class ministry which was limited to five or ten churches and ignoring the mature leaders who were doing the actual work of the ministry in all the churches. In other words we were not being fair either to the churches or to these young seminary students.

The decision: We must take theological education to the natural leaders in the local congregations. Rather than try to uproot these older men and women and send them away to school, which would be costly and detrimental, we should take the professor, materials, and classes out to them. So began the search for the best possible tools and arrangements for an extension system which would focus on the needs of the students. Centers were established in churches at strategic points throughout the country, depending on accessibility and local interest. Classes were held at times convenient to the students, and the professors traveled to these centers. It seemed that weekly contact between student and professor was an optimum because it gave the student sufficient time to work through a reasonable amount of material and yet it did not leave him too long on his own. Larger periodic gatherings at the centrally localed rural headquarters in San Felipe permitted the students from different parts of the country to meet together, to gain a broader perspective of the Seminary and the church, and to participate in specialized, brief training sessions.

As the program developed, several dimensions of the extension concept have become clearer. Most people first think of extension in *geographical* terms. We take theological education back to where the churches are--up in the cool highlands, down on the hot costal plains, in the fertile coffee belt and over in the arid North, in the large capital city and the major commercial towns. More important is the extension into different *social and cultural* contexts. The weekly meeting is not dominated by some artificial, hybrid environment set up by the institution and obliterating the diverse backgrounds of the students; rather each extension center sets its own environment and the professor relates to the students on their terms. Since the program is geared primarily to the mature leaders of the congregations, these men and women truly represent the life of their communities; they are never uprooted. This is particularly important in

Guatemala, which although physically small is culturally rich
and diverse, with perhaps 8 different sub-cultures and with over
50% of the population divided among 14 major Indian tribes.
Extension to us means also *academic* broadening to include the
various levels of church leaders and their communities. In most
rural and even urban areas primary schooling is the norm; we
train most of our students at that level. In some town and city
churches secondary schooling is the norm; this is our second
level of courses. Nationally there are a number of professional
men and a few pastors with university studies; these men and
women serve in strategic ways in our own denomination and in the
evangelical movement and in society; so we also have a university
level program. But these levels do not compete, for they are all
fully recognized as ministerial training in what has been
referred to as the functional parity of different academic
levels(9). There is also an *ecclesiastical and theological*
dimension to extension. Instead of isolating and training
exclusively candidates for the ministry, we encourage clergy,
candidates, and laymen to study theology together with no dis-
tinctions. The door to the pastoral ministry is open to all;
many are encouraged to develop their gifts; and all are
considered ministers.

These are structural changes that together make up a profound
process of contextualization. We don't even pretend to know
what patterns or kinds of ministry will develop in the future as
the extension program increasingly opens the door to the full
participation of the believers in the ministry, the recognition
and training of local, natural leaders, and the expression of
multi-cultural values and traditions. But we already have a
very diverse, enlarged, representative student body of 250 in a
constituency of about 15,000 adult members (instead of a select,
privileged group of 10 or 15, the average in the previous
residence program). These men and women are young and old,
mature leaders and new Christians, pastors and candidates for
the ministry and laymen, Indians and Ladinos, rural and urban.
They are basically oriented to their own communities and congregations; they support themselves and pay for their texts and
other fees; most of them are not dependent on the church for
their present studies or for their future ministry. The
majority of our students do not seek a full-time pastoral
ministry, but there are already (in ten years) far more fulltime church workers and pastors among the extension students and
graduates than there are among the graduates of the former
residence program (of 25 years), and many are serving in congregations that could not afford to employ a residence seminary
graduate(10). The natural process is for a man (often several
in one congregation) to prove himself by his dedication and
effectiveness, gradually take on more responsibilities and
preparation, and at some point along the way be selected by the

members as a leader (ordained or non-ordained, salaried or non-salaried) of his own or another congregation.

II. THE METHODOLOGY OF THEOLOGICAL EDUCATION--
CONSCIENTIZATION

A second fundamental concern of theological education today is methodology. The extension model requires new educational methods, and the movement has begun to stimulate creative experimentation and serious reflection on the nature of the educational process and some research into the effectiveness of theological training programs. This should lead to more profound and more fruitful changes in methodology in the future.

As we mentioned at the beginning of this paper, the radical critics of modern schooling go beyond the usual discussions of curricula, personnel, teaching techniques and meterials, etc. They are concerned not only with teaching and learning but with "growth, dignity, antonomy, freedom, and the development of the full range of human potentialities"(11). They focus on the person and demand a humanization of our educational systems.

Once again we can compare the problems of development, general education, and theological schools. Although the Third World nations have thrown off the most obvious chains of imperialism, they are in danger of perpetuating a colonized and a colonizing mentality. It is still widely held in Latin America, for example, that only massive infusions of foreign capital and technology are capable of solving many of the basic social and economic problems. Rural villagers persist in the forlorn belief that the national government can and should solve their problems. And the miserable workers of the coffee plantations abjectly accept the traditional understanding of reality according to which any individual initiative is hopeless and worthless. The status quo is eternal; society is controlled and determined by others; the individual is predestined, locked in place by circumstances. What is needed in these situations is not further outside help but an awakening among the people themselves as to who they are and what they can do.

Educational institutions generally follow a pattern of oppression, also, all the way from kindergarten through university, including the overrun, under-equipped, public schools and the select, upper-class private schools. The entire academic program is laid out without consulting the students. The curriculum doubtless includes much that would ordinarily be of interest to the students, but it is regimented and packaged and delivered in such a way that it becomes unpalatable and irrelevant. Natural curiosity and motivation are lost, so artifical stimuli and discipline are necessary(12). And the student, whether he realized it or not, is forced through six, 12, 16,

or more years of controlled activities which are comparable only
to life in the military or in prison.

One exciting new development in recent years has been the
"open school" concept(13). It begins with the simple but profound premise that children are people. They have different
needs and abilities. They grow up and learn at different rates.
They have their own working patterns and interests. They have
great powers of concentration when working at something that
interests them. They are innovative. They are naturally
curious and self-motivated to learn. They can take responsibility for themselves(14). Rows of desks, schedules, classes,
examinations, and grades can be and are eliminated. Teachers
and parents play new roles--also as people. And the school
becomes a stimulating environment in which the children are
encouraged to follow their own interests, ask the questions
that interest them (and find answers), work out their projects
independently and in groups, and develop their own integrity
and personality as they learn.

Another interesting development today is the whole field of
non-formal education. It makes the important observation that
learning and schooling are not co-terminous. In fact some of
the most complex skills (e.q. one's mother tongue) are learned
outside of school. Studies are now being made of non-formal
programs (e.q. on the job training) which may help break the
hegemony of the educational establishment. Descriptive analyses
point out intriguing contrasts between formal and non-formal
education. The tendency of formal school programs is to depend
upon motivation within the content, have poor clarity of
objectives, experience a low level of appropriate instructional
technology, base validation on tradition, and offer symbolic
rewards. The tendency of non-formal programs, on the other hand,
is to find motivation within the learner, have a higher clarity
of objectives, experience a high level of appropriate instructional technology, base validation on performance and application,
and offer pragmatic rewards. Formal education is a ladder
reaching from one grade to another. Non-formal education
enables people to meet their needs and do their jobs more
effectively(15).

Pablo Freire, the leading Third World educator, has developed
a methodology and a philosophy called conscientization. He had
worked out his concepts primarily in relation to adult education
(more specifically alphabetization). Traditional education is
domesticating; it treats the student as an object, a thing to be
shaped or filled, an animal to be trained by rewards or punish-
ment. Freire begins with the person; he enters into dialogue
with the person in order to learn with him about his world. As
the person reflects upon his problems, faces them, and takes

action to solve them, he becomes more truly human. He becomes
conscious of his own nature and of his own capabilities; he
becomes a creative subject, the author of his own destiny, a
free participant in society. In this process no one teaches
anyone; people learn together in the real world(16).

Faced with the radical critique of traditional schooling and
the new approaches to education, theological educators are today
being challenged as never before to evaluate and change their
methods and programs. We must ask whether our institutions are
vehicles of oppression or liberation, of domestication or
humanization, of indoctrination or conscientization. And we
will want to consider the innovations of the extension movement
and the possibilities of the extension model in the search for
a new methodology for theological education.

Obviously the present state of theological education in the
Third World is very disappointing. Traditionally, of course,
seminary professors have been theologians and not educators,
concerned with research and content, not with methods and
communication. As scholars they have been beyond criticism.
Bible institute professors have been the purveyors of sacred
truths and thus equally beyond criticism and unencumbered with
methodological concerns. What goes on in these institutions is
still almost entirely domesticating, the imposition of a
curriculum made up of a certain number of required courses, the
transferral of pre-packaged subject matter primarily through
lectures, and production of graduates who will believe and
perform as the institution and the churches desire.

It would be dishonest to pretend that the extension movement
has broken with all that is domesticating and irrelevant in
theological education. There is in fact some evidence that the
extension approach is being used to indoctrinate and control
more efficiently and widely than ever before. Nevertheless the
change in structures in the extension model, which we have considered above, opens the way for the formation of a methodology
of conscientization.

In Guatemala the shift to extension brought into play a whole
new set of factors which in turn led to new methods. Once the
decision was made to meet with the students in each center just
once a week, it became evident that we could not possibly give
them the course content in the class time available (one to
three hours). They had to get it on their own, so it was
imperative to develop self-study materials. Lectures were
eliminated. It was also soon evident that the extension students
had a different perspective toward their studies. The majority
were involved in the ministry already, and almost any subject
they studied had direct application or significance for their

immediate situation(17). Then, too, these factors produced a
wholely different class experience. Having studied the basic
content of the courses before coming to class and being able to
relate the ideas and skills they were studying to a living
situation, the weekly sessions of professor and students came
alive. Again and again the professors were surprised and
inspired by the spontaneous discussion and grappling with real
issues that occurred almost constantly in the extension
centers(18).

As the program has developed, we have come to analyze and
understand more clearly the significance and potential of the
extension model, and these new insights coincide at many points
with the methodology of the open school, non-formal education,
and motivation. The students choose to study and they study
because the program is useful to them in their ministry, not
primarily because they want to pass their exams and get a
diploma. Teacher and students meet as colleagues in the work
of the church, sharing content and experience and learning
together. The teacher realized that the students are the ones
out on the front line doing the work of the ministry week by
week, day after day; the students realize that the important
thing is not to memorize their notes but to get on with the job.
Although the curriculum appears to be a traditional list of
courses, it functions very differently. The students take only
as many courses as they want, and they can choose the ones they
want. There is no pressure to take them all, to finish in a
certain period of time, or even to graduate. To some degree
extension claims to do less and is therefore able to do more.
We realize that the basic formation of Christian leaders is a
function of the Holy Spirit in the life of the individual at
home, in society, and in the church; we merely extend to them
the tools of theological studies so that they can perfect their
gifts and be recognized for what they are and for what they
do(19).

Special mention must be made here of programmed instruction,
since it has been widely promoted as an integral element in the
extension movement. In Guatemala we investigated programmed
instruction for practical reasons. We wanted to facilitate the
learning process for students who had to get the basic content
of their courses on their own. We resisted strongly the
behaviorist psychology which is behind much of the early
literature in this field. But we adopted certain basic
empirical principles: learning proceeds best from the known to
the unknown; learning depends on prompt use of newly acquired
information, concepts, or skills; learning increases when
appropriate use of the new material is confirmed; and learning
effectiveness is directly related to the perceived relevance of
the material in the life of the learner(20). We were greatly

stimulated by the discipline of defining for each course the
specific objectives, the target population, and the strategy and
steps required for the learner to advance from his beginning
position to the desired goal. We recognized the value of programming's built-in self-evaluation. The students' ability is
carefully measured at the beginning and at the end of each
course, and the program is repeatedly revised until the students
reach the desired level of performance; since the content is
laid out systematically, it is possible to identify and change
the weak links in the program. We believe that programmed
instruction can be an effective tool for theological education--
by extension and otherwise. But even more important we believe
that this kind of learning analysis, course development, and
evaluation is necessary in theological education in general--not
just for programmed materials. Programmed materials should not
be considered the only method or the solution of all the problems
of theological education. Care must be taken to maintain
objectives and procedures that are humanizing, not domesticating.
And the necessary investment must be made to develop, test,
revise, and publish quality materials.

All in all the extension model opens up intriguing possibilities for a new methodology in theological education. Having
broken the traditional elitist structures, the next logical
step is to change the domesticating methods of the past. In
the extension movement we are faced with new factors; a new kind
of student; new relationships between study and service, students
and teachers, the institution and the local church; new motivation and validation. And these given realities are leading us
toward a new understanding of the nature of theological education. They make possible and necessary a methodology of
conscientization for ministry in our churches.

III. THE CONTENT OF THEOLOGICAL EDUCATION--LIBERATION

The third and last fundamental concern of theological education that we shall consider here is content. Perhaps we should
have dealt with this point first, for this is where we find the
missiological basis for the other two. But it is in this area
of content that the extension movement has contributed least.
So we shall here present primarily a challenge to the extension
movement.

Radical critiques of contemporary societies, education, and
churches call in question not only our structures and our
methodology but above all our concept of man. They challenge us
to present a message of liberation. Liberation means self-
discovery and self-expression, self-determination and self-
development. It is a message for the human being that may be
conceptualized in words but must also be expressed in action.

In our contemporary world there is no more vital subject than liberation. It has been the cry of Third World nations, of youth, of women, of racial minorities, of the poor, and of the workers. In each case it represents the basic human need for identity and self-realization. Colonized peoples have to throw off foreign rule not only to get rid of the imperialists but also to prove themselves and to be able to write their own history. The black power movement in the U.S. is significant not only because it has gained legal rights and economic benefits for the blacks but primarily because it has given the blacks a certain amount of self-respect and self-confidence. Women's liberation is a continuing struggle for the full acceptance of 50% of the population as people. And the rebellion of youth is an afirmation of the freedom to reject values and standards of the past and to assert new values and standards. The demands of the poor and the working class must be interpreted not only in terms of the distribution of material goods but in terms of the social and spiritual dimensions ofhuman nature.

What then is the message of the schools? We have already noted that the structures and methodology of our educational isntitutions are essentially oppressive. The message being proclaimed, if indeed there is a message, seems to be: Go to the school in order to get a better job in order to earn more money in order to buy more things. Man is merely part of the economic system, a cog in the machinery of production. His purpose is to produce and consume. And the fact that he is being exploited and learning ot exploit is ignored.

And what is the message of the churches? Consider the protestant-evangelical-pentecostal movement in Latin America. The Marxist critique is all too true. We preach a message of individual salvation which utterly ignores the social sins, the terrible injustices and the inhumanity of man to man which are so prevalent. And within the protestant churches themselves there is little that can be called liberating. The local church is not only a refuge from the problems of life; it becomes another oppression enclosing and controlling the life of its members. Standards of behavior are largely negative and strictly enforced. In some cases styles of dress are restricted. Doctrine is taught as propositional truth to be accepted and defended, not to be questioned or discussed. And the almost daily worship services occupy most of the members' free time(21).

On the other hand there is hope for the future. The churches of Latin America have demonstrated tremendous vitality and growth. They proclaim a message of personal liberation, and this message is being accepted by the masses and at all levels of the population. Great emphasis is placed on the conversion experience, which is an act of self-determination. Significant changes take place in the life of the believers, especially in the home and in personal ethics. The current spirutualization of the Biblical message is obviously distorted, but the Bible is recognized as the absolute authority for faith and for all of life.

Now the question arises, What role could the extension movement play in the liberation of Latin America? It has already brought thousands of local leaders into the orbit of theological education for the first time; these men and women represent the grassroots of the church and all sectors of society. They study as they lead the churches; their theological growth is interpreted and applied in the local context. As they experience liberation themselves, they are in a position to bring about liberation in their churches and in their communities.

The Presbyterian Seminary of Guatemala is relatively conservative with regard to curriculum content. Nevertheless it is interesting to note at many points and in many ways a potential for liberation. The following illustrations suggest how even elementary and traditional theological materials can contribute to liberating action and reflection through an extension program.

Consider first the formation of basic skills. Probably the greatest need felt by the leaders in our churches is the ability to study and use the Bible independently (in the full sense of the word). The Bible is without question the basic sourcebook. Most of our students have no libraries; they are called upon to expound the Bible constantly; and they must base their entire ministry upon its teachings. Therefore we have discarded most of the usual introductory, historical, survey, and exegetical courses. The students work intensively through four selected books of the Bible (in Spanish) in order to develop their ability to do inductive Bible study on their own. If they reach the objectives of these courses, they will be able to discover for themselves the nature of the book, its historical background, and its structure; they will be able to take any passage and observe what it says, interpret what it means, and apply its message to their own situation; and they will be able to develop sermons and group study guides and investigations in Biblical Theology. As the students learn these skills, they will be liberated from tradition and ignorance and also from textbooks and schooling. They will be able to learn on their own and think for themselves. They not only learn a method of Bible study; they develop an approach to the Bible which gives them the freedom and the responsibility to create their own methods of Bible study(22).

Another important and urgently needed skill in our churches is the ability to lead without imposing. Many have pointed out the futility of vertical, one-way communication, which is so dominant in the protestant churches in Latin America. In most congregations the preaching pattern is maintained in all the regular services, prayer meetings, youth programs, and Sunday school. This kind of tradition is not easily challenged; it is not changed through exhortation or though books. Change must come through a new experience and a new understanding. Our extension students carry out their entire study program in small circles of group study in their local situation. This is a new experience for many; it brings new understanding of leadership and people, learning and truth, communication and community. And this approach is beginning to make its impact in the life of the congregations as the students try to break out of the old patterns of authoritarian leadership and formal programs.

A third essential skill in the ministry is the ability to train others. Without this ability, the leaders are continually overburdened, and the programs of the churches are excessively dependent upon one or two or three people. We have felt that the Seminary cannot and should not attempt to train all the leaders for the local Sunday schools, women's societies, deacons and elders, etc. But we have been able to simplify some units of the regular Seminary courses so that our students can teach them locally. For example one unit of the Christian education course is a brief training course for Sunday school teachers. All of our students study this unit, and a number have taught it in their churches to prospective teachers. The national women's organization has developed a short course for leaders in their organization. We offer this unit in our regular program in order to train local leaders to train others. This two-dimensional arrangement can be applied to courses in doctrine, homiletics, evangelism, etc. It makes the learning experience for our students much more meaningful and effective. It develops skills that are essential in the ministry. And it opens the way for the development of more leaders.

Liberation has to do with basic skills, and it also has to do with ideas and perception. As the program develops, we discover particular issues and concepts that are vital for the churches' understanding of their own situation, for solving their problems, and for determining their own future. One of the fundamental misconceptions that has been passed on from the Roman Catholic heritage and from the protestant missionary movement is a platonic understanding of the material and the spiritual. This underlies the pietist outlook toward religion, the exclusively individualist approach to salvation, and the general unconcern for social issues. It explains the strong

prejudice against programs of welfare and community development
in the churches. The people of Guatemala, including the
members of our churches, obviously have urgent physical and
social needs. One lesson of a course in inductive Bible study
deals specifically with the basic concept of "Flesh and Spirit
in Romans 8." We have simplified this lesson in popular terms,
and the students and others have used it over and over again in
their churches, in conferences, and in other situations.

One of the controversial issues in the churches today is
modern styles. Some churches have tried to prohibit mini-skirts
and slacks for women and long hair for men. The youth in these
churches either conform or rebel. A crisis has resulted in
which two young people's societies are almost dissolved. The
problem is not easy solved, because it represents deep prejudices
and a kind of loyalty to the Bible. We have developed a group
study guide based on the specific texts that are used to support
these standards. As our students discuss this issue and as we
use this study guide in the churches, we hope to develop not
only an understanding of Paul's instructions concerning styles
of dress but also a new outlook toward the authority and
application of the Bible. This will help the churches free
themselves from their prejudices and from the literal imposition
of Bible teachings. We believe that these controversies can be
a liberating experience which will lead to a new outlook toward
other problems in the future.

Liberation in theological education takes place through the
development of basic skills and concepts, but it has to do
fundamentally with people. The most rewarding part of our
experience has been to watch the development of Moisés Alvarez,
Benjamín Jacobs, Mardoqueo Muñoz, Matías Monterroso, Angel
Becerra, Juan Estrada, Miguel Chacaj, Lidia de Mansilla, Samuel
Mejía, Gilberto Cabrera, José Romero, Julio Paz and his wife,
Silvestre Laines, Olga de Ramírez, Hugo Alvarado, and many
others. Florentín Sontay, a young latinized Quiche Indian,
lived in Coatepeque with his wife and family, worked as an
itinerant salesman, carrying his merchandise to three or four
nearby markets each week, and he was active as a deacon and
preacher in his church. He was able to give three off days
weekly to his theological studies, completed the entire program
in just three years, and has been serving as a fulltime pastor
for the past six years in areas which had not been able to
support a pastor. Angel Martínez was in his 30's and had a
large family, owned and administered three fincas (coffee, sugar
cane, cattle), and had recently been converted (and liberated
from alcoholism) when he began his theological studies in the
San Felipe extension center. He is now an elder and for the
past three years he has directed the Synod's community development program--without salary. He served for a time recently as

Mayor of San Felipe, is president of a large cooperative in the
area, and has raised a prophetic voice for liberation in the
whole church and in the communities where he works. Margarita
de López and her husband Raúl attend Seminary classes at Central
Church in the capital. She has been active, especially in the
Sunday school, ever since childhood, and now she is president of
the national women's organization of the Presbyterian Church.
She prepared a panel on the controversial matter of women's
dress for the recent annual women's conference and is beginning
to raise questions about the role of women in our denomination,
which excludes them from ordination (as elders or pastors) and
from the government of the church.

    Space does not permit more examples of the people who come
through or are now in the extension program--the many church
workers who have become the pastors of Suchitepéquez, North, and
Pacific Presbyteries, the first Mam Indians to be graduated from
our Seminary, the elders of the Centro América Church, the
professional men and women in the university level center in
Guatemala City, the group of pastors in Occidente Presbytery who
took the new course in pastoral psychology and had to rethink
their whole ministry, the outstanding young leaders in the
Progreso Church, the group in Coatepeque that has run a half-
hour, daily Gospel radio broadcast for the past six years,
officers of presbyteries and the Synod and other organizations
and boards, etc. It is only as we get to know these men and
women, their circumstances, their ministry, and their study
experience that we can begin to see the real significance of the
Guatemala extension program(23). These and others like them
around the world are the ones who can bring about basic changes
in their churches and communities, renewal of the whole understanding of the ministry, and the formation of a living relevant
theology for and of the people of God. These people, who are
beyond the reach of traditional seminaries, make extension an
exciting and essential alternative model for theological education today.

    As we come to the conclusion of this presentation, we must
bring together the three basic concerns that have been analyzed:
the structures of theological education, the methodology of
theological education, and the content of theological education.
It should be evident that the most advanced courses in the
theology of liberation will be useless if the basic structures
of our institutions are elitist or if our methodology is
domesticating(24). Rather we must build structures that respect
and incorporate local values and leadership. We must deal with
our students as human beings who can solve their own problems
and lead their congregations. Then we can explore with them the
meaning of the Biblical message in their ministry today. Contextualization, conscientization, and liberation are essentially
one process, one experience, one movement.

God has raised up His people in every village and town and city, in every sub-culture, in every sector of the population. He has given many gifts and provided many leaders, most of whom have had little or no training. Through the extension model these men and women can develop their skills and their under-standing of the Gospel; they can genuinely lead their congrega-tions in their missionary task; they can experience and proclaim and demonstrate the Biblical message of liberation in their diverse situations.

We all recognize that the heart of the Gospel is redemption, and redemption is synonymous with liberation(25). Western Christianity has narrowed and distorted this concept so that it means primarily liberation of the individual from personal sin and condemnation. But the historical basis of this concept is the liberation of the Hebrews from slavery in Egypt, an event which was at one and the same time religious, cultural, political, and violent. We live in a time when this message of liberation is anxiously awaited by people everywhere. This message will not be effective if it is proclaimed by political demagogues or by intellectual theorists or by religious elites. It must be proclaimed by God's people through their liberating action in the world.

NOTES

1. Ronald and Beatrice Gross, ed, *Radical School Reform* (New York: Simon and Schuster, 1969), p. 13.

2. Wayne C. Weld, ed, *Extension*, Vol. I, No. 6, p. 3.

3. Ralph D. Winter, *Theological Education by Extension* (South Pasadena: William Carey Library, 1969), Book I is an anthology showing how the movement began. The first inter-national workshop at Armenia, Colombia is reported on pp. 148-178.

4. Orlando Fals-Borda, "Colombia: A Mortgaged Nation," transl. from "Colombia Hipotecada" (Geneva: May 10, 1969), describes how his country was chosen to be a model for development in Latin America. For five years (1962-1967) Alliance for Progress funds poured in, intended to bring about basic social changes. The actual effect was this: "the country was mortgaged to save the ruling class."

5. This imperialism is often unintentional. For example, a TV
   station wishes to develop programs with indigenous music
   and art. But it may cost them $2000.00 to prepare one half-
   hour program compared with $500.00 to buy and translate a
   prepared program from the U.S. showing U.S. cultural values.

6. Ivan Illich, "The Futility of Schooling in Latin America,"
   reprinted from *Saturday Review* (New York: April 20, 1968) in
   Alternatives in Education, CIDOC Cuaderno No. 1001
   (Cuernavaca: 1970), p. 66/7: "Schools grade and, therefore,
   they degrade. They make the degraded accept his own
   submission. Social seniority is bestowed according to the
   level of schooling achieved. Everywhere in Latin America
   more money for schools means more privilege for a few at the
   cost of most, and this patronage of an elite is explained as
   a political ideal. This ideal is written into laws which
   state the patently impossible: equal scholastic opportunities
   for all." "The resulting steep educational pyramid defines
   a rationale for the corresponding levels of social status.
   Citizens are 'schooled' into their places." See also by the
   same author *Deschooling Society* (New York: Harper and Row,
   1971).

7. Roland Allen, "The Case for Voluntary Clergy," *The Ministry
   of the Spirit* (Grand Rapids: William B. Eerdmans, 1970),
   pp. 155-159. Allen questioned over 40 years ago the wisdom
   of imposing Western patterns of professional training and
   support for the ministry in non-Western countries. He
   recognized the necessity and the value of ordaining local,
   natural leaders.

8. *Ministry in Context* (Bromley: The Theological Education
   Fund, 1972), p. 20: Contextualization "means all that is
   implied in the familiar term 'indigenization' and yet seeks
   to press beyond. Contextualization has to do with how we
   assess the peculiarity of Third World contexts. Indigenization tends to be used in the sense of responding to the
   Gospel in terms of a traditional culture. Contextualization,
   while not ignoring this, takes into account the process of
   secularity, technology, and the struggle for human justice
   which characterize the historic moment of nations in the
   Third World."

9. Winter, *op. cit.*, pp. 29-35.

10. *El Seminarista*, (San Felipe: Seminario Evangélico
    Presbiteriano de Guatemala), January and February, 1973,
    includes a survey of the extension graduates from 1965 to
    1972. Of the 38 graduates, 18 are pastors, 15 are

evangelists or church workers, and 5 are laymen. Since the extension program began in 1963 many more pastors and church workers have participated in the program. But the majority have always been laymen. A much lower proportion of laymen are expected to graduate, as this is often not their goal.

11. Gross, *op. cit.*, p. 17.

12. See especially the works of John Holt: *How Children Fail* (New York: Dell Publishing Co., 1964), *How Children Learn* (New York: Dell Publishing Co., 1967), and *The Under-achieving Child* (New York: Pitman, 1969).

13. Edward B. Nyquist and Gene R. Hawes, *Open Education: A Sourcebook for Parents and Teachers* (New York: Bantam Books, 1972), contains a wide selection of the writings by key authors in this field plus bibliography.

14. This description was taken almost verbally from Appendix A of the Bylaws of the Integrated Day Center, the only open school in Guatemala.

15. This paragraph is based on papers and addresses by Ted Ward, specialist in nonformal education at the College of Education, Michigan State University.

16. Paulo Freire, *Educación Liberadora* (Medellín: Editorial Prisma, 1972), pp. 23-35; *Pedagogía del Oprimido* (Montevideo: Tierra Nueva, 1970), pp. 75-99; *Cultural Action for Freedom* (Harvard Educational Review, Monograph Series No. 1), pp. 27-52; *La Educación como Práctica de la Libertad* (México: Siglo Veintiuno, 1972).

17. Traditional seminaries have tried to provide practical application of theological studies through field work, internships, clinical training, etc., but they always project the student into these situations artificially. In extension the student is solidly rooted in his own home, church, and community.

18. Ted Ward, *The Rail Fence: An Analogy for the Training of Professionals* (Holt: Associates of Urbanus, 1972). Originally written as a model of secular training programs in the U.S., this article has been widely used as an explanation of the basic elements in theological education by extension.

19. There are of course many variations of the extension model. One creative experiment is described by George Patterson,

"Modifications of the Extension Method for Areas of
Limited Education Opportunity," *Extension Seminary*, No. 4,
1972. The focus of this program is upon church planting
by lay pastors who are semi-literate and who barely
realize that they are enrolled in an institution.

20. Ted and Margaret Ward, *Programmed Instruction for
    Theological Education by Extension* (CAMEO, 1970), p. 9.

21. Christian Lalive d'Epinay, "Protestant Churches and the
    Latin American Revolution," transl. from *Cristianismo y
    Sociedad*, Año VI, Nos. 16 and 17, 1968, p. 21-30. See
    also his *El Refugio de las Masas* (Santiago: Editorial del
    Pacífico, 1968).

22. We have prepared three lengthy, programmed texts which
    attempt to do this: F. Ross Kinsler, *Inductive Study of
    the Book of Jeremiah* (South Pasadena: William Carey
    Library, 1971), *Inductive Study of the Book of Mark* (South
    Pasadena: William Carey Library, 1972), and *Estudio
    Inductivo del Libro de Romanos* (San Felipe: Seminario
    Evangélico Presbiteriano del Guatemala, 1974).

23. F. Ross Kinsler, "What is Extension?" *Extension Seminary*,
    No. 2, 1970, pp. 1-4, describes the students in two
    presbyteries at one particular time.

24. Several of the "high level" protestant seminaries in
    Latin America are involved in the formation of a theology
    of liberation, but they are out of touch with and have
    lost the confidence of the churches. Similarly radical
    movements such as Iglesia y Sociedad en América Latina
    (ISAL) have gone so far out in their thinking as to have
    almost no effect upon the thinking of the churches.

25. Several Latin American theologians have explored and
    applied the Biblical concept of liberation for our time.
    One of the clearest and most helpful exposition is by
    José Míguez Bonino, "Theology and Liberation," transl. from
    Fichas de ISAL, Año III, No. 3, 1971, pp. 2-5.

5

Open Theological Education

Theological education by extension came into existence in response to a vast, urgent need that was not being met by traditional seminaries and Bible institutes, viz. the training of mature, local church leaders who were (and are) largely excluded from residence programs. The movement spread rapidly not only to meet that need but as an alternative pattern of theological education, covering the whole field, i.e. preparation for candidates for the ministry, lay leadership training, continuing education for pastors, etc. Some theologians, educators, and anthropologists began to believe that extension could not only extend theological education to many more people but also reach specifically the people who should be reached and do a more effective job by teaching them in the context of their own churches and communities. From the beginning, there was fuel of controversy, and polarization has taken place in varying degrees and forms. In general, however, the challenge and issues raised by the extension movement have provoked a healthy and necessary process of reflexion, evaluation, and change, and many theological educators on both sides are now seriously and radically considering ways to improve their work. The dialectic is moving toward a new synthesis in which all are becoming increasingly open to new concepts and experiments and innovations in theological education(1).

At this historic moment perhaps the most significant insights coming to us from other educational fields can be grouped under the heading "open education." For some time we have noted that the theological education by extension movement runs parallel to or is part of a worldwide revolution in education, and we have

drawn valuable support and useful models from non-theological
fields. The present article will make use of concepts and
models of open education that can be very helpful in the field
of theological education, particularly with a view to going
beyond the residence-extension polemic.

First, we shall consider the structure and methods of
theological education on the basis of a case study, the Open
University of Great Britain. Then we shall look at what is
going on in the widely discussed open primary schools in order
to stimulate our thinking with regard to motivation and
curriculum design in theological education. Third, we shall
analyze the role of the student and the role of the teacher in
theological education in the light of a model worked out by two
open school educators. Finally, we shall borrow from open
education philosophy in a consideration of evaluation and
validation in theological education.

It would not be presumptuous to say that theological education not only has much to learn from other fields of education
but also something to contribute. We shall gain much from the
new developments in open education specially. But we should
keep in touch with these developments also because we can
contribute significant insights and models from our own
experience. The extension movement in particular provides a
viable model for non-theological educators to look at both in
Third World countries, where traditional schooling can reach
only a tiny minority of the population, and in the industrial-
ized nations, where there is widespread disillusionment with the
schooling establishment.

The primary purpose of this article is to encourage residence
and extension theological educators, through the formation of a
new concept which we shall call "open theological education," to
join forces in the unending search for new structures, methods,
and models for better service to the churches in the development
of genuine leadership and the sharing of ministry among the
whole people of God. Included in each section are practical
suggestions that can be used to introduce open education concepts to people who are related to theological education.

I. STRUCTURES AND METHODS

A. The Open University of Great Britain(2) is a bold step
forward in higher education and a fascinating case study for all
who are interested in new structures and methods of adult
education.

Apparently the idea of an Open University began to take shape
in 1963, and preliminary decisions were made by the British

government in 1966. By 1969 huge allocations were going into
the project, the bulk of the staff was recruited, and course
production began in earnest. In 1970 applications were
received for the first year of classes in 1971. 43,444 people
applied, although only 25,000 students could be accepted. By
1974 the facilities had expanded, and the enrollment of students
in accredited degree courses was well over 40,000.

The Open University offers 3 programs: undergraduate, post-
experience, and post-graduate. The vast majority of the
students are taking the basic university courses under six
faculties: Arts, Maths, Science, Social Sciences, Technology,
and Educational Studies. The post-experience courses are for
advanced knowledge or updating in specific fields for people
who do not wish to study for a degree. The University plans to
offer post-graduate studies for advanced degrees, including the
Ph.D.

It is exciting to see how the Open University has broken with
traditional structures and methods of higher education in order
to achieve its primary goal: openness to people. The British
educational system was until recently one of the most selective,
class-conscious, oligarchical in the world. Now the Open
University proudly opens its doors to people of all walks of
life and designs its programs especially for those who are
older, fully employed, and tied down with family and other
commitments. Whereas previously less than 10% of the population
reached the universities after scaling the schooling ladder, now
anyone can apply directly to the Open University with no formal
educational qualifications. Now not only the young and the
privileged but also working people can obtain a university
education.

This particular experiment in higher education brings
together imagination, heavy economic investment, and the best
educational and technological resources available anywhere.
Obviously few organizations or even nations have at their
disposal such resources. But the striking lesson of the Open
University is its openness to new methods and structures. This
can and should be emulated everywhere, especially where resources
are very limited.

The Open University program is built around the student who
is over 21 (an experimental group 18-21 is being tested), is
probably employed full-time, and studies mainly at home in his
spare time. "The most important element in the instructional
system is the correspondence package, which most students
receive every week." A full credit course is made up of 32
weekly units; each unit includes study material and assignments
and takes 10 to 14 hours to complete; some exercises are

are programmed and include feedback, while others are sent in
for checking by computer or for marking and comments by a tutor.
Weekly radio and television programs are integrated into the
home study materials, especially for lower level courses. There
are about 300 study centers all over the country, equipped with
television and radio receivers and in some cases replay
facilities and computer terminals. At these centers students
meet in the evenings with tutors and counsellors for help and
supervision. Another essential part of the instructional system
is summer school; lower level students are required to spend one
week in residence for each full course. This provides an intensive study experience on a university campus, allows staff and
students to meet together and share group study, and provides
science and technology students an opportunity for laboratory
work. The latter are also provided home experiment kits for use
during the year, and these include chemicals, equipment, and
specially designed instruments.

In short the Open University combines correspondence courses,
radio and television, tutorial help, extension centers, and
short periods of residence in an integrated, decentralized program of higher education. This varied system is represented by
the following diagram, taken from one of the manuals of the
University.

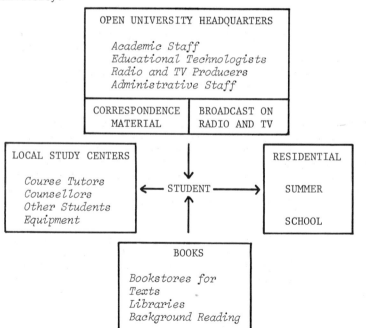

Through this open structure the institution has been able to offer a university education to the whole population of Great Britain, not just the privileged few. In addition the Open University states, "We are also open to new ideas in the field of teaching methods and technical innovations." At the heart of the program an Institute of Educational Technology has been established to prepare and revise constantly the course materials and methods through a process of evaluation. Since the program is decentralized and accessible to all and far more economical than traditional university training, it will continue to grow. It is already the largest university in Great Britain; if it remains open to new structures and methods, it may one day reach more people than all the other universities put together.

B. The value of this case study for theological education is self-evident, especially at the present stage in our discussions over residence and extension. Rather than defend one way or make simplistic contrasts between 2 ways of doing theological education we should consider many possible alternatives and combinations and search for the most effective structures and methods for each situation. If the governmental and educational authorities of Great Britain, with almost unlimited resources at their disposal, felt free to use correspondence and home study as well as extension centers and residence for a fully accredited system of university education, surely theological educators can lay aside their prejudices and see the value of different structures and methods. If theological educators will look for more open structures and become more open to the use of different educational methods, their programs will doubtless become much more diverse and reach far more people in the future.

The Presbyterian Seminary of Guatemala maintained a traditional 3-year residence program for 25 years. It had become increasingly evident that this program was not meeting the needs of the churches--for several reasons. The structure limited the student body to a handful of young unproven men; it uprooted them from their communities and sub-cultures and homogenized them for an urban, middle class profession; then it sent them out to poor, mostly rural congregations. Naturally the maladjustments, frustrations, and losses were many. In 1963 the Seminary initiated its extension structure. In 4 years the enrollment grew from 6 to 200; the students now remain in their varied contexts and study parttime; they do not become economically dependent on the churches either for their studies or for future service; they are generally mature, experienced leaders; and they are able to relate theological studies to ministerial practice as never before. This change in structure brought about changes in methodology. Faculty members meet with local groups just once a week for 2 to 3 hours; self-study materials

(workbooks to accompany the textbooks) guide the students
through the basic course content at home; the weekly center
meetings are discussion seminars which review and clarify the
material studied during the week and integrate it with the
student's life and ministry.

The Guatemala experiment soon became the model of dozens of
extension programs all over Latin America. The needs were
similar, and they were very great. Probably 80% of the protestant congregations throughout the continent were led by men
with no theological training. The traditional Bible institutes
and seminaries were producing a limited number of graduates who
largely competed for the few, more prosperous churches.

The extension movement is important for 2 fundamental
reasons. First, it has opened up theological education to
local church leaders in a way that has never before been
possible. Not just candidates for the professional ministry
but elders and deacons and ordinary members, minority groups,
working people, people of different academic levels, young and
old, all have access to theological training, which means that
they can develop their gifts and become fully incorporated into
the ministry of the body of Christ. Second, the extension movement is important because it has broken the established
traditions and opened up new possibilities for theological
education. Just as extension structures and methods have been
able to meet certain needs as never before, we may in the future
discover other structures and methods that will complement or
surpass the work of both residence and extension seminaries.
At this moment extension leaders are tempted to think that they
have the only valid system and to try to impose it on every
situation. But the real challenge of today is to remain open
to new possibilities.

Openness to new structures and methods should be a stimulating, if at times disconcerting, challenge to all of us. The
following is a simple workshop exercise which can be used to
present this challenge to a group of theological educators or
churchmen. First, make a simple survey of the leadership needs
of a specific region or country and define an appropriate goal
for theological education in that region. Let the participants
themselves come up with the description and the goal. Second,
make a list of the resources available to the churches in that
area for leadership development and training. The group should
not limit its thinking to the traditional concept of an academic
institution; they may include the resources of the local church
(such as the Sunday school), publications and other means of
communication, regional church gatherings, etc. To stimulate
their thinking you may point out cases where the growth of
congregations and the spontaneous development of leaders is

inversely proportional to the formal theological training
available. Third, analyze the factors that limit the possibilities for theological education programs in that region. The
participants may come up with economic, geographical, cultural,
ideological factors, etc. There may not be sufficient funds to
set up and run a residence program; distances may be too great
and transportation too difficult for an extension program; the
local leaders may be illiterate or too busy to study more than
2 or 3 hours a week. The final stage in this exercise is to
design one or more possible programs of theological education
for the region with the resources available and within the given
limitations. Be sure to encourage the participants to be
original and creative and not confine their thinking to existing
patterns. For the earlier steps in this analysis you may ask
the participants to work out their ideas individually, then
discuss their findings together. For the final stage it may be
more effective for them to work out their proposals in small
groups, then compare the results.

All of us need to think through periodically the possibilities
for theological education structures and methods. We should
analyze our own programs and reconsider our own situations, and
we should study what others are doing in other places. As
theological education becomes more open, new models with new
structures and methods will lead us to greater diversity and
greater service(3). In the past theological education has been
debilitated by two serious faults: a structure and methodology
which limited its benefits to an exclusive minority and a
mentality which accepted only this structure and methodology.
Today's challenge is to open our minds to new structures and
methods and to build structures and discover methods that will
open up theological education to the whole people of God.

II. MOTIVATION AND CURRICULUM DESIGN

A. The concept of the open school or open classroom(4) is
more controversial than the concept of the Open University, and
it deals with issues that are more complex. The following
analysis is based on articles and personal experience related to
open primary schools. It will focus on motivation and curriculum
design and lead to a consideration of this aspect of theological
education.

Walk into an open school, and you will see immediately that
it is different. No rows of desks... and no rows of pupils
listening to a teacher. No bells and no schedule of classes.
In fact, few or no classes at all. And perhaps no grade levels.
It may seem as if there is considerable confusion, certainly
much more free moving about than you have ever seen in a
traditional school, and probably more noise than you would think

proper. There will be a large quantity and variety of materials on display, laid out on tables and shelves, or simply piled up within reach. And lots of talking is going on all the time. Each child probably works on 2 or 3 major projects during a given day and makes regular use of books and magazines, art materials, programmed instruction, games, plants and animals, etc. Most notable, if you think about it, will be the amount of individual involvement--active, self-directed, and sometimes supervised.

The overall content of what is studied in an open school is not so different from what children study in other schools. But the curriculum design is very different. To a great extent the curriculum of a traditional school is closed; the state, the school, and the teacher determine beforehand the courses to be offered, the texts to be used, the calendar and schedule of classes, and the specific content and procedure of each period. The open school curriculum begins with the conviction that each child has his own interests, learning style, abilities, and needs. And it offers him the opportunity to study different things--on his own, with a friend, or in a group--as these interests develop. It is to a large extent open.

The Integrated Day Center in Guatemala City occupies a large 10-room house with its 52 students, 3 full time teachers and a kindergarten teacher, 3 assistants, a secretary, and several parttime helpers (mothers), plus a dog, a goat, a guinea pig, and about 20 mice. The curriculum focuses upon 5 learning centers: for math, science, reading, art, and life, which combines language arts and social studies. Each center (one or two rooms) tries to stimulate interest and provides materials for exploration and study. In the math center, for example, you will find beans, pebbles, scales, geo-boards, cusinaire rods, liquid measuring devices, some math games, and math books; on the walls you will see graphs, number puzzles, questions to provoke your curiosity, and reports on math projects. Each student begins the day by planning his schedule with the help of a homeroom teacher. He will check the master schedule to see if there is a special movie, play practice, or a committee meeting; he will probably include a special class in math or "life" or science (there is one special class for each age level in each of these areas each week); he will not forget to water his plants up on the roof; and his homeroom teacher will generally encourage him to include some time for all 5 learning centers. These activities laid out before him, he then goes off to the different centers to take up material he has been working on regularly, to browse through magazines and books, or to carry on a long-term project.

Educators have long recognized that motivation is the vital key to learning, and open classroom educators have demonstrated

how to relate motivation to curriculum design. Rather than
pre-determine and then impose a program on the students regard-
less of their interests, it starts with their interests, allows
them to plan their learning experiences, and encourages them to
broaden and deepen their whole field of interests. Rather than
subject the students to a rigid schedule of classes, courses,
and grades, it offers them a world of learning opportunities,
allows them to choose their own subjects, and generally
encourages them to give as much time as they need for any
given project. Rather than assign material to be copies or
read and "learned," homework to be done slavishly night after
night, and exams to be taken and courses to be passed, it places
at their disposal a stimulating environment, as many educational
materials as possible, and teachers who can actually work with
them as personal advisors in the different learning centers.
Rather than push 20 or 30 or 40 students through a set program
in lock step, the open school curriculum is designed to guide
each one along an individual path toward his own goals.

Many questions remain unanswered in this brief description of
open schools, and it is not possible to deal with them all here.
Some of the more basic issues will be touched on in the following section as we consider the role of the student and the role
of the teacher and in the final section as we deal with evaluation and validation.

B. The open school approach to motivation and curriculum
design can be very suggestive for theological education.
Obviously residence and extension seminary programs fall under
the criticisms of open school educators, with a few belated
exceptions. And both residence and extension theological
educators can learn something basic about curriculum design from
the open schools.

The typical seminary or Bible institute has a long list of
courses, generally divided into standard categories or departments, probably not integrated or coordinated, based on obscure
reasoning, and only tenuously related to the practice of the
ministry. Even the rash of curriculum revisions that has
characterized some institutions in recent years is mostly just
a reordering and rearranging of the same old stuff to be passed
on to the students gratuitously. Founders and leaders of
extension programs, faced with the possibility of designing
completely new curricula, have frequently tied up the old course
material in new, more rigid, programmed packages. Theological
curricula are largely closed and uninspiring.

What should be the natural motivation of ministerial candidates as they study the Gospel story from Genesis to the 1970's,
from Adam to Abraham to Moses to David to Jesus to Paul to
Augustine to Aquinas to Luther and Calvin to Wesley to Barth

and Bonhoeffer (in whatever order), from the woes of Jeremiah to
the scandals of Watergate, from the spontaneous expansion of the
Apostolic Church to church planting in nearby villages or suburbs
today, from the First to Twentieth Century gnostics and
judaizers, etc, etc. What a world of fascinating material for
the theological student to explore, investigate, correlate, and
incorporate into his own life and ministry! But we have
destilled all this appetizing material into heavy textbooks and
dry lectures or mechanical manuals. We have determined what the
student must study, the order in which he will "take" it, the
exact number of hours he will give to each subject, and the
specific exercises and examinations he will have to go through.

Open school educators have noted that young children learn a
fantastic quantity of information and skills in the pre-school
years but that by the time they have been in school for 3 or 4
years their natural curiosity and learning drive have to a great
extent been killed. Isn't this what happens in seminaries and
Bible institutes also? After 3 or more years of theological
processing, relatively few graduates continue any regular
program of self-motivated study throughout the rest of their
ministry.

One way of introducing the idea of an open theological
curriculum would be to hold a workshop in which faculty members
and students would be challenged to design alternative ways of
presenting the curriculum as a whole, department areas, specific
courses, and/or inter-disciplinary studies. Before assigning
each group or individual a task, it would be helpful to describe
and discuss an open school program (as above) and perhaps give
some more specific examples from the 3-R's or in the field of
theological studies. The basic principle which should be
incorporated into each project is to begin with the student's
interests/concerns/problems/needs.

Following are some brief examples that may be useful to
stimulate further exploration. In the area of Bible, instead of
requiring all students to study certain books of the O.T. and
N.T. according to prepared syllabi, let each one choose the books
that he would like to study (individually or in teams), work out
his own methodology (with an advisor), and present his findings
to the class, indicating especially how he plans to use this
material (and the methods) in his ministry. In church history
rather than force all the students to go through the entire
text chapter by chapter, each student could study a specific
period, a great person, a specific controversy or problem, etc.
In theology each student could investigate a specific doctrine
or doctrinal issue that he is concerned about and develop a
presentation of that issue for use in the class and in his
church. In Christian education separate units could be planned

on the Sunday school, group dynamics, small group Bible studies, the family, community problems and Christian witness, youth activities, leadership training, etc., and the student could select any 4 or make up his own units. A course in ethics could be designed so that the students would form teams to investigate and report on different moral questions or problems they are facing.

Opening up the theological curriculum should foment the student's natural motivation, and, as most educators agree, motivation is the *sine qua non* of learning. What the student wants to learn, chooses to investigate, discovers for himself, analyzes, relates to his own life and ministry, and presents to a class will be far more significant and permanent and useful than what someone else tells him to learn, investigates for him, and explains to him. Some skills and areas of knowledge require more systematic development and guidance than others. Traditional and programmed texts, lectures, and other materials and methods are not necessarily excluded by any means. But it is quite evident that the effectiveness of theological curricula will be directly proportional to their openness to the student's interests.

Theological education by extension faces a peculiar challenge in this area. On the one hand extension students are generally highly motivated, and their motivation is primarily directed toward service in the churches. If they are leaders already, they must deal constantly with the practical problems, basic concerns, and multiple needs of the ministry. This provides an excellent basis for the theological curriculum. On the other hand the extension structure gives them only limited time for study and very brief contact with fellow students and teachers. If the extension center meeting is held for just one 2-hour period per week, it is very difficult to deal with the many, diverse interests of all the members of that group.

In an extension center the students are generally encouraged to take the same courses in order to make optimum use of class time, but at least the group can decide what courses to take and their sequence. The course content may be largely programmed or prepared for home study; this is to enable the students to cover the basic material at their own convenience and to free class time for discussion of student concerns, usually in relation to the courses. The group may decide to suspend the regular coursework at any time in order to deal with problems they are facing; there need be no set calendar and no rush to finish the courses. The main focus of the program should be not what goes on in the class but what is happening in the churches.

An open theological curriculum--in residence or by extension--
should be based on the students' interests, problems, and needs.
It should begin with their needs and respond to their interests
as they develop. It should help them solve their problems and
carry out their ministry. As we open up the theological
curriculum, we should tap an artesian well of motivation in our
students that will carry their learning experiences well beyond
the classroom, courses, and graduation.

III. THE ROLE OF THE STUDENT AND THE ROLE OF THE TEACHER

A. Probably the most crucial aspect of open education is
the relationship between student and teacher. The role of the
student and the role of the teacher are both radically changed.
Defining these new roles is not easy; working them out in actual
practice is of course even more difficult. It is high time that
theological educators and students begin to struggle with these
issues and try to redefine their roles.

The description of open school curricula in the previous
section brings out the fact that open schools are student-
centered. The student is active not only in the sense of
participating in the learning experiences but also in determining the content, direction, sequence, and pace of these learning
experiences. This description can easily fall into the popular
concept that all learning systems can be located along a
continuium with "teacher-centered" at one end and "student-
centered" at the other end. According to this simplistic
analysis, if the student takes on greater responsibility, the
teacher must take less responsibility. Or if the teacher takes
an active, authoritative role, the student necessarily plays a
minor, passive role.

But the open school is as much teacher-centered as it is
student-centered. In fact, the teacher is required to play a
far more active, creative, demanding role in an open classroom
than he does in a traditional classroom, where the schedule,
course work, and materials are all laid out for him ahead of time
and all the students follow the prescribed program simultaneously.
Open school advocates are as much concerned about liberating the
teacher from an oppressive, closed system as they are about
liberating the student. They are trying to develop a person-
centered environment in which both students and teachers are
thinking, feeling, active, growing human beings.

To express this concept and differentiate it from other kinds
of schooling, the following model was designed(5). Instead of
placing student and teacher at opposite ends of one continuum,
it presents the role of the student and the role of the teacher
as separate though related factors. The student may play a

relatively active or passive role in the learning process, and
the teacher may play a relatively active or passive role in the
learning process also.

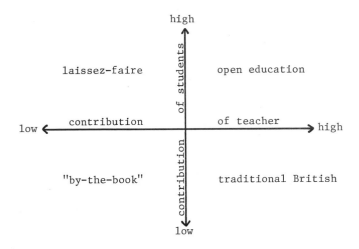

The originators of this model locate open schools in the
upper right-hand quadrant because both teachers and students are
profoundly involved in the development and direction of learning.
They place laissez-faire or free schools in the upper left-hand
quadrant because the children largely determine what goes on in
the classroom, and the teachers are limited to understanding and
responding to the children and accepting whatever they decide to
do. For the lower right-hand quadrant they suggest the traditional British schools as typical because there the teacher is
often an active professional who chooses carefully his
curriculum materials, diagnoses the students' progress, develops
his own way of teaching, and may emphasize topics that interest
him; the student plays a correspondingly minor role in decision
making, curriculum development, and class direction. The lower
left-hand quadrant is characterized as "by-the-book" and refers
to those classrooms where both students and teachers slavishly
and mindlessly accept and go through the prescribed classes,
texts, exercises, examinations, etc., day after day, year after
year, whether or not they are interesting, reasonable, relevant,
or meaningful. Perhaps few schools should be located in the
extreme corner of any quadrant. It is more likely that the
majority will be found converging toward the center with some
aspects crossing over into neighboring quadrants. But the model
is a useful device for conceptualizing and analizing the role of

the student and the role of the teacher in different educational systems, and it helps to bring out the special contribution of open education.

What then is the role of the teacher in an open school? There is no easy formula, but several functions should be mentioned. (1) The teacher prepared an environment where learning can take place. Since the students are not required to study a particular set of courses and materials, the teacher makes available equipment, literature, things that will catch and hold their interest. Since each student is encouraged to follow his own path to learning, there must be many and diverse materials available. It is not possible and it is not necessary ot have unlimited resources, but the teacher must be sensitive to the nature of the materials he does find. Much has been written on the use of common things such as sand (wet and dry), water (for measuring, etc.), and objects to be found in every basement or attic. An open school teacher has an enormous task making provision for learning. (2) He is also an advisor who counsels, guides, and extends the learning experiences of each student. If the students were left on their own in a classroom with all these materials and instruments, they might be careful, creative, dedicated to learning, but it is more likely that their interest would soon wander, materials would get strewn around and mixed up, objects would break, conflicts would develop. The teacher is a very necessary partner who helps the student identify his interests, decide on a project and a fruitful path of investigation, see the potential value of the materials that are available, and go beyond the learning implications that are at first evident. Here again the open school teacher's responsibility is very complex and demanding. Instead of following neatly defined paths of learning sequence in science, social studies, etc., he has to be able to break into these fields (and interrelate them) at any given point. (3) In order to carry out these teaching functions the teacher himself must be deeply involved in these learning events. If he is simply trying to entertain the student by putting attractive objects and activities before him, he will soon be exploited by the student and run out of material. If he is an authoritarian figure always insisting that the student keep working, he may never learn what the student really wants to do. If he is only superficially interested in the student's projects, the student will soon find out and lose interest or break off contact. The open school teacher must be warm, honest with the students, and excited by what goes on in the classroom as he himself discovers new relationships, works on new projects, and sees new possibilities for learning. In other words, the teacher must be a growing person in order to help others grow.

The open classroom provides a genuine opportunity for students and teachers to be active, creative, growing people. The demands on both are formidable; the relationship is complex; the problems are many. But as students and teachers work out these roles, learning can take place at the highest level of human existence.

B. What is the role of the student in our seminaries and Bible institutes, and what should his role be? What is the role of the teacher in our theological institutions, and what should his role be? The model designed for analyzing open schools can be useful to us as we analyze our present situation and as we look for ways to improve our work. The experience and experiments of open schools may help us redefine our roles and work out these roles as we move toward the formation of more open theological education.

The 2-dimensional model showing the contribution of the student and the contribution of the teacher in the educational process could be presented for discussion at a workshop for theological students and professors. The participants should try to locate their own institution(s) somewhere in the model, and they could also consider how other institutions compare with their own. There may be differences of opinion; in many cases there will be no simple answer; there will probably be some crossing over from one quadrant to another. This analysis could lead to a second session in which small groups would make a study of the student factor or the teacher factor. In other words, one group would list the ways in which the student is active and the ways in which he is passive, then try to come to some consensus as to the present role of the student in their institution(s). Another group would do the same with regard to the role of the teacher. These groups should then come together to share their conclusions and draw up some guidelines for student-teacher relationships in the future.

In some ways theological education is very different from and has tremendous advantages over primary education. The students are (or should be) adults, and they are seeking training for a vocation to which they are committed. They already have (or should have) practical experience in the churches, and for years they have observed others in the practice of the ministry. To a large degree they know (or should know) what they need and are motivated to work toward that goal. This is an ideal situation in which students and teacher can sit down together and work out a plan of study that will respond to their expectations and fulfill their needs. The teacher, following the pattern of the open school teacher, should prepare resources for study; he should serve as an advisor, counseling, guiding, and extending the learning experiences; and he should be deeply involved in these learning events. Since the teacher himself is committed to the same vocation, he should have no difficulty identifying

himself with the students as a partner in the learning process
and a colleague in the ministry.

The sad truth of the matter is that we have largely ignored
and depreciated this fundamental relationship between students
and teacher. Following the ways of traditional schools and
society, we have kept the professor on a pedestal and the
students at his feet (physically, psychologically, spiritually,
and even economically). We have continued to domesticate the
students, making them recipients of knowledge rather than invest-
igators, imitators rather than creators, dependent rather than
independent thinkers. And we have passed on to them a non-
functional image of the ministry by which they strive to become
our successors in our institutions or our emulators in the
churches, repeating this stagnant relationship rather than
creating dynamic ministry in the body of Christ.

Those who work in theological education by extension have the
greatest opportunity for breaking this tradition... and they
must carry greater blame if they fail to do so. (1) As soon as
you become involved in extension teaching, you realize that your
role has to change radically. Class time is reduced to one
period (2 or 3 hours) per week in each center; it is impossible
to get across even the basic course content in that amount of
time; lectures are eliminated entirely. The professor has to
become a provider of study materials, and since he does not have
to stand in front of students for several hours a day he actually
has time to prepare them. Faced with the task of placing in the
students' hands all that they will need—not just information and
concepts but a learning sequence for self-study—he is forced to
go more deeply than ever before into the subject matter itself
and into the nature of learning. (2) The change to extension
also means a striking change in the student body. There are
still young men preparing for the professional ministry, but
they are not living in and dependent on the institution. The
majority of the students are married and have families and
support themselves working fulltime. Most have had experience
in society. You meet with them week by week not to discuss
irrelevant theological controversies or memorize facts but to
deal with the life and mission of the church. Much of the
course material is "old hat," but it comes alive as these
students relate it to their own experience in the churches.
Because they bring to the class a wealth of practical experience
and have studied the lesson content on their own before class,
they become full participants in the discussion. The professor,
instead of being the source of information, becomes a participant
also and an advisor, counseling and guiding the students;
responding to their concerns, and learning with them. (3) The
extension structure gives us a new, living context for doing
theological education. The professor does not have to drum up

interest in his subject and try to relate it somehow to the
local church. He simply goes out to where the action is and
meets with those who are doing the job. This isn't an "academic"
exercise; the success and sometimes the survival of the churches
depend on these men and women. There is no trouble getting the
professor involved in these learning events; he is as much
inspired by these encounters as the students are.

The importance of this kind of a relationship is not just
pedagogical. The way we teach determines to a large degree the
way our students will lead their congregations. Church leaders
are called not to do the work of the ministry but to "equip the
saints for the work of ministry, for building the body of Christ."
If we are able to develop an open relationship with our students,
they will be far more likely to develop an open relationship with
their fellow members in the churches.

IV. EVALUATION AND VALIDATION

A. No consideration of open education would be complete
without some discussion of the thorny problems of evaluation.
And no program can be validated unless there is some way of
looking at the overall results. In this final section we shall
consider some examples and concepts of open school evaluation
and then compare them with what we are doing in theological
education.

Traditional schools depend almost entirely on the proverbial
carrot strung out in front of the student and the perhaps more
forceful whip hovering close behind him. The whole educational
system is permeated by these two extrinsic stimuli. If you miss
a class or don't pay attention in class, forget to do your
homework or lose your notebook, fall down on an exam or rouse
the teacher's ire, you may get a low grade or fail the course;
if you flunk several courses, you will be held back a grade; if
you drop out of school, you are considered a drop out from
society. On the contrary if you keep on your toes and do the
extra assignments and please the teacher, you can come out near
the top of the class, pass the courses with flying colors, move
on up the academic ladder year after year, and finally graduate
"with highest honor." As if this were not enough, there are
parents who reinforce the system with attractive rewards and
severe punishments at home and laws that make absence from
school a criminal offence. This whole scheme works because
society is built the same way; everyone is trying to climb the
economic, professional, prestige ladder. Schools are *preparation
for life*.

Open school educators challenge this system from top to
bottom(6). School should not be a beginning cog in the social

machine. Children should not be at the mercy of our adult rat
race. Learning should not be manipulated through threats and
appeasement. The classroom should not be an education factory
where children are forced to sweat out a 6-hour day (up to 8 or
10 with homework and other activities) in competition with their
friends. So open schools throw out examinations, grades, and
report cards--at least in their usual forms.

Open schools start with the premise that schooling is not
just a preparation for life; *it is life* for those people who
happen to be 6 to 18 years old. Society may dictate that
children go to school during those years, but everything
possible must be done to make those years happy, loving,
peaceful, an end in themselves; not a drudgery, a tunnel, a
necessary evil, a ladder to climb, an almost unending series of
obstacles to be hurdled on the way to adult life. Quite
obviously if a person has not learned to enjoy life during all
those years of schooling, he has little chance of enjoying it
later on. If he has been formed primarily by competition and
artificial stimuli in school, he will probably perform the same
way thereafter.

Examinations, grades, and report cards can be eliminated with
the stroke of a pen. But what should be put in their place?
How do open schools evaluate their work? There is no simple
answer, although we can say that open school evaluation fits
into the framework of curriculum design and student-teacher
relationships that have been described above. Open schools are
concerned about much more than the academic, intellectual
development of the child.

The Integrated Day Center in Guatemala uses several methods
of evaluation that involve students, teachers, and parents. The
most basic and constant level of evaluation is the daily work
relationship between student and teacher. As a teacher listens
to, observes, advises, and helps a student, he is in fact
considering the student's attitude toward himself and others,
his interest and progress in learning, his comprehension and
capabilities. He talks over these matters with the student
from time to time as opportunities arise. The student takes
pride in his work not because of grades, not primarily in
comparison with others, but as the achievement of his own goals
and the expression of his own personality and ability. In
specific areas of systematic learning, such as reading and math,
he makes use of programmed materials that allow him to measure
his own advancement step by step. At the end of the week the
students all write a brief note home to their parents indicating
what they have done during the week. This enables them and
their parents to see and perhaps discuss what they are learning.
At the bottom of this note the homeroom teacher may add some

comments--but never a grade. Twice each term the teachers sit
down with the students one by one to write up a more complete
evaluation of their participation and progress and feelings in
the different learning areas and in school in general. Later
the parents go over their children's evaluation with the
teacher.

Perhaps it is too early to say whether open education is a
success and will replace traditional schooling; those who enter
into the movement (parents, teachers, students) will have to
validate it for themselves. The following personal testimony of
one family may be helpful. Paul is 9, fairly cooperative, and
interested in learning. He spends a great deal of time with one
special buddy working on projects, talking about all kinds of
things, or just fooling around. Babs, his favorite teacher,
believes that one way to judge the effectiveness of the program
and of a particular child's learning experience is to watch his
degree or level of involvement. She is fascinated by what kids
learn through play, conversation, and friendship. One day,
though, when she saw Paul wandering about the back yard, she
suggested, "Don't you think you'd better get to work on something Paul?" His answer, expressed with some seriousness and
some humor, was, "Babs, I'm thinking!" Fair enough, she
decided, for she does not want to fall into the trap of making
kids keep busy just to be busy or of believing that if they are
busy they are learning something or of reinforcing the popular
idea that school is for work (a drag) rather than play (fun).

John is just 11, a hyperactive child, bright, but still has
trouble reading, which makes learning difficult in several
areas. At the other schools he attended he was being left
completely behind, as has happened to thousands of hyperactive
children, not for lack of intelligence but because of a
physiological inability to sit still and pay attention to what
the teacher was presenting hour after hour, day after day. The
danger was that he should begin to think he was dumb or react
to the system in other harmful ways. Now at the IDC he is free
to work as long as he wants on any project; he can get up and
move around as long as he doesn't bother other children; and he
can receive special, personal attention. As far as learning to
read and write, the best they have been able to do is let him
stay home for the first hour every day and study with his
mother, but even that has been very helpful. He is gradually
getting over the hump in reading and everything else.

Beth is 12, small, pretty, and intelligent, also very
independent and perhaps opinionated. She was getting to hate
school, especially the arbitrariness of the program and the
uselessness of so much memorization. At the IDC she has progressed in all subjects at least as much as she did in the

other schools, and now she likes school. One of the first
things that happened was that she "discovered" reading; she just
"took off." Her teachers didn't pay much attention to this,
except to talk with her once in awhile about reading too much
and slighting other activities. Then toward the end of the
second semester one teacher went around asking each student how
many books he had read during the term. To everyone's surprise
Beth had read at least 46 books. Not only that, but she now
reads faster than her father. Since she loves to read, this one
ability is, we believe, more valuable than a Ph.D. The sequel
is also exciting. Although Beth soon learned to love reading,
she disliked writing, even to report on the books she was
reading. Then she and her girlfriend began writing projects--
without the teacher even knowing, much less suggesting it. She
wrote an 85-page book on "The Amazing Advenchers of the the
Mice Family," complete with introduction, 13 chapter headings,
illustrations, and her own binding and cover.

These experiences are what validated the open school for one
family. Obviously other children have different experiences;
that's just the point. In fact, it is interesting to note that
these experiences happened not so much because the school
planned them, but because it let them happen--and that
traditional schools would not have let them happen. Learning
experiences like these go so far beyond examinations, grades,
and report cards as to make them insignificant. They awaken in
parents and children as well as teachers a sense of challenge,
a call to involvement, and an appreciation of the demands and
nature of genuine education. They even pose the possibility
that our children, rather than just fit into the socio-economic
machinery some day, or turn out as non-conformists and misfits,
may actually become creative, independent innovators, capable
of changing society.

B. In the light of the above concepts and examples we must
raise serious questions about theological education. How do we
evaluate our course work? And how do we validate our programs
as a whole? The open school provides a perspective from which
to criticize present practices and form new criteria.

One prominent educator who knows and is sympathetic to the
work of theological education, after participating in workshops
and consultations in the U.S. and Third World countries, came to
the conclusion that our seminaries and institutes teach students
to memorize lists--because that is what we ask for in our
examinations, which are the principal method of evaluation in
our institutions. Others have expressed concern over the widespread drive for higher and higher academic standards: raising
entrance requirements, lengthening bibliographies, and
emphasizing accreditation and degrees. They point out that

this tendency is obviously contrary to N.T. values, especially
for Christian leaders. Some have in recent years repented of the
heavy investments made over the past 25 years in theological
education, especially in the Third World, precisely because they
have contributed to the formation of elitism in our institutions
and in the churches and to the decontextualization of the
ministry. The values of secular schooling have to a great
extent permeated the theological education establishment.

It might be useful to present the problems and challenge of
evaluation to theological educators and churchmen in a workshop
experience. You could discuss with them first the need for
evaluation; let the participants list several reasons for
evaluating their programs. Then discuss with them the dangers
of traditional methods and systems of evaluation; you might use
arguments such as have been presented here. Finally give them
an assignment like this for small group study: "eliminate
examinations and grades and design an entirely new system of
evaluation." As they discuss evaluation, they will of course
have to define the goals of theological education and the mission
of the church.

When we try to judge or validate our programs as a whole,
what do we look for? Generally we look for results in terms of
effective ministry, and this probably has little correlation
with good grades in seminary(7). It may even turn out that the
students who work hardest for grades are the least effective, on
the long haul, in the ministry. Certainly there is an enormous
gap between the church history exam or the theology paper or
even the weekly exegesis assignment and the actual practice of
the ministry. What is needed, probably, is a detailed analysis
of the roles of church leaders, a fundamental revision of the
curriculum in keeping with those roles, and then a new system
of evaluation that will enable students to measure their
progress in terms of effective ministry.

As noted in the previous sections of this paper, theological
education by extension presents a unique situation and unique
opportunities. The program itself is not preparation for
ministry but in-service training. It's relevance can be tested
by present experience, not just by conjectural future application. It can be validated by students, teachers, and the
churches themselves as they participate in study and ministry
together.

The Extension Bible Institute in northern Honduras has
developed a program for men of very limited educational background that is in some ways very similar to open education(8).
There is no established curriculum, only small, one-week units
that are developed and used as the students confront specific

specific problems in their work, which is to raise up new congregations. These brief study units are inter-disciplinary, problem-centered, and programmed for self-study. The professor meets regularly with three men to discuss their work and place in their hands study materials as the needs arise. These men teach the same materials to another 20 students in eight centers, who in turn teach another 25 men in remote villages. The extension education chain is actually a chain of church planting. There are no examinations, no grades, no diplomas; no one ever graduates. Evaluation is entirely focused on effective ministry. The task will be completed only when every village and suburb of northern Honduras has a thriving congregation. The program is being validated by the establishing of new congregations and the growth of old ones.

Examinations may be useful, even in open education, if they are understood within the framework of personal growth and effective service rather than as competition for grades and prestige. But personal interviews, group discussion, questionnaires, and other methods are also necessary. In Guatemala we have discovered that most extension students are not very interested in competition or grades, although those who are church workers are concerned about graduation, which is usually a requirement for ordination and fully recognized pastoral ministry. We try to maintain the focus of our work, as professors and students, on effective service in the churches.

Our Inductive Study of the Book of Romans(9), for example, is programmed to meet one of the greatest needs in our churches; our students want to learn how to study and use the Bible. As a pre-test they are asked to describe how they would investigate the book of Romans for use in their preaching and teaching ministry. Then they discuss in terms of specific objectives how they could study Romans and other books of the Bible inductively. The first group of lessons deals with the book of Romans as a whole; the second division presents procedures for studying and using paragraphs; the final division goes into Biblical theology. Evaluation is carried out informally through weekly discussion of the lessons and their application. Many of the students use the book of Romans in their preaching and teaching and share these experiences with the class. At the end of each major division the students work out a completely independent study of new biblical material in order to demonstrate (to themselves primarily) their ability to do inductive Bible study on their own. There is a final written evaluation designed to bring out the potentiality and the practicability of inductive study and to point out the weaknesses in the program. Real validation of the course depends upon the students' getting "turned on" so that they will study and use the Bible (not just Romans) effectively in their future ministry.

It may take some time for theological education, even
theological education by extension, to break with traditional
methods of evaluation and find new methods that are appropriate
and effective. Meanwhile, we may have to "play the game" of
examinations, grades, and diplomas, even though we find the real
values elsewhere and even as we develop other criteria. But we
must not forget that the traditional methods can be detrimental
to the whole educational system and prejudicial to basic biblical
values. Just as open schools are searching for new, more human
ways to validate their programs, open theological educators must
find new, more Christian ways to validate their programs.

CONCLUSIONS

A. Theological education stands today at an important
crossroads. The tension between residence and extension
adherents is symptomatic of deep-seated crises and unprecedented
opportunities. There is an economic crisis; it is doubtful
whether traditional seminaries and Bible institutes can meet
rising costs even in the U.S.; and it is evident that this
system, which has been exported to the Third World, is not
financially viable there. There is a pedagogical crisis;
theological institutions as well as other educational establish-
ments are being challenged as never before; classrooms must
become more human, and schools must place themselves at the
service of the people. There is an ideological crisis; the
elitism and dependency fomented by our institutions are under
direct attack. And there is a biblical crisis; the professional,
oligarchial, clerical pattern of the ministry is being replaced
by the N.T. concept of the body of Christ, in which there are
many gifts and all are called to minister. Theological institutions must change.

On the other hand theological education faces new, unprecedented opportunities for service to the churches. Cassette
recorders, transister radios, off-set printing, and other means
of communication can make educational material available to
thousands of local church leaders at minimal cost--among sparce,
rural populations as well as in urban areas, throughout India
and Brazil as well as England and the U.S. Educational
technology is producing a growing array of self-study materials
and equipment that can be placed at the service of theological
education. New educational systems, such as the Open University
of Great Britain, provide models that suggest fascinating
possibilities for future development in theological education.
All these factors are breaking down prejudices and bringing
about increasing acceptance of innovation and openness to change.

To hold on blindly to traditional ways and vested interests
at this historic moment would be suicidal. To invest our energy

in polemics between residence and extension theological education
would be myopic. The possibilities are much wider, and the
stakes are much higher. We are challenged to join forces, not
dissipate them. We are called to open up theological education
for today and for the future.

B.   In this paper we have made use of the experience,
concepts, and models of open education. Open educators are
dealing with the fundamental concerns facing our schools and our
society, and their perspectives are specially provocative for
theological education. Their criticisms hit hard, for our
institutions have imitated many of the fallacies and incorporated many of the values of secular school systems. But if we
are ready to face these criticisms, we may also be able to
utilize the insights and contributions of open education. We
can at least find out what is happening in open education(10),
introduce these ideas to our theological faculties, and
experiment with these models.

At the same time we should look for additional experiences,
concepts, and models in other educational fields and in other
sectors of contemporary culture. The field of non-formal
education is bringing together fundamental insights into adult
education that may be decisive for the formation of school
systems and development programs in the future, especially where
economic resources are limited. Agricultural extension programs
have long pioneered with decentralized training, adoption and
diffusion techniques, literature and radio, and the role of
technical advisors. Industry and the military have an enormous
reservoir of experience with on-the-job training. Radio and
television have been harnessed for educational purposes at the
alphabetization, pre-school, primary, secondary, and university
levels. Some countries are training unschooled para-medics
empirically in their own cultural environments. The cooperative
movement is an important educational process which deals with
fundamental social and economic problems as well as specialized
orientation.

The open education movement offers some of the most significant contributions to educational development today, but it
certainly is not the only source of insight and innovation. It
is time that theological educators look beyond the professional
academic model developed over the past 200 years in Europe and
the U.S. as they plan for the future.

C.   In our analysis of open education we have considered four
major factors: structures and methods, motivation and curriculum
design, the roles of student and teacher, and evaluation and
validation. These four factors are interrelated and should be
integrated in the formation of any educational program. Thus the

open classroom curriculum requires new relationships between
student and teacher and also a new approach to evaluation. On
the other hand many open schools fall under serious criticism
because they are so costly that only wealthy countries or upper
class people can afford them, i.e. they are structurally closed.
Conversely theological education by extension has been revolutionary in opening up theological education to the whole people
of God, but many extension programs impose a closed curriculum
through traditional methods of teaching and evaluation. A
truly open educational system, theological or otherwise, must
find ways to deal with all four of these factors.

D. In order to introduce open education to theological
educators, students, and church leaders, we have made some
suggestions for workshop experiences dealing with each of the
four major elements presented in this paper. The literature on
open education contains many more practical suggestions that
can easily be adapted for use at seminaries and Bible institutes.
In fact, examples taken from the regular school subjects can in
many cases be utilized and the application of these examples left
for the paritcipants themselves to work out. As new theological
models, games and simulations, projects, and group exercises are
developed for presenting open theological education, these
should be circulated also.

E. Throughout this presentation we have noted the special
significance of the extension movement in theological education.
Up to now its importance lies primarily in the fact that it has
transformed the traditional structures and methodology of many
seminaries and Bible institutes. Its contribution will be far
greater in the future, however, if it will take advantage of the
momentum for change by continuing to introduce new concepts of
curriculum design, student and teacher roles, evaluation, etc.
In fact, the basic changes in structure and methods that have
already taken place lead quite naturally to these other changes.

If the extension movement continues to grow and experiment,
there is no telling where it might lead and what it might
achieve. In just eleven years it has taken root and extended
its branches around the globe; it now includes perhaps 200
programs with 20,000 students on all six continents(11). In
another eleven years it could grow to 1000 programs and 100,000
students. Models and materials and methods developed in Latin
America have been adapted and have sparked new variations in
other situations. Workshops are being held constantly in many
different places, covering different aspects of the task--among
professors and administrators, students, and church leaders.
Many extension theological educators are now involved in a
dynamic process of reflexion and change. The extension movement
is producing increasing openness in theological education.

F. The final conclusion of this paper is a recommendation
regarding the name "theological education by extension." No
doubt this name has served a worthy purpose. It has identified
the movement we have just described, indicating its nature and
purpose, i.e. to extend theological education geographically,
culturally, academically, ecclesiologically, etc. And it has
captured the imagination of thousands of church leaders with a
new vision of what theological education should and can do, i.e.
provide training for the whole people of God and enable many
more members to be fully incorporated into the ministry and
mission of the church. But the purpose and vision of this
movement go far beyond a simple change in structure (the word
"extension" seems to imply just a change in structure). And
we need to bridge the gap between extension and residence and
join forces in the search for more adequate and more effective
programs of theological education.

Paulo Freire has pointed out that the term "extension" can be
not only inadequate but detrimental(12). His analysis
associates the extension concept with transmission, condescension,
messianism, cultural invasion, manipulation, etc. It is easy to
see that in popular usage the word extension can give the idea
of extending and imposing something that has already been
determined, designed, and fabricated. This raises serious
questions as to the nature of theological education by extension
and as to the wisdom of using this name.

It is certainly true that some extension programs have merely
extended the old system of theological education so as to impose
it on more people. But the challenge facing theological education today is to take an open attitude to structures and
methods and to design programs that will be open to the whole
people of God, to take an open attitude toward curriculum
design so as to build on the students' interests and needs and
motivation, to take an open attitude toward the role of the
student and the role of the teacher so that both can become
fully involved in determining and developing the learning
experiences, to take an open attitude toward evaluation and to
discover more relevant, more human, more Christian ways to
validate our programs. If theological education by extension
should take on this enormous, unending challenge and join
forces with theological educators of all traditions, then
perhaps we should look for a new name. The name which comes
very naturally out of this study and which expresses this vision
is: "open theological education."

NOTES

1. Ralph D. Winter, ed., *Theological Education by Extension* (South Pasadena: William Carey Library, 1969), documents the extension movement up to 1969. Ralph R. Covell and C. Peter Wagner, *An Extension Seminary Primer* (South Pasadena: William Carey Library, 1971), gives a much shorter resume. The *Extension Seminary* (San Felipe, Reu., Guatemala) is a quarterly newsletter which circulates current thinking and news.

2. Information about the Open University was obtained from the Director of Information Services, The Open University, Walton Hall, Walton, Bletchley, Buckinghamshire, England.

3. In the U.S., for example, there is an oversupply of seminaries and seminary graduates for the professional ministry. If one seminary were to invest its entire resources in an open, decentralized program, it could reach tens of thousands of local church leaders and perhaps revolutionize the ministry.

4. Charles E. Silberman, ed., *The Open Classroom Reader* (New York: Random House, 1973) is the most extensive sourcebook on open education to date.

5. Anne M. Bussis and Edward A. Chittenden. "The Teacher's Manifold Roles," *The Open Classroom Reader*, pp. 213-232.

6. One of the most incisive radical critics of contemporary U.S. schools and society is John Holt. See especially his *Freedom and Beyond* (New York: Dell Publishing Co., 1972). See also the writings of Ivan Illich.

7. Paul Goodman, "No Processing Whatever," *Radical School Reform* (New York: Simon and Schuster, 1969), p. 98: "The evidence is strong that there is no correlation between school performance and life achievement in any of the professions, whether medicine, law, engineering, journalism, or business."

8. George Patterson, "Let's Multiply Churches through Extension Education Chains," *Extension Seminary*, No. 3, 1974, and "Modifications of the Extension Methods for Areas of Limited Education Opportunity," No. 4, 1972.

9. F. Ross Kinsler, *Estudio Inductivo del Libro de Romanos* (San Felipe: Seminario Evangélico Presbiteriano de Guatemala, 1974).

10. Edward B. Nyquist and Gene R. Hawes, ed., *Open Education:
    A Sourcebook for Parents* (New York: Bantam Books, 1972),
    contains a wide selection of writings by key authors in
    the field plus bibliography.

11. Wayne C. Weld, *The World Directory of Theological
    Education by Extension* (South Pasadena: William Carey
    Library, 1973), contains data about many but by no means
    all of the existing extension programs. Included also is
    a bibliography of literature about the movement.

12. Paul Freire, *¿Extensión o Comunicación?* (Montevideo:
    Tierra Nueva, 1973).

6

Theological Education by Extension: Service or Subversion?

INTRODUCTION

The extension program of the Presbyterian Seminary of Guatemala is now in its fifteenth year. The program has grown, stabilized, made many adjustments. The infra-structure needs strengthening; the curriculum is being revised; most of the instructional materials should be reworked. But the results of these 15 years are overwhelmingly positive--at least in terms of traditional expectations. On completion of the current academic year (November, 1977) there will be a total of approximately 85 extension graduates, of which 45 are serving fulltime as pastors and church workers (not yet ordained); another 15 occupy important leadership positions in their congregations and presbyteries as laymen, licenses preachers, or ordained pastors; 10 others are pastors and outstanding leaders in other churches here in Guatemala or in other countries. Current enrollment stands at about 250 students in 20 extension centers scattered around the country; efforts are being made to expand into three major Indian areas plus two frontier situations with the help of volunteer adjunct professors. During this 15-year period a total of about 1000 students have participated in some course of study--in a national church which has about 20,000 baptized adult members, 90 organized churches, and 300 congregations.

Yet there is still strong opposition to the whole idea of theological education by extension right here in Guatemala among some of the most outspoken and powerful leaders of the Presbyterian Church. They no longer attack the extension program directly; they have to concede what it has achieved.

But they insist that the Seminary should reopen its residential program to meet the priority need for "adequate" preparation for those who are "really" called to "the ministry." We have pointed out that the Seminary's previous fulltime residential program reached only 264 students during its 25-year history, that just 52 were graduated and only 15 are currently serving the Presbyterian Church of Guatemala, six of them as fulltime pastors. Nevertheless these pastors of the old guard persist in their "high" views of the ministry; they insist that pastors need special, separate training. They fear that extension is weakening the ministry and undermining the church.

We have chosen here to deal directly with this question, Is theological education by extension a significant service to the church or is it a subversive threat to the church and its ministry? In this study we shall try to deal with the complaints and analyze the on-going opposition to our extension program in Guatemala. But we shall also refer to the extension movement in general, which continues to experience varying degrees and kinds of resistence around the world.

In a recent conversation with the executive secretary of an association of theological schools, he expressed surprise that we still face opposition here in Guatemala after 14 years of extension and noted that in other places there now seems to be no conflict. My response was to point out that there are serious differences between the advocates of extension and residencial training, that ecclesiastical structures and hallowed traditions are being challenged, that conflict and controversy may in fact be good signs. It, on the other hand, extension is easily incorporated within the established system--as training for "laymen," for those who cannot get to a "real" seminary, or for "lower" levels--perhaps no essential changes in the status quo are taking place.

Orlando Fals Borda, a brilliant Colombian sociologist and Presbyterian elder, has recommended the recuperation of subversion as a useful, dynamic concept. Given the unjust, exploitive socio-economic-political structures of Latin America, any move to help the poor gain basic rights, land, or power is labeled as subversive. We may argue in a similar way that the churches in Latin America and elsewhere are dominated by the clergy, by ecclesiastical structures that place power and privilege and initiative in the hands of a few, and by inherited or imported patterns of theological education and ministry that stifle indigenous, popular leadership. From this angle, too, we must raise the question as to the role of theological education by extension. Should it merely serve the given structures and vested interests of the established system of the ministry? Or should extension subvert those interests and structures?

The following paragraphs suggest some ways in which the extension movement may provoke radical change, not to destroy the church or its ministry but rather to undermine its perpetual tendencies toward hierarchization, legalism, traditionalism, dead orthodoxy, and unfaith. This kind of subversion, it will be argued, is healthy and necessary. It is dynamizing. It will most probably, as we have seen in Guatemala and elsewhere, occasion opposition. *Theological education by extension may in fact render its greatest service to the church and its ministry by challenging existing structures.*

I. HOW SHOULD WE CONCEIVE OF THEOLOGICAL EDUCATION?

The opposition to extension here in Guatemala and elsewhere seems, in the first place, to be built on a certain vision of what theological education should be. We really need to take seriously the ideals and the reasoning that make up that vision, the concerns that lie behind the complaints, and the important issue of academic excellence in ministerial training.

The traditional vision of what a seminary should be continues to carry considerable weight in some circles. Our older pastors, especially, would love to see even a tiny group of bright, dedicated young men at the seminary fulltime, living in special forms, attending classes daily, spending long hours in the library and with their professors, and enjoying a close fellowship of worship, work, and recreation. If they have offered their lives in service to God, it is reasoned, they should be given the best opportunity to prepare themselves. If they have their whole lives before them and are to serve fulltime in the ministry, the church can well afford to give them three years of fulltime preparation. Extension training, which is parttime, often sporadic, tacked onto the daily routine of work and home and church activities, can hardly be an acceptable substitute. These doubts about extension increase as more and more people all around us advance up the education ladder and as other churches build bigger and more impressive theological institutions.

The desire for academic excellence is certainly worthy of consideration. Our critics believe that fulltime, residential training is far more adequate preparation for "the ministry," i.e. for pastors; they call for upgrading the level of training and tightening or increasing course requirements; they want the seminary to provide a different or at least a longer program for candidates for ordination. In response we have questioned whether academic excellence, as it is commonly understood, is very relevant to the ministry as it really is or as it should be. In Guatemala, most of Latin America, and much of the Third

World, schooling is primarily a vehicle of escape from poverty,
and it alienates people from their own families, communities,
and cultures. The purpose of the seminaries and Bible
institutes is to prepare leaders for service among all the
congregations, especially among the poor, but we have seen over
and over again that they too are instruments of alienation and
elitism. Throughout the Third World there is an enormous drive
for more schooling, and theological institutions everywhere are
moving up the education ladder. The end of the process is
greater specialization and professionalization with abundant
benefits for these who reach the highest ranks.

We can never take lightly the intellectual seriousness of our
task in theological education, but we must define our objectives
in terms of the life and mission of the church. Ninety percent
of the people of Guatemala are extremely poor; 60 percent are
illiterate; and less than 1 percent have completed secondary
school. The Presbyterian Church of Guatemala has many congregations in rural areas where plantation workers earn less than
a dollar a day and peasant farmers struggle to subsist on tiny
plots of land, in the towns and cities where trade flourishes
and artisans and professional people concentrate and schooling
is more prevalent, and among the vast Indian populations where
Spanish (the "national" language) is spoken only by a small
minority. No seminary could "form" pastors for this diverse,
growing church; few graduates of traditional seminaries would be
able to adapt to the exigencies of most of these situations;
most of the congregations will never provide "professional"
salaries.

It is our understanding that the congregations themselves can
and must form their own leaders and candidates for ordination.
The seminary's role is to provide study tools and tutors and to
design training programs that will enable these men and women to
develop more effectively their gifts, to reflect more critically
upon their ministries, and to lead their people in more faithful
service and witness. We insist that the seminary must offer
functionally equivalent training for the ordained ministry at
widely separated academic levels (entrance with primary,
secondary, and university schooling); in fact we are in the
process of adding an even "lower" level in response to obvious
local needs. Similarly we have resisted earnestly all attempts
to separate courses for "ministerial candidates" from courses
for "laymen" in our struggle to break down the false dichotomy
between clergy and laity. Whereas contemporary Western society
and Guatemalan education place great value on degrees, levels,
faculty, buildings, schedules, we have tried to reverse this
process and emphasize growth in service in the congregations.

Although at times--such as annual graduation services--we put
on the paraphernalia of academe in order to maintain credibility

for our program and for our graduates, we are dedicated to the deinstitutionalization of theological education. We are looking for new guidelines for academic excellence. Our faculty is not deeply concerned about "original research"; we would rather divest ourselves of the professorial image in order to relate with our students as colleagues in the ministry and in theological reflexion. We--students and teachers--are not directly involved in international theological debates, but we are all vitally engaged in the problems of our church and in the needs of our people.

Aharon Sapsezian has said that our seminary has "committed institutional suicide." Peter Savage describes this new vision of theological education as "pedagogical conversion." We are in the process of breaking some of the assumptions and subverting some of the pretensions of schools in general and of theological institutions in particular. We are trying to open up rather than close the door to ministry, to challenge rather than discourage people of all ages, levels of schooling, social and economic status, ethnic and racial background to respond to God's call. This process may also help the churches to throw off the bondage of a professional clergy, the ideology of the middle classes, the legalisms of the past, and the cultural forms of a foreign church and an alienated society.

II. WHAT IS OUR UNDERSTANDING OF THE NATURE OF THE MINISTRY?

The opposition to extension is not merely a criticism of the educational model. It is rooted in and strongly committed to a certain understanding of the ministry. We must explore that concept of the ministry, examine its validity, and ask whether theological education by extension can and should support it.

The idealism surrounding the Presbyterian ministry in Guatemala flows no doubt from several sources: the highly competent, highly motivated, "spiritually" oriented missionary; the all-powerful, authoritative Catholic priest; and the highly visible, outspoken "ladino" leader of plantation, political party, and community organization. A pastor is expected to have above all a deep sense of call, a self-image that places him in a unique sphere of service, dedication, and sacrifice. His integrity and authority should not be questioned. He is the spiritual leader of his congregation, the axis around which the life of the church revolves. The people cannot grow spiritually beyond the level of their pastor. He is the prime mover, orientor, and advisor for all the programs of the church. He is the preaching-teaching elder, who must expound God's revelation, maintain discipline, and lead the congregation. In Presbyterian church order a pastor must preside over the local church governing body (the session), and only pastors are authorized to administer the sacraments.

Given this image of the ministry, it was probably inevitable that our extension program would cause not only disappointment but righteous resentment. The image is so strong that some of our extension graduates themselves have joined the opposition, agreeing with the older pastors that extension training is inadequate. At presbytery and synod meetings certain persons have been eager to pick up any indication of incompetence on the part of our extension students and graduates; at last year's plenary assembly one of the synod executive officers inadvertently used the word "mediocre." The facts show of course that extension graduates and students now lead most of the churches throughout the whole denomination, including the largest ones, and several have been elected as presidents of their presbyteries and of the Synod. But they do not quite fit the idealized image; in fact they unconsciously call into question that very image.

The older pastors feel very strongly that they were called to serve fulltime in the pastorate and that anything less is a denial of their calling, even though most of them have not been able to carry out that ideal. They believe that candidates for "the ministry" should abandon secular employment and give themselves wholly and "sacrificially" to theological studies and later to the pastorate. On a number of occasions when the seminary's report, with its long list of students, has been presented in a presbytery or synod meeting, someone has asked which students are candidates for the ordained ministry, implying that they are the only ones that really count. They want the seminary to provide a kind of training which would make our graduates stand head and shoulders above their congregations—in spiritual power, biblical knowledge, and theological competence.

This writer, for one, believes that the true role of theological education by extension is not to try to fulfill the expectations of that image of the ministry but rather to transform it. The concept of an omni-competent spiritual leader has no basis in the New Testament, and it has never been effective, at least not in Guatemala. Rather we should seek to build up the ministry of each congregation as a body. The present pattern of authoritarian leadership must be replaced with an emergent, plural, corporate leadership of the people. The ineffectual, top-down style of communication must evolve into an experience of dialogue so that the people can grow in their understanding of the Gospel and begin to relate it meaningfully to their own lives and to the needs of their neighbors.

Extension is a necessary alternative for theological training because it enables us to break into the heirarchical patterns of the past, to encourage local leaders to develop their gifts, to allow them to gain recognition as pastors and teachers as well as deacons and elders, and to build a plural, collegiate ministry of the people.

We insist that God's call to ministry is to all followers of Jesus Christ, corporately and individually, wholly and equally. This approach to theological education may be labeled subversive both by its enemies and by its supporters because it does promote radical changes in the nature of the ministry.

III.   WHAT CONSTITUTES THE CHURCH?

The question about the role of theological education by extension goes beyond the matter of educational models and concepts of the ministry to the nature of the church. The opposition to extension is based in large part upon a set of ideas about the church, and the legitimacy of extension must be posited in terms of these concerns.

More than 25 years ago Emil Brunner wrote *The Misunderstanding of the Church*, which he called "the unsolved problem of Protestantism." The problem is still with us. The question remains, what is the church?

The vision, ideals, and concepts of the church held by our worthy opponents here in Guatemala are not always clear, but the assumptions are none the less definite. There is an easy identification between the true church and the Presbyterian church-- and other, similar, Protestant groups. The church consists of those who have "accepted Christ" and become members. The primary dimension of the church is the local congregation, and the main expression of the life of the church is cultic. Every congregation in Guatemala meets weekly for an average of six or more worship services, some of them for the expressed purpose of prayer or teaching, one supposedly for youth and another for women, but almost all follow a stereotyped pattern of hymns, prayer, Scripture reading, and preaching. The church exists to carry on this routine faithfully and to add as many new people as possible. The local, regional, and national ecclesiastical structures and all the other organizations and institutions of the denomination exist to perpetuate and expand this program.

According to this view of the church, the seminary is called upon to supply each congregation with a pastor who will carry on the worship services, visit the members so they will not slacken in their attendance, evangelize others so that the membership will increase, and perhaps attend preaching points which will eventually become churches. The seminary should prepare these pastors to strengthen their congregations' denominational loyalty, doctrinal convictions, biblical knowledge, moral standards, and organizations.

According to our Reformed tradition the church is based on the correct preaching (and hearing) of God's Word and administration of the sacraments of baptism and the Lord's Supper. In Presbyterian Churches around the world only ordained, relatively highly educated pastors are authorized to administer the sacraments and preside over the local session, thus constituting the church in that place. Because of their high calling and training pastors need salaries, and their salaries should in some way reflect their training and calling. In Guatemala and in many other countries this has meant that most congregations could never have pastors, become recognized as "churches," and be free to develop their own style of ministry and concerns for mission. It has meant that much of the business of the organized churches (with pastors) and higher ecclesiastical bodies has revolved about the selection and support of pastors.

Now we must ask whether theological education by extension is simply another way of building up this kind of a church with these kinds of institutional concerns. At first glance it appears as if extension does indeed provide many more pastors to carry on these functions and strengthen this concept of the church. Perhaps many extension programs are doing just that. On the other hand we believe that extension is beginning to infiltrate these traditions and structures and to lay the groundwork for radical change.

The first step is to ensure that the churches' leadership represents the whole church, is responsible to the people in the congregations, and does not create a financial burden for the members. Extension allows the congregations to choose their natural leaders as pastors by enabling them to fulfill the academic requirements for ordination. It provides abundant opportunities so that all the congregations can have ordained pastors, either with or without salaries and at all levels of salary.

The second step is to focus the churches' programs on the needs of their people. As we meet with our extension students to study the Bible, church history, pastoral psychology, etc., we come again and again to the conclusion that the congregations are not meeting the needs of their own members, much less community needs. We know that every home and every individual life has its heavy burdens and urgent concerns, its dreams and illusions, but these matters are hardly ever shared or dealt with. The preaching and teaching, the many worship services, and the ponderous organizational machinery continue to proceed unwittingly and unheedingly onward. Now in extension we are

sitting down with local leaders and beginning to reflect upon
the real and felt needs of our people and to discuss how to meet
those needs in the light of the Gospel.

The third step is to introduce changes into the life of the
congregations--changes in the regular worship services and other
activities, changes in the way the Bible is studied and taught,
changes in organization and planning, changes in the ways the
members and leaders relate to each other. In the past our
students have complained that in the seminary we discuss great
ideas for the renewal and mission of the church but that in the
congregations and presbyteries these ideas are often squelched.
This situation is beginning to change because our extension
classes include a broad selection of the churches' leaders,
i.e. the people who are capable of making radical changes at the
grassroots and at all levels of the church's life.

A fourth step is to restructure the life of the church and its
ministry. This is particularly urgent--in our own situation--
for the Indian churches. The Quiché Presbytery has discovered
that the congregations that have no trained, ordained, paid
pastors are growing fastest. Rather than impose the old structures and standards they have decided to authorize outstanding
leaders to serve the sacraments, ordaining them as local
pastors. The Mam-speaking congregations are in the process of
forming a new presbytery in which they hope to change the requirements for organizing a church, redesign the ministry according to
indigenous patterns, and make the sacraments available to every
congregation. The remote Kekchi congregations have been growing
very rapidly under local men apprenticed to a wise old leader of
the people; they too will soon organize their own presbytery.
These exciting developments are not the result of theological
education by extension, but extension has helped to shape the
thinking that is allowing these basic changes to take place, and
it provides the means whereby local leaders can form sound
biblical, theological criteria as they determine their own
destiny in the church.

IV. HOW IS THE CHURCH TO CARRY OUT ITS MISSION?

We have followed a logical progression from theological
education to the ministry and the church. Our fourth and final
question deals with the mission of the church. Due to the
limitations of this paper we shall not attempt to define the
nature of that mission here but rather focus on the instrumentality of mission. In the final analysis the controversy over
theological education by extension involves fundamentally
divergent conceptions of the way in which the churches are to
carry out their mission in the world. Extension leaders must
consider whether their task is to support or subvert traditional
beliefs about training for ministry for mission.

Ron Frase, a former Presbyterian missionary to Brazil, has
written a stunning analysis of ministerial preparation in his
doctoral dissertation, "A Sociological Analysis of Brazilian
Protestantism: A Study of Social Change" (Princeton Theological
Seminary, 1975). He points out that the Presbyterian Church of
Brazil has been committed to a highly trained ministry, that
this commitment has produced rigid institutional structures and
seriously hampered the church's ability to respond to the
Brazilian situation, and that this whole development is the
result of a definite missiological concept. In 1847, just a few
years before the first missionaries were sent to Brazil, the
Board of Education stated succinctly in the Minutes of the
General Assembly of the Presbyterian Church in the U.S.A., "The
basis of all operations of the Board of Education is that a
pious and well qualified ministry is the great instrumentality
appointed by the Head of the Church for the conversion of the
world." At that time the Presbyterian denomination had 500
churches without pastors in the U.S., and yet it continued to
advocate--at home and abroad--a highly educated ministry in the
firm belief that Christ himself had appointed these "ministers"
to carry out the church's mission. Frase comments that other
churches were not held back by this concept and by the
concomitant structures and thus were able to respond more
effectively to the needs of the people both on the U.S. frontier
and in the interior of Brazil.

Although they would perhaps not state their case quite so
strongly today, the opponents of theological education by
extension in Guatemala and elsewhere are heirs to this understanding of how the church is to carry out its mission. This
explains why they fervently defend the traditional, elitist
approach to theological education and the hierarchical,
professional model of ministry.

A recent event in the life of the Presbyterian Church of
Guatemala may serve to illustrate how pervasive and convincing
this conception has become. On February 4, 1976 Guatemala
suffered its most devastating earthquake in recorded history.
23,000 people were killed; many more were injured and widowed or
orphaned; and one million were left homeless or with badly
damaged houses. A group of leading pastors and a few laymen in
Guatemala City immediately formed a Presbyterian emergency
committee (CESEP) to assess the needs and find and distribute
aid to the victims, especially Presbyterians. Two missionaries
took special interest in the pastors whose manses or homes had
fallen, and this became one of the more appealing projects as
large quantities of funds began to pour in from the U.S. and
elsewhere. A year after the earthquake, when this committee
reported to the plenary assembly of the Synod, they revealed
openly and without any sense of wrong that they had distributed

$24,165 among 310 laymen whose homes were destroyed or damaged (average: $78 per family), $38,300 to 26 pastors who had suffered losses (average: $1473), and another $30,000 to 6 leading pastors in the capital city area ($5000 a piece) who had not lost any property in the earthquake--and most of these 6 were members of the CESEP committee.

The point of this story is that the people most involved in the incident were quite convinced that what they did was right-- in view of their understanding of the special place and role of the ordained pastor in the church and in God's mission to the world. At a moment of extreme crisis and vast human need, these pastors could actually improve their lot ($5000 is about 5 times as much as an average pastor earns in a year) and accept reconstruction money even if they had had no house of their own. The treasurer of CESEP, one of the most highly respected laymen in the Presbyterian Church and at that time Moderator of the Synod, apparently approved of what happened, although he expected nothing for himself. Missionaries helped get the money and cooperated with the emergency committee; the liaison person in the U.S. approved the budget; and the donors in the U.S. were eager to help the pastors. Even the representatives of the churches at the recent Synod meeting raised few questions and did not censure the members of CESEP, although they knew that many of their members had suffered great losses and had been given much smaller amounts of aid, if any, by this committee. The only possible way to contemplate this whole affair is to recognize that the ordained ministry is conceived of as the great instrumentality "appointed by the Head of the Church" to carry out God's mission in the world. Within this frame of reference what happened was not only justifiable but probably inevitable.

According to this "elevated" concept of the ministry, the churches should do everything within their power for the prepara- tion and support of their pastors. Seminaries are sacred places, seedbeds for the formation of God's chosen servants. It is easy to see why theological education by extension is depreciated and rejected by many. But by the same token it is easy to see that extension has great potential for radical change not only in the ministry but also for the renewal of the churches for mission. It may also be argued that the churches' mission in the world will always be gravely distorted unless the members in the churches, the whole people of God, are given access to theological education and the ministry.

The Presbyterian Seminary of Guatemala, with almost 15 years' experience of extension, has barely begun to challenge the old structures of the ministry and to change the churches' under- standing of mission. But now 250 people representing the whole

spectrum of the churches' membership study theology each year in
the context of their own homes, congregations and communities--
instead of 10 or 15 privileged youth set apart at a seminary
campus. Probably 75 percent of these students have no intention
of becoming ordained pastors, but they are eager to study in a
system which offers no relief from the demands of daily life and
employment, and they expect to serve their congregations
voluntarily the rest of their lives. At least 50 students are
Indians, second class citizens in a country which is striving to
obliterate their languages and cultural values through "social
integration." Perhaps another 50 are women, members of a
church that deprives them of ordination as either pastors or
elders, which means that they are disenfranchized from the
entire ecclesiastical governing structure. The great majority
represent the poor and could never attend a traditional seminary.

We readily confess that there are still major gaps in the
curriculum, instructional materials, personnel, and organization
of our extension program, although we know it is superior to the
earlier residential program. And we hesitate to guess what will
be the future shape of the churches' ministry, although we know
the options are now much greater than they were. We strongly
believe that the Seminary is now serving the churches and
strengthening their ministry and mission by breaking out of the
confining, debilitating patterns and concepts of the past.

CONCLUSION

Change is always difficult, especially in the realm of
religious beliefs and ecclesiastical structures, above all in
relation to the ordained ministry, due to aged traditions,
vested interests, established patterns of dependence, and sacred
taboos. Many a discussion of critical issues has floundered or
been dismissed by a simple reference to "the call" or by an
appeal to the sacrifice, dedication, or spirituality of "the
ministry." The extension movement here in Guatemala and elsewhere has taken on a task which is difficult and complex, for
it is attempting to revolutionize not only theological education
but also the ministry, the church, and its mission in the world.
The outcome--after almost 15 years--is by no means certain.

We have suggested that this task may be understood as subversion. The word "subversion" usually carries very negative
overtones; it means to undermine or to overthrow. It may,
however, be used to refer to a positive, dynamic process of
renewal and transformation from within. Another word that has
been used in recent years to express the same fundamental concept
is "contextualization." The concern of theological educators in
many places is to liberate our institutions and chruches from
dysfunctional structures in order to respond in new ways to the

Spirit of God in our age and in our many diverse contexts. Theological education by extension is a tremendously versatile and flexible approach to ministerial training; it is also now a spreading, deepening movement for change, subversion, and renewal.

More questions than answers are evoked by this paper and by the extension movement. Can we finally abolish the persistent dichotomy of clergy and laity in our various ecclesiastical traditions--with the help of theological education by extension? Surely there are not two levels of calling or service in the ministry. Is ordination, as it has been practiced over the centuries, really valid? Perhaps there should be a parity of ordination--or one basic ordination--among deacons, elders, pastors or priests, and bishops. Or perhaps every adult Christian who is willing to serve God's purposes should eventually be ordained for ministry. Why is there such a great distinction between Christian education and theological education? It seems--from the perspective of theological education by extension--that there should be a progressive continuum of service and preparation in ministry in the context of the local congregation and society. How can the churches employ pastors, preachers, administrators, etc., without becoming dependent on them and ruled by them? Paying salaries for fulltime work in or for the churches is not bad in itself; our problems lie in the matrix of theological education-ordination-the sacraments-the ministry-salaries-the professional role. What should be the content of theological curricula if we do decide to subvert the existing structures of theological education and the ministry? We have avoided any discussion of content here, but it could be argued that the medium itself is the most significant message. Our task is to place the tools of theological reflection in the hands of the people of God so that they will be able to clear away the centuries of theological, ecclesiastical, and liturgical residue and begin to theologize, to build a much more vital, corporate ministry, to renew the church from its roots, to move out in liberating mission to all people.

In this paper we have focused quite specifically upon one local situation, but our concern is for the worldwide Christian movement, which owes so much both positively and negatively to its Western heritage. The writer is obliged to point out particularly that the professional, academic model of the ministry is far more entrenched in his home country and in his own church than it has yet become in Guatemala. The United Presbyterian Church in the U.S.A. probably spends $200 million of its annual income, to support pastors; it contributes $7 million, just 1.5 percent of its income, for mission and service and ecumenical relations around the world.

Our purpose is not to criticize fellow ordained pastors either in Guatemala or in the U.S. or elsewhere. It is rather to call in question the basic structures of the ministry, which we have all accepted and propagated to some degree, and to recommend radical changes. Although we did not build these structures, we--both clergy and laity--are accomplices, and we are all stewards of the church and its mission under God.

In recent years the churches have raised a prophetic cry for justice amidst the oppressive structures of our societies, and Christians are identifying themselves increasingly with liberation movements. José Míguez Bonino (*Doing Theology in a Revolutionary Situation*) and others have suggested that we may have to redefine the church in terms of these missiological concerns and in terms of para-ecclesiastical or even non-religious groups committed to human liberation. Certainly the churches and their seminaries will have little credibility in today's ideological struggles if they continue to foster elitism and privilege within their own ranks. Theological education by extension opens up an avenue for the churches to transform their own structures, placing power and initiative in the hands of the whole people of God. This in turn may enable the churches to become a servant people, counter communities whose prophetic message is accompanied by living witness and liberating ministry.

PART
II

Regional Issues and Adaptations of the Extension Movement

7

Dialogue on Alternatives in Theological Education:
Latin America

Latin America has been the scenario of convulsive movements and revolutionary change for some time. In recent years it has gained a worldwide hearing for its theology of liberation. In ecclesiastical circles the Latin American Pentecostals have become a focus of attention due to their fantastic growth and indigenous ways. And the theological education by extension movement, which first developed in Latin America, has now spread to all six continents.

The purpose of this paper is to describe and analyze recent developments in theological education in Latin America with special reference to the extension movement. The following pages must of course be limited and selective, based on the writer's perspective, knowledge, and experience. We have put down in writing some of the factors and events that converge in the extension movement in Latin America today with the hope that these reflexions will contribute to the current dialogue on alternatives in theological education here and elsewhere.

The emphasis on extension in the following presentation is due to the writer's personal involvement in that movement, but it is also due to the truly amazing growth of extension through-out Latin America and the world during the last ten years. The Theological Education Fund made theological Mandate (1970-1977). In July, 1976 the T.E.F. Committee held its annual meeting in Costa Rica. In his report of that meeting Thomas Campbell, a member of the T.E.F. Committee and the Dean of United Theological Seminary in Minneapolis, U.S.A., wrote:

Theological Education by Extension is now clearly established as the most vigorous alternative creative form of
preparation for the ministry. It may soon outdistance
residential patterns of training as the dominant form of
training for the ministry. (See the *T.E.F. Report for
1976*, p. 11.)

In the first section of this paper we shall take a very
cursory look at traditional patterns of leadership formation in
Latin America among Roman Catholics, the historic Protestant
churches, independent missions and churches, and the Pentecostals.
Then we shall examine some of the cultural and ideological
factors at work in Latin America that further explain the need
for alternative approaches to theological education. The third
section deals directly with the extension movement in Latin
America. And the final section summarizes some of the continuing
concerns in the search for alternatives in theological education.

I.   TRADITIONAL PATTERNS OF LEADERSHIP FORMATION

A. *The Roman Catholic Church*

No discussion of Protestant developments in Latin America
would be adequate without some mention of Roman Catholic
antecedents or counterparts, for that church has dominated not
only religious life but culture in general for almost 500 years
in this region, and even today 90 percent of the population is
considered in some sense Catholic. Latin American Catholicism
includes a wide range of movements and leadership patterns, but
we shall mention only three major kinds of leaders and their
preparation: the priests, catequists, and lay brotherhoods.
The following observations are focused on Guatemala, which is a
microcosm of Latin America.

There are two main structures for Catholic religious life at
the local level. Within the hierarchical pattern the parish
priest has absolute authority, for he alone can dispense the
sacraments, the means of grace and salvation. The priests
appoint as their assistants catechists, who help run the parish
programs, especially in the absence of the priests and in the
less accessible communities which the priests visit only once a
month, once a year, or even less frequently. The other main
structure of Catholic life is the *cofradía* (confraternity or lay
brotherhood or sisterhood), which is led by local people and is
concerned primarily with the care of the images of the saints
and their festivals and may not be tied to and subject to the
priest.

Following Catholic tradition elsewhere the Catholic Church in
Latin America provides formal training for the priesthood through

a network of minor and major seminaries. In Guatemala this system has never been very successful in providing national priests, either Latin or Indian. Apparently there are now only about 600 priests in the whole country, an average of one per 10,000 people, and 500 of these priests (83%) are expatriates. (Among the Protestant denominations there are probably 4,000 congregations with 1,000 ordained pastors, an average of one per 600 constituents, and at least 90 percent of the pastors are nationals.)

Not only is there an extreme shortage of Guatemalan priests; the nature of the priesthood is seriously distorted, and this is directly related to the training process. Candidates are selected and set apart at a very young age, pass through a long educational process which alienates them from their own communities and culture, and are made to be the "spiritual fathers" of the Church with no reference to the members and no real testing of their leadership ability. Through this process even the Guatemalan candidates become "foreigners." They are educationally and religiously far "above" the common people; they do not do any physical work; they are to be reverenced, served, and obeyed.

The catechists are altogether different from the priests whom they serve. They are local people, and they never lose their cultural identity. Their training varies, but it is entirely functional and non-formal. A local priest meets with his catechists regularly or at least occasionally to instruct them for their tasks, to discuss problems as they arise, and to plan special events such as religious festivals, weddings, baptisms, and funerals. At one end of the scale catechists may go through serious biblical studies and do some of the preaching, especially where Indian languages are used; at the other end of the scale they may be simple errand boys virtually ignorant of the supposed meaning of the religious symbols, terms, and liturgy. There must be 20 or 30 times as many catechists as priests in Guatemala and in Latin America as a whole, but they are totally dependent on the priests.

The *cofradías* represent another very different, entirely local, autonomous structure. Many towns have one or more *cofradías*, each of which is responsible for the care of a "saint," the annual festival of that saint, and the carrying of the image of the saint in stipulated processions. In Indian communities, where the *cofradías* continue to hold great social importance, all male adults are expected to serve progressive one to three-year terms off and on throughout their lives. There is an ordered and ritualized process of induction and service as ordinary members, then as junior stewards, and finally as the steward of the saint, and the different *cofradías* are themselves graded according to the importance of their saints in the town pantheon. The men who reach the top and serve as the steward of a saint exercize great influence as chief organizers of their *cofradías* and also speak for them at the town assemblies. On completion of this responsibility they become town elders or *principales*. Although this pattern is in one sense hierarchical, it is radically different from the ecclesiastical structure in several important ways. Access to positions of prestige and influence is gained only by responsible service at all the lower levels. Selection is based on group consensus and carried out by the upper leaders in the structure; no one volunteers or offers to be a steward or an elder. Service is not remunerated; rather than provide income or economic advantages it requires great sacrifice in time and energy and money. The steward of a saint is required to provide meals and provisions for all his members at the time of the festival and a house for the image during his term of service.

In recent years conflicts between the priests and the *cofradías* have increased as reformist priests have tried to downplay the saints, deemphasize the processions, oppose superstition and traditional practices, and even to remove the images from their church alters. But the *cofradías* represent the people; they provide for widespread participation of the people in the religious and social life of their communities; and they have developed a process of leadership formation which is functional and entirely indigenous. The catechists also maintain close ties with their people, but they are neither chosen by them nor responsible to them.

It is easy to see that the Protestant churches have been influenced by Roman Catholic patterns of leadership, and it would be tempting to suggest ways in which the Catholic Church could benefit by basic changes in its structures. Unless changes are made, that Church will probably continue to lose ground rapidly.

B. *The Historic Protestant Churches*

Rather than survey the traditional training patterns among the different Protestant denominations in Latin America, we shall try to get at the critical issues by looking at an in-depth study of the Presbyterian Church in Brazil as analyzed by Ronald Frase in his dissertation, "A Sociological Analysis of the Development of Brazilian Protestantism: A Study in Social Change" (Princeton Theological Seminary, 1975), p. 411-425. This case is typical of the historic Protestant churches throughout Latin America in that the Presbyterian Church was in many countries the first or among the first to be established and its influence has been especially strong in the matter of ministerial preparation.

The Presbyterian Mission carried with it from the U.S. and
implanted in Brazil--as it did in Guatemala and around the world
-- a deep concern for a highly educated clergy. The seriousness
of this concern was stated in the Minutes of the General Assembly
of the U.S. Church in 1847, just a short time before the first
missionaries were sent to Brazil: "A pious and well qualified
ministry is the great instrumentality appointed by the Head of
the Church for the conversion of the world." And further "our
standards make high literary attainments an indispensible
qualification for the sacred office." With this kind of a
rationale the establishment of high level seminaries with a
classical curriculum (including Greek and Hebrew) become a top
priority of the Mission and later of the Presbyterian Church of
Brazil.

Frase enumerates some of the ways in which "the Reformed
legacy of a highly trained ministry proved to be an obstacle to
the spontaneous expansion of the Presbyterian Church of Brazio."
(1) It was impossible to provide pastoral care for the many new
congregations that were springing up, and many opportunities for
growth were lost. (2) The high level seminary training tended
to alienate the ministerial candidates from the people in the
congregations were largely illiterate, rural, poor. (3) Because
the congregations were largely among the "ignorant classes,"
they could not be organized or support a pastor or offer the
sacraments to the new believers. (4) Many presbyteries were
unable to provide seminary training for new candidates for the
ministry. (5) Although the congregations were often able to
maintain active programs led by lay leaders, the judicatories in
the Presbyterian form of government (local sessions, regional
presbyteries and synods, and the national General Assembly) had
great difficulty because they required minimal representation by
ordained pastors as well as elders (laymen).

In retrospect it is all too clear that the Presbyterian Church
of Brazil was hamstrung by the exigencies of a highly trained
ministry and clergy-dependent church structures as it faced the
challenge of receptive communities throughout that vast country.
Frase comments at several points that the Baptists were able to
respond much more effectively because of greater flexibility in
the requirements of ordination, pastors who were able to identify
more easily with rural life and with the lower classes, and the
autonomy and economic viability of the local congregations.
Within the Presbyterian Church attempts were made to develop a
lay ministry, lay evangelists, and alternative training programs,
but these efforts were blocked by "an incipient clericism
fostered by an ecclesiology which placed effective power in the
hands of the clergy at the expense of the laity."

The problem we are dealing with here is not just pragmatic,
but missiological and theological. Although the Presbyterian

Church of Brazil did continue to grow, scores of congregations
were deprived of pastoral care, the sacraments, and effective
teaching. The church failed during a critical historical
period to expand into hundreds of neighboring communities. And
an elitist understanding of the ministry was established which
will no doubt limit gravely that church's ability to grow, to be
renewed, and to serve for many years to come. In fact the
Baptists themselves--not to mention the Lutherans, Methodists,
Anglicans, and other historic churches--have today largely
accepted the standards and privileges of a professional, highly
trained clergy in Brazil.

There seems to be a profound, unresolved contradiction in the
historic churches' approach to theological education. We know
that Jesus' ministry was one of complete self-giving, humiliation,
and sacrifice. But our seminaries and ecclesiastical structures
elevate candidates for the ministry above the common people, form
in them values and needs which the people are unable to support,
and give them transcendental, permanent status and privilege in
the churches. We know that Paul described the church as a body
in which all the members are essential, though diverse, and he
ascribed the ministry to the whole body. But we have made the
ministry dependent on the ordained pastor, and we deprive the
rest of the members of the training and the authority to carry
out the most elemental and essential responsibilities of the
ministry.

Looking at Latin America as a whole, one would have to say
that the challenge is as great and the problem as critical today
as it was in Brazil 50 or 100 years ago. In the 21 Spanish and
Portuguese speaking countries (including Puerto Rico), the
historic denominations are at present maintaining only a handful
of traditional, university or high school level seminaries--
with heavy subsidies from abroad. The major centers are in
Puerto Rico, Mexico, Argentina, and Brazil, and even these are
facing crises with low enrollments and very high costs. The
Theological Community of Mexico, for example, is a cluster of
five seminaries representing seven major ecclesiastical traditions with millions of dollars invested in facilities, but
enrollment dropped below 25 this past academic year. The
Advanced Evangelical Institute of Theological Studies (ISEDET)
in Argentina has the most distinguished faculty in Latin America
and is sponsored officially by eight major denominations, but
last year it graduated only four students in theology and nine
in music. While these denominational seminaries are struggling
to survive in the rarified atmosphere of higher theological
studies, putting out a total of perhaps 100 graduates per year in
the entire region, the Protestant and Pentecostal churches
continue to grow rapidly and form an estimated 5,000 new churches
every year.

C. *Independent Missions and Churches*

The historic denominations--Presbyterian, Anglicans, Baptists,
Lutherans, Moravians, and Methodists--were the first Protestant
groups to send missionaries into Latin America, but during the
last 30 years conservative evangelical, fundamentalist, and
independent missionaries have become the overwhelming majority.
Although the number of missionaries does not even closely
correlate with the size of the churches in Latin America, these
younger ecclesiastical traditions are an important component of
Latin American Christianity, and they too have made significant
contributions in the field of theological education.

On the one hand the non-historic groups in Latin America are
noteworthy for the number and diversity of their leadership
training programs. There are perhaps 400 to 500 Bible institutes,
night Bible schools, Bible correspondence programs, and short
term institute programs of various academic levels and doctrinal
emphases throughout the region, each with its own local color,
advantages, and disadvantages. The short term institutes and
correspondence programs reach tens of thousands of local church
leaders, but usually they do not provide a very profound or
systematic preparation, and generally it is not recognized for
ordination. The night schools and residential Bible institutes
are more demanding academically; they provide training for large
numbers of students, many of whom go on to occupy leadership
positions in their churches; the courses are by and large much
less sophisticated than seminary courses, i.e. more practical
and functional and at times simplistic and mechanical.

On the other hand there is a strong drive toward the "upgrading" and consolidation of training among these programs and
their constituencies. The common, uncritical belief is that
more training is better and that higher levels are more effective.
Short term institutes become residential institutions; primary-
level Bible institutes begin to require one, two, or three years
of secondary preparation; more advanced theological institutes
become seminaries; and correspondence programs are considered to
be very inadequate or worthless. The dominant model or ideal is
the full-fledged residential seminary at or near the university
level. This trend follows the example of the historic denominations and leads to the formation of an elitist view of theological
education and the ministry. It means that more and more training
will be provided for fewer and fewer people, and local leaders
will no longer have access to training and no longer be accredited
for "the ministry."

The Central American Mission-Church provides a typical example
of this process. Just a few years ago their Bible Institute in
Guatemala City proudly became the Central American Theological

Seminary, requiring secondary schooling for entering students
and relegating lower candidates to their institute in the nearby
town of Chimaltenango. The Robinson Bible Institute, which had
been established to train Indian church leaders and had once
taught courses in the Indian languages, now became the Guatemalan
Bible Institute, requiring first a primary diploma and adding
very shortly some secondary schooling. Far out in the hinterland
the Barillas Bible Institute serves several Indian populations,
which in most areas are more than 90 percent illiterate, but this
institution now uses Spanish and is beginning to set up formal
requirements. Apparently this is progress. But most Indian
church leaders do not have sufficient Spanish or enough basic
skills to enter any of these institutions, and they could not
afford to leave their families in any case. Church leaders in
the Department of Chimaltenango complain that they cannot afford
to hire graduates of the Guatemalan Bible Institute, which is
located there. And no one knows where the graduates of the
Seminary will be able to serve aside from a few administrative or
teaching positions subsidized by the mission—or in some other
profession.

The same tendency toward institutionalization and upgrading is
evident throughout Latin America, fostered by competition among
the theological institutions themselves and by the growth of
schooling in general. The results are questionable. The most
outstanding non-denominational seminary in the entire region is
the Latin American Biblical Seminary, which is located in San
José, Costa Rica and has over 100 fulltime students enrolled in
university-level theological studies. It rightly boasts an
outstanding, Latin-dominated faculty and curriculum, but it
requires a foreign subsidy of perhaps 80 percent of its total
costs. This seminary is unapologizing in its commitment to
evangelism, evangelical Christian faith, and the evangelical
churches, but recent surveys indicate that fewer and fewer
graduates are serving as pastors. The seminary has taken great
strides toward an ideological commitment to the poor and to
radical social change, but its own faculty and by and large its
graduates are part of the privileged upper and middle classes.
And this seminary, because of its "success," serves as the envied
model for all the other up and coming evangelical seminaries in
Latin America.

D. *The Pentecostals*

It is a well-known fact that 70 percent to 80 percent of the
Protestants of Latin America are Pentecostals and that the
Pentecostal churches are growing by leaps and bounds. Christian
Lalive d'Epinay, Peter Wagner, Kenneth Mulholland and others
have described in detail the fascinating way in which these
churches develop indigenous leadership through in-service

training, apprenticeship, or "street seminaries." Actually the
Pentecostals of Latin America have employed all the methods of
theological education that we have considered thus far, but
their extraordinary growth is no doubt related most directly to
their non-formal training programs.

Among the Pentecostals of Chile the ministry is at once
hierarchical and democratic--somewhat like the Catholic
cofradías we have mentioned. On the one hand every believer is
expected to participate in the evangelistic witness of the church
from the moment he is converted. And any convert may become a
pastor if he demonstrates the gifts and dedication and fruits
necessary for a successful ministry. On the other hand there
are many stages or levels of ministry, and few reach the top and
become fully recognized as pastors. The normal process is to
proceed from street evangelism to Sunday school teaching and
occasional preaching, to responsibility for a preaching point,
and then to the beginning of a new church. Only after successfully fulfilling all of these responsibilities and finally
building up a congregation to the extent that it can support him
financially is the probationer promoted to the pastorate. Within
this system training is entirely non-formal. There is no
theological institution; there are no "students" enrolled; there
are no fees, no "teachers," no courses, no "examinations" or
marks. Yet the essential functions of training for ministry are
carried out with tremendous effectiveness. The on-going ministry
of the church is itself the training program; all the members are
involved, learning as they participate in the varied ministries;
the teachers are those who have advanced further up the leadership ladder; the curriculum is alive and functional; advancement
is based on real learning and effective service.

It is easy for outsiders to find fault with this approach to
leadership formation and to this ecclesiastical pattern.
Biblical content and theological reflection may be very weak;
historical understanding may be very limited; and formal training
in the human sciences totally lacking. The pastors tend to be
powerful *caudillos*; splits are common; and heresy is a real
danger. On the other hand these churches are growing spontan-
eously; the ministry is truly an expression of the whole people
of God; the leaders identify socially and culturally with their
people; and training is a means to service rather than personal
advancement, economic gain, or intellectual upgrading.

The Assemblies of God in Brazil, an indigenous Pentecostal
church with some ties to the Assemblies of the U.S. and Sweden,
is the largest non-Roman church in Latin America with two to
three million members. Traditionally this church has been
opposed to systematic theological training; about six years ago
they opened the door to Bible institutes; now large extention

programs are taking shape in at least two areas. Ronald Iwasko,
a missionary located at Fortaleza who was initiating one of
those extension programs, reported in January 1976 that there
are about 40,000 workers among the Assemblies of God in Brazil,
ranked in ascending order as helpers, deacons, presbyters,
evangelists, and pastors. He estimated that the denomination
would within five years have 5,000 pastors and workers studying
by extension within their democratic-hierarchical structure of
ministry. History will determine whether it is possible to wed
the effective indigenous leadership pattern of the Pentecostals
with modern educational technology through theological education
by extension.

II.   THE NEED FOR ALTERNATIVE APPROACHES
TO THEOLOGICAL EDUCATION

A. *Diversity of Cultural Contexts*

What is needed in Latin American theological education
today is not simply an indigenous pattern of leadership formation or a new educational technology but, in the first place,
a deeper understanding of the diverse cultural contexts in the
region. This writer is not equipped-nor does space allow--to
analyze the multitudinous racial, cultural, and linguistic
patterns of Latin America. Rather we shall focus upon one of
the basic contrasts and conflicts facing us here in Guatemala,
the Ladino-Indian setting, in order to illustrate the importance
of the cultural context in the formation of theological training
programs. This particular matter is probably the most important
cultural issue facing the churches in Guatemala, Ecuador, Peru,
Bolivia, and parts of Mexico, Honduras, Nicaragua, Panama,
Colombia, Chile, Paraguay, and Argentina.

The Mayan peoples of Guatemala and Southern Mexico number
about five million, and they steadfastly maintain distinctive
cultural patterns--their own languages, belief systems, dress,
and economic life--even after 500 years of Spanish-Ladino
dominance. Missionary anthropologists have described the marked
contrast between Indian and Latin patterns of leadership, and
they have urged missions and churches in this region to take
seriously these differences. Unfortunately these studies, which
have been available for 10 to 25 years, have not been widely
disseminated, and serious errors are being repeated again and
again in the churches and in their training institutions.

In the dominant Latin culture schooling is becoming
increasingly important as the gateway to leadership. In Indian
society formal schooling has never been significant; in fact it
was practically non-existent until recently; the ability to
read and write is still not essential; leaders are prepared and

selected through the experience of service. In Latin society
youth and virility are admired, and young men can occupy leadership positions. In the Indian communities the men work their
way gradually up to leadership positions; maturity is essential.
Latin society approves and awards individualism, and those who
assert themselves usually become leaders. Indians do not approve
of assertiveness, and those who stand out or speak out are
rejected as leaders. Latin leaders are generally highly visible
and audible. Indian leaders are usually quiet, stand in the
background, keep a low profile. Latin leaders tend to rule or
run their organizations by force of personality or will.
Indian leaders tend to lead their communities through group
consensus.

The implications of this oversimplified contrast in culture
patterns and values are readily evident for theological education. Traditional residential seminaries and Bible institutes
are not recommended for Indian situations because they cater to
young people rather than mature leaders; they emphasize books and
theoretical knowledge rather than experience and responsible
service; they take candidates out of their communities and make
them stand out from their peers rather than helping them to
emerge within their group. Brief institutes and extension
programs, on the other hand, are effective training models
because they can fit and heighten the normal processes of
leadership formation in the congregations.

One wonders how many Bible institutes and seminaries--or for
that matter extension programs and other alternatives--have
been implanted in Latin America wholly or partially oblivious to
the local cultural patterns and values. In how many places are
youth being drawn away from their communities never to return
and serve their own people, or to return and clash with the
traditional authority system, or to impose their own leadership
and foreign customs, or to be ignored and rejected by their own
people. This is no small or isolated concern. It may be one of
the most decisive factors in the growth and effectiveness of the
churches not only in Indian areas but throughout Latin America.

At the same time we must allow for and indeed call for a
critical stance beyond indigenization. What if the churches'
leadership among the Indian peoples becomes stagnant because
only the older men are allowed to rule and perhaps they are
unwilling to learn and to grow? What are we to say about the at
times overbearing, arbitrary, and manipulative rule of Ladino
leaders? Theological education, like the Gospel itself, must
adapt to and infiltrate indigenous leadership patterns to the
extent that it can eventually transform them from within. But
only when church leaders, theological educators, and students
are well established within their cultural contexts can they

expect to make changes that will be appropriate, acceptable, and
enduring.

B. *Social, Economic, and Political Realities*

The second dimension of our concern for alternative
approaches to theological education deals with the social,
economic, and political realities of Latin America. It is not
uncommon in theological circles in this region to hear the
question, What are the ideological presuppositions of your
program of theological education? Paulo Freire has made us all
aware that there is no neutral, a-political approach to education; ideological commitment--one way or another--is unavoidable.
As capitalism and military repression continue to reign unabated
in Latin America, theological educators and churchmen are being
forces to analyze their own stance and engagement in the
struggle for liberation. Theological education, in its
structure and methodology as well as its content, must either
serve or challenge the status quo.

The structures of domination and exploitation in Latin
America are well known and well documented, as is the complicity
of the Christian religion. The 16th Century conquest raped the
Native American peoples of their gold and their land, their
dignity and their independence, and in time their languages and
their culture. The Roman Catholic form of Christianity was the
ideological tool and part of the rationale of the New World
Empire, for it taught the subjugated peoples to obey their
conquerors in obedience to God, to keep the 10 Commandments,
especially the eighth ("Thou shalt not steal"), which meant to
reverence the right of the conquerors over the land they had
expropriated, and to work hard and peacefully--for the benefit
of their lords. The second conquest or neocolonialism began in
the 19th Century, took the form of modernization and liberalism,
and led to the internal and international dominance of
capitalism. At this time Protestantism invaded Latin America,
in some cases (such as Guatemala) at the direct invitation of
liberal, reforming governments, who saw in the new religion both
both a counterweight to reactionary Catholic power and a moral
force to promote the new ideals and enterprises--with its
personal piety and discipline, its concern for medical and
educational services, and its teachings concerning hard work and
private property. We come now to 1977 and find that the
structures of colonialism and neocolonialism are still entrenched
and that both Catholicism and Protestantism are still, with some
notable exceptions, serving the interests of the upper classes
while apparently identifying themselves with the poor. Ninety
percent of the fertile land is in the hands of a few families
and corporations, although in most countries of Latin America
eighty percent of the people live off the land. Many are

plantation workers (serfs), sharecroppers, or migrant laborers; most are landless. Two-thirds of the people are undernourished and close to starvation; half suffer from infectious or deficiency diseases. Both the natural resources and labor are being sold off cheaply for the benefit of the upper classes and the wealthy nations. As the oppression of the masses becomes increasingly intollerable, political and military repression becomes increasingly necessary to maintain the status quo. The churches continue to carry on their routine of worship and personal religion, apparently uncaring...or ignorant..or impotent.

Less well known but equally well documented is the role of education in relation to these structures, and this leads us to a reevaluation of traditional patterns of theological education. Closely parallel and tied to the steep social-economic pyramid of Latin America there is an educational pyramid, the new ideological tool which subtly and effectively promotes and justifies the horrendous injustices and exploitation of the system. The schools are so effective, as Ivan Illich has pointed out, because they reach out into all sectors of the population, tying them into a process of apparent advancement, while in fact they leave the poor basically in the same disadvantaged position relative to the level of schooling they attain. In all of Latin America less than three percent of the people ever reach the universities, and these few come from and/or enter into the benefits of wealth and power. The rest continue to struggle upward, accept with resignation their lower positions on the ladder, but hope their children or their grandchildren will one day arrive at the top. The subtlety lies in the illusion and the achievement of personal progress, in which the people accept and willfully collaborate with the structures of exploitation.

We noted earlier that the Bible institutes and seminaries are engaged in a similar process of upgrading. Some of the more enlightened seminaries are becoming very aware of and outspoken about the structures of oppression and exploitation in Latin America; they carry on serious research and produce erudite theses, speak eloquently about conscientization and the poor and liberation. But they themselves are elitist structures; they too alienate their students from the masses; their teaching and prophesying, in as much as they are earnest and sincere, must call into question their own existence. Alternative approaches to theological education are urgently needed, approaches that will break the upward spiral of the educational pyramid and make available the tools of theological reflection to the people of God without forcing them into the mold of the world's elitist, oppressive structures.

C. *Development at the Grassroots*

Many have commented that most of the talk about development,
the debates about liberation, and even the prophetic voices of
theologians in Latin America are futile because they never have
much real effect among the people. Books and articles are
published, congresses and seminars are held, governments change
or are overthrown, but the poor remain poor, are getting poorer
and more desperate, and are more numerous every day. What
prospects are there then for development at the grassroots level--
which must be the key to all genuine development? And what does
this process suggest for those of us who are involved in the
churches and in theological education?

Local communities, both rural and urban, reflect the same
dynamics which we have just considered, for they are an extension
of the same hierarchical structures of privilege and power. In
Quetzaltenango, for example, a farmer or worker must work an
entire week to earn the $5.00 it costs him to see a doctor for
10 minutes. Not only that but hundreds of thousands of these men
in the Western highlands of Guatemala are forced to go down to
the fertile coastal region for months at a time to work on the
coffee, cotton, and sugar plantations at sub-minimal wages so
that the wealthy and/or absentee landlords can export these
products at low enough prices on the world market in order for
Guatemala to earn the exchange credits to bring in petroleum
products, cars, television sets, and other luxuries for the
upper and middle classes. And the entire trade process is in
the hands of people who are in a position to rake off benefits
far in excess of the workers' salaries. So this rich, agricultural country does not produce enough basic foods for her own
people, and the working classes continue to live at bare subsis-
tence levels, with endemic malnutrition, and excessive levels of
disease and infant mortality.

David Werner has spent the last 12 years helping to form a
rural health care network in western Mexico, and he has brought
together penetrating insights into the problems and solutions of
grassfoots development in two major papers and a circular letter
(dated January 1977, available from the Hesperian Foundation,
Box 1692, Palo Alto, California 94302, U.S.A.). Werner narrates
laconically how rural health services have in recent years--
inspite of and because of huge investments of aid money--gone
from bad to worse. Years ago, before modern Western medicines
and professionals reached the villages there was quite an array
of empirical community healers, herb doctors, bone setters,
traditional midwives, and spiritual healers. With the growth of
national health departments and medical schools, they "tied to
stamp out this motley work force." To replace it they began to
train more doctors, only to discover that Western-style,

city-trained M.D.s were far too expensive and refused to serve
in rural areas, so this created a surplus of poorly trained
doctors in the cities. Then they tried to require graduating
medical students to spend a year in the villages, but found that
they were ill prepared both by their training and by disposition;
they were often resentful, irresponsible, or corrupt. Next they
tried mobile clinics, but these created further dependency and
unfulfilled expectations, national health authorities have
recognized the need for a holistic approach to health problems
with a whole range of participants in a pyramidal health team,
including local, auxiliary health workers, but even these new
programs can be terribly paternalistic and initiative-destroying
and serve finally to perpetuate the status quo.

In a recent study tour through Central America and northern
South America Werner and his colleagues visited almost 40 rural
health programs in order to find out what is happening and what
works effectively. They discovered that these programs tend to
fall somewhere along a continuum between two diametrically
opposed poles:

1. Community supportive *programs or functions are those
which favorably influence the long-range welfare of the
community, that help it stand on its own feet, that
genuinely encourage responsibility, initiative, decision
making and self-reliance at the community level, that
build upon human dignity.*

2. Community oppressive *programs or functions are those
which, while invariably giving lip service to the above
aspects of community input, are fundamentally authoritarian,
paternalistic, or are structured and carried out in such a
way that they actually encourage greater dependency,
servility and unquestioning acceptance of outside regula-
tions and decisions; those which, in the long run, are
crippling to the dynamics of the community.*

Throughout Werner's analysis the key question or challenge
is: "How can more people become responsibly involved in caring
for their own health?" And in his response the village health
worker becomes not the auxiliary or lackey of the trained
professional but rather the basic, primary agent of health
care. He is chosen by his people; he knows them and understands
their problems; he is responsible and responsive to them; he can
live among them within their life-style and economic level. He
can, if given the opportunity and minimal tools, learn to help
them meet 97 percent of their own health needs--and refer them
to others for the rest. In fact, Werner insists, the village
health worker is more qualified than the M.D. "to deal effectively
with the important sicknesses of most of the people." The health

team pyramid is still necessary, but it must be turned on its
side so that the people and their local health workers come
first and the professional doctor is no longer on top.

Health is, however, more than the treatment and prevention of
disease, and the village health worker is, in Werner's conception,
more than a paramedic. Far more basic to the physical, emotional,
and social well-being of the people are such matters as the
distribution of land and wealth, education, and politics. The
village health worker is in a position not only to help his
people in terms of their immediate needs; he himself is an
example to his neighbors that they can learn new skills and take
new responsibilities to improve their life; he gets his people
to work together; he awakens in them a wider sense of their
human potential and ultimately of their human rights. "The
chief role of the village health worker, at his best, is that
of liberator."

At this point it becomes very evident that the problems of
community health are inextricably bound up with the structures
of oppression and exploitation which we mentioned earlier...
and with all aspects of human need. Inevitably the medical
profession and power groups oppose the more effective community
health programs and their local promoters. But the central
role of the people and their leaders in solving their own health
needs and in resolving the whole range of human development
needs, including the "spiritual," is unquestionable. Theological
educators, especially in the Third World, must take seriously
these fundamental concepts in order to avoid the drastic effects
of Western professionalization, institutionalization, and
commercialization in the ministry.

The parallel between medicine and the ministry as professions
is painfully evident. In the U.S. the ministry was the first
profession way back in the colonial period; the seminaries and
their accrediting associations still seek to maintain their
standards and prestige on a par with the medical schools.
Fortunately the Protestant missions and churches in Latin
America have never been able fully to build up the professional
ministry to that extent--although, as we have seen, there is a
strong trend among all groups in that direction. Several years
ago a Guatemalan newspaper published a survey of all the medical
doctors in the country, indicating that 85 percent of them
lived and worked in the capital city among 15 percent of the
national population, with 15 percent of the doctors serving the
other 85 percent of the people, most of whom in the rural areas
received no professional attention whatsoever. Surveys of
seminary and Bible institute graduates in different parts of
Latin America reveal similar, though not so drastic, results.
This is one of the basic reasons why many churches and theological
institutions are initiating extension programs.

Theological education holds as essential key to the effectiveness of the ministry in the churches and in their communities--
in the widest possible sense. If we continue to build up the
assumptions, the institutions, and the structures of the professional ministry, we run the risk of fostering dependence among
our members, we make an elite out of our pastors, and we will
continue to leave the majority of our congregations without
pastoral care. If, on the other hand we encourage the members
to select their own leaders and develop their own ministry, there
is no limit to what their gifts, dedication, and service can
achieve. One of Werner's urgent concerns is to prepare simple
self-help manuals in fields related to health and community
development on the assumption that *"people with little formal
education have the native intelligence and potential will to
meet most of their basic needs for and by themselves."* He goes
on to assert that the most fundamental of human rights is *"the
right of the people--as individuals, as families, and as
communities--to stand on their own feet, to make their own
decisions, and to care for themselves."* Development at the
grassroots, particularly among the overwhelming poor majority in
every country of Latin America, will take place only when the
people themselves are given the opportunity and the basic means
to handle their own needs for health care, legal concerns,
education, land reform, economic growth, and ministry. This is
the way of true development; this is real revolution; this is
the meaning of liberation.

D. *The Liberation of Theology*

At the annual graduation exercizes of the Latin American
Biblical Seminary of Costa Rica in November 1972 Rubén Lores,
then Rector of the Seminary, chose as the topic of his keynote
address, "The Liberation of Theology." After referring very
briefly to the theology of liberation, he went on to ennumerate
several ways in which Latin American theology needs to free
itself in order to become an agent of liberation. This is
another basic concern of the dialogue on alternatives in
theological education.

At the level of the sophisticated theologians and "higher"
seminaries of Latin America there has in recent years been much
discussion of the need to throw off the North American, European
cultural trappings that have obscured the Gospel and deformed
the churches ever since the missionaries came and to develop a
Latin American theology and a Latin American ecclesiology. This
is no simple task, and it is just beginning to bear fruit. The
more liberal, leftist expressions come from the movements "Church
and Society in Latin America" and "Christians for Socialism."
Many of the more conservative and moderate spokesmen belong to
the "Latin American Theological Fraternity." Both mainstreams

are limited by their own classical, Western training, but both
are dedicated to the search for a new understanding of the
Kingdom of God in a world of unconscionable injustice and massive
poverty. Both tend to be philosophical and verbal, but they are
seeking to develop a new hermeneutics out of their own engagement
in Latin America's struggle for liberation.

At the level of the "lesser" theological schools and of most
of the pastors of Latin America theological reflection is still
largely bound up with fundamentalism, negativism, and legalism.
While assuming naively and affirming vociferously the absolute
literal authority of the Bible, they often perpetuate traditional
beliefs and practices that are clearly condemned by the prophets
and apostles and attacked by Jesus himself. One of the most
glaring blights of the many Protestant groups is that they are
fragmented, schismatic, competitive, and proselytistic, yet they
continue their separate ways self-righteously and pride themselves on being anti-eccumenical. They set themselves off from
the world in artificial judgmental ways (no drinking, smoking,
dancing, or fiestas), while affirming that salvation is by grace
alone and particularly for sinners. Most still refuse to participate in politics and in community organizations, insisting that
their mission to their neighbors is purely evangelistic. They
continue to maintain an anti-Catholic, ghetto posture in an era
in which many Catholics are not only friendly to Protestants but
eager to share their needs and to learn how to study the Bible.
The Protestant movement in Latin America is vital and growing,
but its theology is to a large extent in bondage. If it is not
liberated, it will in the long run cripple the churches and
destroy their witness to the Gospel in this large region which is
so receptive today.

At the level of the common people in the congregations there
is an inordinate preoccupation with the holding of and attendance
at innumerable *cultos* (worship services), as if this were the
primary or the only expression of the Christian life. No doubt
this stems from the popular concept of "spirituality" over
against the material and mundane. There is a strong sense of
the obligation to evangelize one's neighbor, but too often this
is an impersonal concern for "lost souls" rather than a genuine
expression of love for people. The radical, simplistic break
with Catholicism seems to have produced an inverted, internalized
model of the same basic fallacies in popular, Latin American
protestantism. And the transcendental emphasis on the conversion
experience has pushed all other dimensions of the Christian faith
into varying degrees of insignificance. Theological reflexion,
in this setting, is not even encouraged.

Theology needs to be liberated from its bondage at all these
levels in order to enable the churches to hear God's Word more

clearly, to follow His Will more nearly, and to pursue His
Mission more effectively in Latin America. Theological education
is the main instrument for the liberation of theology, and as we
have intimated in other sections of this paper theological education must take place at all levels of the churches' life. The
sophisticated theologians and "higher seminaries" must communicate their concern for a Latin American theology and ecclesiology
with the Bible institutes and pastors and with the common people
in the congregations. The pastors and Bible institutes must lead
their people out of the dungeon of fundamentalism, negativism,
and legalism into an understanding of Christian liberty and
liberation. And the common people must begin to reflect critically on their own religiosity and to pursue actively and
creatively the meaning of the Gospel in their own homes and
communities, their work and daily life, as well as in their
churches. We suggested earlier that this process of theological
renewal cannot take place from the top down, because that order
of things is itself an expression of bondage. On the other hand
all these levels and structures must be involved in the process
of liberation. The solution may come through a new approach to
theological education which will challenge all sectors of the
church simultaneously. There is no doubt in this writer's mind
that the churches in Latin America offer the greatest potential
for integral human liberation--greater than any political or
ideological movement--beginning with the tens of thousands of
groups of believers in practically every city, town, and village
in the region and including the admittedly inadequate ecclesiastical and institutional structures that have been imported and
adapted from other continents. But the question remains, How can
theological education best respond to the movement of God's
Spirit and to the needs of God's people and to the challenge of
Latin America today?

III. THE EXTENSION MOVEMENT

A. *The Birth and Growth of Theological Education
     by Extension*

Many people both inside and outside of the extension movement
have been quick to warn that extension is no panacea or magic
formula capable of solving all of the problems that theological
education faces today in Latin America or anywhere else. But it
is fascinating to see the ways in which theological education by
extension is capable of responding to the problems of traditional
patterns of leadership formation (Section I) and to the need for
alternative approaches to theological education (Section II)
which we have considered in this paper. Many of the currents
both in the churches and their institutions and in the Latin
American context are forcing theological education into an
elitist, hierarchical, institutionalized, academic mold. It is

increasingly evident that a reversal of this trend is essential
for the health of the churches and--if the churches are to
become instruments of liberation in their communities--for the
salvation of the peoples of Latin America. The extension movement, if it continues to grow as it has during the last ten
years and if it continues to pursue this vision, may become a
significant part of that long awaited, desperately needed
revolution of the Spirit.

It is not necessary to recite again the history of the
extension movement. Rather we shall consider some of the
issues and problems that have arisen since the first pilot
project was launched in Guatemala 15 years ago, with the hope
that these observations will be instructive to others who are
passing through the same struggles here in Latin America and
elsewhere. Those who are interested in reading the story in
detail and the documents that were written during the early
stages will want to refer to the following major works and their
bibliographies:

Ralph D. Winter, ed., *Theological Education by Extension*,
South Pasadena: William Carey Library, 1969.

Ralph R. Covell and C. Peter Wagner, *An Extension Seminary
Primer*, South Pasadena: William Carey Library, 1971.

Wayne C. Weld, *The World Directory of Theological Education
by Extension*, South Pasadena: William Carey Library,
1973.

Kenneth Mulholland, *Adventures in Training the Ministry:
A Honduran Case Study in Theological Education by
Extension*, Nutley: Presbyterian and Reformed Publishing
Company, 1976.

1. Perhaps the most important lesson to be learned from the
Presbyterian Seminary of Guatemala is simply that it is possible
for an institution to break with tradition and go against the
stream. Upon arrival in Guatemala in 1964, when the extension
program was in its second year and still rather experimental, we
heard many discouraging comments. "The Seminary is closed."
"It's a failure." "You have come to teach at the Seminary?
What for?" Obviously the changes were not understood or approved
by all. As time went on and more and more students were enrolled,
as explanations were repeated and reports of results began to
come out, criticism dwindled, but there has remained to date a
very strong, though reduced opposition in the church, mainly
among the older pastors of the denomination. This tension has
caused much agony, especially within the faculty, and at times
it looked like the entire enterprise would crumble like a house

of cards. But we have come to see the inevitability and the real meaning of this struggle. Our Presbyterian Reformed tradition--and many other traditions as well--has elevated the ministry to a sacred status, so that the church should provide the best possible training for ministerial candidates. Our Western tradition has elevated schooling over non-formal education, and everyone assumes that fulltime study in an institution is superior to any other system. Put these two axioms together and the residential seminary becomes the most important institution of the church, the mother of the pastors who in turn are the fathers of the churches. Theological education by extension has come on the scene not only to provide an alternative approach to ministerial training but also to challenge the established assumptions about training and about the nature of the ministry itself. It affirms that local leaders can and should be equipped and authorized to lead their congregations in ministry, for the ministry is a function of the body of Christ. It undercuts the power and authority of the clergy as a separate caste by opening the door to ministry to all. We have come to see that we are engaged in a process of service and of subversion, and in this process opposition is perhaps a good sign.

2. Interest in extension has spread like wildfire. James Emery published a first major article on "The Preparation of Leaders in a Ladino-Indian Church" in *Practical Anthropology* in 1963. News of the new concept was shared through the meetings and bulletins of the regional association of theological schools (ALET). Personal correspondence with people in different parts of Latin America increased each year, and visitors began to come to observe and discuss our program. James Hopewell, then General Director of the Theological Education Fund, published articles about extension in ecumenical circles as early as 1965. Ralph Winter initiated a small bulletin, *Evangelical Seminary*, in 1966, and in 1970 this publication was stabilized under a new name, *Extension Seminary*. By 1967 new extension experiments were taking shape in Honduras, Guadeloupe, Ecuador, Mexico, and Costa Rica. Then came the first extension workshop at Armenia, Colombia in September of 1967, followed in 1968 by major workshops in Ecuador, Bolivia, Brazil, and the U.S. By this time the movement was in orbit and ready to circle the globe. All of this came about through a dynamic process of communication, the sharing of a new vision of the renewal of the church for mission through the training of local leaders.

3. The chief tool for hammering out the concepts, structures, methods and materials for the new approach to theological education was the workshop. At Armenia (1967) the focus was on "The Extension Seminary and the Programmed Textbook." All but two of the theological institutions in Colombia--and others from Mexico, Central America, Ecuador and Panama--were represented, and during

this workshop they formed the Union of Biblical Institutions of
Colombia and initiated plans for the preparation of programmed
texts through CLATT and CATA. The workshop at Cochabamba,
Bolivia (1968) attracted 121 delegates, representing all the
institutions in that country and also several in other countries;
they studied extension methodology and programmed instruction in
greater detail and advanced plans for the Spanish Intertext
Project. The first workshop in Brazil, held in Sao Paulo (1968),
drew 65 people representing 23 theological instititions and led
to the formation of the Evangelical Theological Association for
Extension Training (AETTE). Over the years scores of workshops
have been held throughout the region, and they have provided
much of the impetus for the launching of extension programs, the
writing of extension materials, the training of extension
directors and teachers, the development of educational concepts
and strategies, and the evaluation of existing programs. The
value of these experiences, when committed people engaged in an
innovative movement meet and work together, should not be
underestimated.

    4. One of the more serious problems of the young movement has
been the preparation of self-study materials. From the very
beginning it was evident that extension required the preparation
of a new kind of study textbook to cover virtually the entire
theological curriculum and that this endeavor would call for an
enormous investment of skilled personnel. The only possibility
of providing many materials in a short time was through a joint
venture. The Spanish Intertext Project, conceived at Armenia in
1967, was a grandiose scheme involving on the one hand an ad hoc
list of institutions scattered throughout Latin America and
enrolled by Peter Wagner as members of CLATT to approve of new
manuscripts for publication. On the other hand an editorial
committee called CATA was organized to enlist, train, and guide
writers through various stages in the preparation of programmed
workbooks. The process broke down for a number of reasons. In
the first place most of the people who volunteered or were asked
to prepare these materials had neither the technical skill nor
the background knowledge nor the time to do an adequate job. In
the second place the specialists who were asked to serve as
technical and content advisors were unable to take on the tedious
job of evaluating manuscripts. In the third place few writers or
institutions ever went through the necessary, time consuming
process of field testing and revision. Finally, when CATA and
CLATT were replaced by ALISTE at Medellin, Colombia in 1972, it
was decided to give up the old plan as unworkable and to share
as widely as possible the efforts of individual writers and
isntitutions.

    5. One of the most controversial issues of the extension
movement has to do with the matter of programmed instruction.

Philosophically or ideologically no one seems to approve of
B. F. Skinner's behaviorist view of education, yet many who are
involved in extension see the necessity of planned, carefully
guided learning sequences. At one point, after considerable
debate, it was decided to accept in principle the need to put
all the materials of the Spanish Intertext Project into a programmed format, but only one book was ever completed. In Brazil
AETTE has applied programming more widely and successfully, and
for a time extension and programmed instruction were used as
synonyms in that association. At the Presbyterian Seminary of
Guatemala only four or five of our 20 courses use programmed
materials, and we continue to encourage others to use varied
formats.

6. The question arose early in the movement as to whether
extension was or should be a fixed, well defined way of doing
theological education. On the one hand there was a tendency to
call any decentralized program extension, but this definition
was so diffuse it gave little guidance as to the nature of
ministerial training. On the other hand some innovators were
going way beyond the guidelines drawn up in Guatemala, and no
one wanted to limit their creativity. There is general agreement
that the purpose of extension is to enable local church leaders
to obtain a solid theological training for their ministries
without interrupting their regular employment, family, and congregational obligations and that the essential ingredients are
systematic home study, on-going practical work, and regular group
seminars. Beyond this minimal definition there are numerous
adaptations, innovations, and additional ingredients. At one
point we prepared a paper on "Open Theological Education" in an
attempt to emphasize that our primary concern is to open up the
structures of ministerial training and make it accessible to all
the people of God.

7. In the early years one of the chief criticisms of the
extension movement was that most of its leaders were expatriates.
In many places the missionaries were the first to hear about
extension, the ones most likely to attend workshops, the ones
with time and resources to begin preparing workbooks, the ones
to be chosen to organize new programs and participate in the new
extension associations. However justified the reasons for
expatriate participation, the validity of the movement depended
on its ability to inspire and incorporate strong national
leaders throughout the region. When the Latin American Association of Extension Theological Institutes and Seminaries was
organized in 1973 it placed a high priority on the development
of new Latin American leadership, and this goal was pursued
arduously and effectively through the ALISTE Project for Training
Extension Specialists, which began with eleven participants in
1974, five more in 1975, and eleven more in 1976. Many of these

outstanding Latin American leaders are now leading the extension
movement locally and denominationally, nationally, and regionally,
directing their own programs, workshops, and the ALISTE organization itself. In Brazil AETTE has also attempted to turn over the
leadership of the movement to national leaders, and it has
developed a graduate level training program for writers of
extension materials. (The ALISTE and AETTE training programs
will be described below.)

8. One of the ambiguous aspects of the rapidly growing
extension movement has been its competitive stance vis-a-vis the
residential seminaries. It would not be possible to identify or
weigh all the factors in the challenges and criticisms that have
flown back and forth; in fact the exchange was inevitable and has
been to some extend edifying. Extension enthusiasts were often
quick to point out the glaring faults of traditional schools and
sometimes made inordinate claims for extension. Defenders of the
residencial programs easily found weaknesses in the fledgling
extension programs and could fall back on the evident substan-
tiality of their own institutions. One of the basic realities
of the situation was that the total resources available for
theological education were very limited, so that the success of
the extension movement depended on its ability to earn a share
of those resources either through cooperation or competition
with the residential schools. This point will be expanded below.

9. Another subtle dimension of the extension movement is its
mystique. As we have noted earlier, the driving force that
inspired the leaders, the workshops, and the countless hours of
hard work was a vision of thousands of local church leaders who
could be reached for the first time through extension training
programs, men and women who were actually leading the vast
majority of the congregations throughout the region with little
or no training of any kind, dedicated, self sacrificing, humble
people who could gain full recognition for their ministries and
be encouraged and enabled to deepen and strengthen the mission
of the church at the grassroots level. This vision and motivation has produced a certain mystique that continues to give the
movement a necessary cohesiveness and dynamism, but it can also
create an uncritical atmosphere which in turn may conceal or
defend serious deficiencies.

10. Statistics never provide an adequate measure of a movement because they are by nature quantitative, but we cannot fail
to mention the somewhat sketchy statistics of the extension movement in Latin America. In his *1976 Supplement* to *The World
Directory of Theological Education by Extension* Wayne Weld reports
a total of 11,566 students in 99 programs in Latin America. (We
know of several additional programs.) This may still be less
than the number of students who attend residential Bible

institutes and seminaries, but it is striking that such a radical change has taken place throughout such a vast region in such a short time. There are still many thousands of local church leaders to be reached, but it is remarkable that now for the first time the churches have an effective way of giving all of them the basic tools of theological education.

B. *Extension and the Theological Education Establishment*

The birth and growth of the extension movement is intimately related to the seminaries and associations of theological schools of Latin America. The Presbyterian Semianry of Guatemala had been a traditional residential seminary for 25 years when it was transformed into an extension seminary, causing considerable upheaval within its own constituency. Most of the seminaries and many of the Bible institutes in the region have now become involved in theological education by extension in one or more ways, though few of them have closed out their residential programs. The Latin American Association of Theological Schools (Northern Region), ALET, came into existence almost at the same time as the Guatemalan extension program and has had to deal with the new perspectives and realities of extension from the very beginning. The other two major associations, ASTE in Brazil and ASIT in southern South America, have more recently taken a deep interest in extension, both because of the growing interest in extension in their areas and because many of their member institutions have extension programs. As was to be expected some of the more prestigeous institutions were at first uninterested or condescending toward extension; then as the controversy over extension heated up some became critical and defensive; at recent theological consultations delegates from some historic seminaries have begun to ask if they still have a significant role to play. Some of these theological schools are in serious trouble--with low enrollments, economic shortages, ideological conflicts, and confusion of purpose. Theological education by extension has grown like topsy and needs help desparately in several areas--the preparation of personnel and instructional materials, the development of curricula, libraries, and audiovisual materials, the strengthening of educational philosophy and methodology, etc. So it seems as if the relationship between extension and the theological education establishment will be very important for both partners in the years to come.

1. In March 1964 Ralph Winter and José Carrera of Guatemala attended the meeting in Mexico City at which the constitution for ALET was first drawn up. The extension program of the Presbyterian Seminary of Guatemala was just a year old, but even at this early date ALET was able to take into account the new perspectives represented by that institution. The new constitution recognized three different academic levels as valid and by inference

functionally equivalent. At subsequent meetings some members of
ALET have pursued the matter of accredition after the manner of
associations in other parts of the world, but here again extension
not only does not fit the usual criteria, it calls into question
the traditional concepts and requirements for academic excellence.
So the accreditation process has been delayed, revised, and sus-
pended. In 1967 Ralph Winter, who during the decisive years of
transition had been a member of the Board of Directors of the
Presbyterian Semianry of Guatemala, was elected for a two year
term as Executive Secretary of ALET, and his first major assignment in that office was to set up the Armenia workshop on "The
Extension Seminary and the Programmed Textbook," to which we have
already referred. The 1969 meeting of ALET in Nicaragua turned
into a hot debate between representatives of traditional institutions and James Emery of Guatemala. (We should note in passing
that two of the three seminaries represented by the opposition
to extension at that meeting have since been closed, and the
third has lost the official support of its own denomination.)
Since that meeting the dialogue has continued in a more construc-
tive way. In 1975 ALET held a joint consultation on alternatives
in theological education with ALISTE, the extension association
for Latin America.

   2. In Brazil greater polarization took place at the beginning,
in part by accident. The meeting which gave birth to AETTE, the
extension association, was unintentionally held on the same dates
that ASTE, the associaiton of theological schools, was meeting in
another city. This was probably due to the fact that the first
promotors of extension in Brazil were from conservative missionary
organizations, and this has continued to color the movement there.
Several institutions have, however, belonged to both associations,
and in recent years there has been increasing exchange between
them. In January 1975 ASTE held a major workshop on educational
technology in Sao Paulo, and the writer was invited to participate in discussions about extension.

   3. The South American Association of Theological Institutions
(ASIT) covers Argentina, Uruguay, Paraguay, and Chile. Perhaps
because this area is somewhat isolated from the rest of Latin
America, it has been slower to adopt extension and by the same
token there has been less controversy. There are extension pro-
grams in all of these countries, however, and when ASIT held a
"Consultation on Extension Education" in Santiago, Chile in
August 1975 many of these programs were represented. This year
ASIT is sponsoring nine extension workshops in the area.

   4. Of greater importance even than the associations are the
major theological institutions in Mexico City, San José, Costa
Rica, Sao Paulo, Brazil, and Buenos Aires. A rapid survey
reveals that most of these institutions are involved in

theological education by extension. In Mexico City the Theological Community includes five denominational seminaries, and
three of them have developed extension programs. Also, the
nearby Presbyterian Theological Seminary and the John Calvin
Seminary have their own extension programs. In Costa Rica the
Latin American Biblical Seminary has long provided training and
resources for extension programs, and it is now launching a
continent-wide extension program at the university level. In
Sao Paulo, Brazil the Methodist Seminary has an extension program, and the Baptist Seminary has an extension program that is
expected to grow to about 1000 students. In Buenos Aires the
Advanced Evangelical Institute of Theological Studies (ISEDET)
and the International Baptist Seminary are both involved in
extension programs.

5. Even with all this information it is difficult to
evaluate the involvement of the theological education establishment in the extension movement. In some cases extension is
merely an appendage of minor importance--for laymen, for lower
levels, or for those who cannot get into the residential program.
In most cases, however, extension is being taken seriously as a
new alternative approach to theological education with a
validity of its own and with insights that need to be applied
in the residential programs. In some cases extension studies
are on the same academic level and interchangeable with residential courses.

6. There are several ways in which the major seminaries are
making important contributions to the extension movement. The
Latin American Biblical Seminary, for example, offers a graduate
degree program of specialization in theological education by
extension. The Baptist Seminary of Sao Paulo offers a similar
program. Professors at several of the seminaries have directed
workshops, written self-study materials, taught in extension
centers, and served as advisors for extension programs. The
Augsburg Lutheran Seminary in Mexico City periodically assigns
one of its professors to dedicate several months visiting
Lutheran extension programs in the region. In these and other
ways the seminaries have not only contributed with their own
resources but they have given moral support and credibility to
the movement.

C. *Major Extension Development Projects*

Latin America's land area and population are divided almost
equally into two blocks, the 18 Spanish speaking countries and
Portuguese speaking Brazil. About 70% of all the Protestants in
Latin America are Brazilians, and the churches of Brazil continue
to grow very rapidly, particularly the Pentecostals, who are by
far the majority. There are two large associations of extension

programs in Latin America; ALISTE covers the Spanish speaking
countries and AETTE Brazil. Each of these associations has in
recent years pursued a major development project for the extension
movement.

1. When ALISTE was organized in January 1973, one of the
primary concerns throughout the Spanish speaking countries was
to find, train, and incorporate new Latin American leadership
for the extension movement. José Carrera, former Director of
the Presbyterian Seminary of Guatemala, was elected International
Coordinator of ALISTE for the first three year term of ALISTE,
and the writer was a member of the executive committee. We
worked out, in cooperation with the Latin American Biblical
Seminary, a four-stage project for the training of extension
specialists. The first stage was an analysis of the local
situation which each candidate was to carry out with the help of
materials prepared by ALISTE in the form of a "Self-Study workshop on Theological Education." The purpose of this stage was
to discover the leadership needs of each church, to prepare the
candidate for more intensive studies in Guatemala, and to
initiate a process of reflection and innovation among his
colleagues so that they would later be prepared to work together
in future developments. The second stage was a three-month
seminar at the Presbyterian Seminary of Gustemala. James Emery
prepared extensive materials (now available in English and
Spanish from Guatemala) for the analysis of the components of
ministerial training programs and for the design of instructional
materials. Each participant worked through these exercises and
wrote up a major project in each of these two main areas for his
own situation. At the same time they observed and participated
in the Presbyterian extension program, and they began planning
and holding workshops on theological education by extension.
The third stage was conceived of as the following year of
application, during which the participants held additional
workshops and worked out their plans for extension back in
their own churches and institutions. The fourth stage was a
return meeting in Guatemala for two to three weeks of evaluation
and further planning.

So far three groups of outstanding Latin American leaders
have gone through this program, eleven beginning in 1974, five
in 1975, and eleven in 1976. They represent a broad spectrum of
Protestantism: five Methodists, three Presbyterians and one
Reformed, three Baptists, three Lutherans, three from the
Evangelical Church of Peru, three from the Christian Evangelical
Union of Bolivia, and one each from the Church of God (Full
Gospel), Church of Christ, Disciples, Apostolic Church, Covenant
Church, and the Moravian Church. They came from nine countries:
seven from Bolivia, five from Guatemala, four from Mexico, four
from Peru, two from Costa Rica, two from Nicaragua, and one each

from Ecuador, Chile, and Argentina. Five of them have not yet
completed their graduate studies at the Latin American Biblical
Seminary; the rest are working in extension (and residential)
training programs, most of them as directors. It would be
difficult to tell what has been the total contribution of these
26 men and one woman to the extension movement throughout the
Spanish-speaking countries of Latin America, but it can be said
that they are now the ones who plan and direct most of the workshops in their own countries and direct the movement throughout
the region.

2. Brazil's extension association, AETTE, was organized in
1968 and now has 40 member institutions plus many individual
associate members. AETTE has held annual assemblies and many
workshops, concerned mainly with the preparation of programmed
textbooks. At the February 1974 assembly AETTE endorsed a plan
for internships in curriculum development which was presented by
Lois McKinney, a curriculum specialists supported by a U.S.
missionary organization, CAMEO. She described the program as
follows:

> The interns commit themselves to an intensive, graduate-
> level learning experience. They study 2 basic courses,
> pursue a reading program, and attend 4 encounters, and
> write an auto-didactic text for theological education.
> The sponsoring institution recommends the intern, provides
> a mentor and an advisory committee for his program, assumes
> the financial responsibilities involved (books, travel,
> sometimes a stipend), orients the preparation of the pro-
> grammed text, and publishes the completed text. As a
> consultant to the program my responsibilities include
> counseling with the interns and the institutions, prepar-
> ing teaching materials (syllabi, study guides, and reading
> lists), planning and leading encounters, and critiquing
> texts as they are being developed. (*Extension Seminary
> Quarterly Bulletin*, Number 1, 1977).

By the end of 1976 44 interns from 18 theological institutions
had participated in the program; seven had finished and ten more
were in the final stages; 20 new interns were expected to enter
the program in 1977. As a direct result of the program the
quality of extension textbooks has improved, and many more are
being prepared by Brazilians. They are now coming out at a rate
of one or two a month. Also, the leadership of the extension
movement in Brazil is passing into the hands of nationals.

3. A third major effort in the development of theological
education by extension and of all kinds and aspects of theological
education in Latin America was proposed by this writer in the
Extension Seminary Quarterly Bulletin, Number 1, 1975. The

proposal is called "Centers for Studies in Theological Education
and Ministry," and it has grown out of the extension movement.
Several years ago we began to realize that increasing numbers of
theological educators and denominational leaders were, because
of extension, becoming involved in a process of reflection and
innovation through consultations and workshops, papers and
bulletins, and experimentation. As this process continues, more
and more fundamental questions are being opened up for discussion
and research, questions not only about the structures, methodology, and content of theological education but also about the
nature of the ministry and about the mission of the church. And
it has become evident that there is a great deal of valuable
information and experience to be shared among those in different
places who are engaged in this process. In order to make the
best use of this situation we suggested that any group in any
particular situation could initiate a research center with little
or no special funding and with no full time personnel. In fact
we realized that some groups were already doing many of the
things which we were proposing.

The Guatemala Center for studies in Theological Education and
Ministry was formally initiated under the Presbyterian Seminary
of Guatemala in July 1975 with the following program areas:
Correspondence, including a network with five different levels,
publications, including the *Extension Seminary* Quarterly Bulletin
and occasional papers, files, exchange visits, meetings of
various kinds and at several levels, workshops, training programs,
including the ALISTE training program, and research and development projects. Several institutions involved in extension in
Mexico have formed another center called Mexican Promoter of Open
Seminaries (PROMESA), which will offer technical advice in such
areas as curriculum design, personnel, materials, funding,
accreditation, etc. The Latin American Biblical Seminary in
Costa Rica will continue to serve as an important center for
research, training, the preparation of materials, and other
aspects of development in theological education for all of Latin
America. The Union of Biblical Institutions of Colombia, which
was founded at the Armenia workshop in 1967 and has been concerned
primarily with theological education by extension, has recently
decided to set up a Center for Studies in Theological Education
and Ministry. Quito, Ecuador is the present headquarters of
ALISTE and may become another center for research; at present
the International Coordinator of ALISTE, Nelson Castro, and the
director of the catalogue of Spanish extension materials, Jorge
Maldonado, are based there. The SEAN team, which has carried
on extensive work in curriculum design and writing extension
materials for people with less than full primary schooling, has
developed an important center in Tucuman, northern Argentina.
In Brazil the most important development and research center is
located at Sao Paulo, which is the headquarters for AETTE and

the writers' internship program. The contributions of all these
and other centers will multiply geometrically as they link
together and share their concerns, problems, experiences, innovations, insights, and materials.

D. *Extension Programs in Latin America Today*

The extension movement in Latin America is now very large and
still growing rapidly, and it is fascinatingly kaleidoscopic.
Apparently the only person who has attempted to keep track of
the many different extension programs in Wayne Weld, who served
for several years in Ecuador and Colombia. In 1973 he reported
a total of 72 programs with 564 centers and 6103 students. In
1976 he reported a total of 99 programs with 1058 centers and
11,566 students, an increase in students of almost 90 percent
in three years.

Country	Inst	Cent	Teach	Cert	Students Dipl	Bach	Lic	Total
Argentina	8	64	42	532	422	60	0	1016
Bolivia	4	37	24	266	42	7	0	365
Brazil	34	242	270	2860	380	77	0	3317
Chile	3	13	21	101	60	10	0	171
Colombia	9	140	113	775	431	31	23	1221
Dominican Republic	2	16	8	58	61	31	0	150
Ecuador	8	77	75	782	151	60	6	1005
Guatemala	7	261	249	1907	331	49	1	2308
Honduras	3	51	40	113	56	25	1	194
Mexico	7	70	92	491	331	124	0	995
Panama	1	6	4	0	36	0	0	36
Peru	5	45	22	195	143	24	0	412
Puerto Rico	1	3	3	0	0	0	21	21
Suriname	1	3	3	6	2	3	2	13
Uruguay	2	6	16	0	42	63	0	105
Venezuela	4	24	24	106	122	9	0	237
Total	99	1058	1007	8192	2610	573	54	11566

*1976 Supplement, The World Directory of Theological Education
by Extension,* South Pasadena: William Carey Library, 1976.

Even these statistics are far from complete. New programs are
being launched every year, and some fold, and many extension
directors are so busy keeping their heads above water that they

don't even report their existence. Weld's list omits Costa Rica, Nicaragua, El Salvador, Belice and Paraguay, and we know there are extension programs in all these countries. He lists 34 programs for Brazil, but AETTE now has 40 member institutions.

It is even more difficult to keep track of what is happening in all these programs, which represent a healthy and creative but bewildering variety of adaptations to meet local needs and circumstances. In the following paragraphs we shall mention several programs which are dealing with particular aspects of the challenge of the extension movement in contemporary Latin America.

1. In Latin America one of the most crucial questions has been, Can and will theological education be adapted to the very low academic level of many local leaders? Tentative surveys have indicated that at least one-third of the men who are in charge of the congregations and preaching points throughout Latin America have received less than full primary schooling, and most of these men have had no formal theological training. In some rural areas they are only semi-literate. As the traditional seminaries and Bible institutes proceed up the education ladder, extension becomes the only way to reach these men with full ministerial training.

George Patterson, a Conservative Baptist missionary in a depressed, rural area of northern Honduras, was one of the first to insist on radical adaptation to meet the challenge of semi-literate leaders. Since study is a burdensome chore and reading very difficult for rural farmers who spend long hours in the fields every day, this program focuses on the task of starting and building congregations. The men who are enlisted in this task meet regularly in groups of two or three or as many as five or six to share their experiences, to talk over the needs and problems that arise, and to discuss materials that have been designed specifically for their tasks and problems. These materials are pocket-sized pamphlets with important content but very simple vocabulary. Each one combines five basic elements: a specific problem in the "student's" life or ministry; biblical, historical, doctrinal, and/or practical information bearing on that problem; questions or some exercize to test the student's comprehension of the new information (with feedback); an assignment which requires him to apply what he has learned; and drawings or cartooning to illustrate the lesson. Each student is required not only to start a new congregation but also to disciple one or two other men who will in turn start other congregations and teach others for the same task. This extension chain had already initiated 30 congregations by 1974; it is capable of penetrating the whole countryside because it places the responsibility and minimal tools for church planting in the

hands of local, albeit semi-literate leaders. The same materials
and basic approach are now being applied in several other
countries. (See Patterson's articles in the *Extension Seminary*
Quarterly Bulletin, No. 4, 1972 and No. 3, 1974.)

Another very significant though very different program has
been designed by SEAN, the Anglican Extension Seminary (Tucumán,
Argentina), for people who have approximately four years of
primary schooling. Due to the lack of programmed materials at
this level, this group has dedicated the last six years to the
writing, testing, and publishing of a brief course for new
believers ("The Abundant Life") and an extensive course for
church leaders and pastors ("The Compendium of Pastoral Theology,
Based on the Life of Jesus Christ According to Matthew"). The
latter is now complete in six volumes of 25 lessons each, and it
is being used in many places and by many different churches
throughout Latin America. Through extensive testing the team of
writers, who reside in Paraguay and Chile as well as Argentina,
have been able to develop a careful technique of programming that
works well at the level mentioned and can also be adapted for
higher levels. The basic theological content areas and skills
are intertwined and integrated around the study of Matthew. The
main aspects of the devotional life and the ministry are
emphasized throughout. Additional aids and orientation for
extension teachers are provided. An English adaptation of the
Compendium is now available, also. (For further information see
the *Extension Seminary* Quarter Bulletin, No. 3, 1975 or write to
Rev. Anthony Barratt, Casilla 134, S.M. Tucumán, Argentina.)

2. Over the past 10 to 30 years several very sizeable
"peoples movements" have developed among the major Indian
populations of Latin America, and this presents another important
challenge to the extension movement. The Mayan peoples of
Guatemala and southern Mexico number about five million and are
divided into several linguistic and cultural families. The
Quiché Bible Institute (Primitive Methodist and Presbyterian)
has developed an extension program among the Quiché people of
Western Guatemala parallel to its residential program. The
nearby Mam Center has recently initiated formal extension training among the Mam people in cooperation with the Presbyterian
Seminary of Guatemala. In Chiapas, Mexico two extension programs
are developing among the Chol people. In the Yucatan Peninsula
the Presbyterian Church has developed a large extension program,
which is directly related to the rapid growth of the church in
that area. These programs utilize self-study materials in
Spanish or Indian languages or both.

The Quechua people, descendents of the ancient Incas, number
at least ten million and are divided into about 50 sub-groups
scattered throughout the highlands of Ecuador, Peru, and Bolivia.

A recent article by Gunter Schulze indicates that the number of
baptized believers among the Quechuas of Chimborazo Province in
Ecuador grew from 315 in 1968 to over 10,000 in 1976. He also
reports that there are 800 men and women enrolled in extension
courses in this area. Similar growth is taking place in other
parts of the Andean Zone, and other extension programs are trying
to respond to the urgent demand for leadership training for the
many new congregations.

The Aymara people form another large Indian population in
Bolivia and southern Peru. In recent years all the churches
working in that area have reported massive conversions, with
entire villages coming into vital, meaningful Christian faith.
Their natural and only course of action is to choose the
accepted community leaders as their pastors. The denominations
which we know have experimented with extension among the Aymara
are: Methodists, Baptists, Lutherans, Nazarenes, Quakers,
Christian Evangelical Union.

3. The extension movement finds its greatest potential growth
and service among the Pentecostal churches, both because of the
size of these churches and because of the dynamic nature of
their ministry. Some groups have opposed formal training in the
past, and most groups have been led largely by empirically
formed leaders. Theological education by extension is essentially in agreement with the Pentecostal pattern and concept of
leadership and will most likely mushroom in these circles in the
years to come.

One of the participants in the first group of ALISTE
specialists in 1974 was Rev. José Luis Barrera of the indigenous
Apostolic Church in Mexico. He was subsequently named Director
of that church's International Theological Institute. Apparently
in the last two years they have launched half a dozen different
extension programs for the training of lay leaders, the preparation of candidates for the ministry, and the continuing education
of pastors. They even planned to train extension teachers by
extension.

Another participant in the first ALISTE group was Rev.
Francisco Son, who was at that time the Director of the Church of
God (Full Gospel) Bible Institute in Guatemala. He initiated an
extension program in 1973, and three years later the first 17
extension graduates received their diplomas. In October 1975 he
presented a paper at a meeting of his denomination's Christian
Education Commission for Central America and Panama, and they
immediately took steps toward the establishment of extension
programs throughout the area. Since then new programs have been
initiated in Honduras, Belice, El Salvador, and Costa Rica.

Earlier in this paper we mentioned that the Assemblies of God
have initiated an extension program in Fortaleza in northern
Brazil. Another one has begun in Sao Paulo in the South. If
these programs are able to capture the imagination of the leaders
of the large mother churches in the major urban centers, they
could expand naturally through their hierarchies and reach many
of the estimated 40,000 pastors, evangelists, presbyters, deacons,
and helpers in that denomination. These three examples--the
Apostolic Church in Mexico, the Church of God in Central America,
and the Assemblies of God in Brazil--should have a tremendous
effect on the other Pentecostal groups throughout Latin America.

4. Another area of strategic importance is extension training
at the highest academic levels. As Ralph Winter pointed out at
the very beginning, extension will be considered a second-rate,
stop-gap approach to theological education unless it is carried
out and fully accredited at the highest as well as the lowest
possible levels. In fact he recommended starting out at the top
in order to gain credibility. Many beginning extension programs
have been pleasantly surprised to find that highly educated,
professional people in their churches are interested in enrolling
in their courses along with students of much less school
experience. Some have included in their plans a university level
theological course. But until recently no institution in Latin
America was dedicating its primary resources for this level.

When Ruben Lores turned over the rectorship of the Latin
American Biblical Seminary at the end of 1974, he dedicated his
sabbatical leave to study the new trends in university education
around the world. When he returned to Costa Rica he set up a
new continent-wide extension program called PRODIADIS, which
would be at the same level and carry the full accreditation of
their residential program. He enlisted the full cooperation of
the faculty in the preparation of study guides, and during 1976
20 students in 11 countries were enrolled in a pilot project.
The program is now open to the public, and with the cooperation
of adjunct tutors and other theological institutions it is
expected to reach hundreds if not thousands of students within
a short time, providing rigorous, university level studies for
pastors and laymen who have never been able to attend a traditional seminary and also for seminary and Bible institute
graduates who want to grow in their understanding of Christian
ministry and mission. Beginning students take four basic
required courses, but the rest of the curriculum is "open."
Under the Seminary's supervision and with the help of a locally
assigned tutor where possible, each student or group of students
will work out its objectives, areas of study, bibliography and
methodology, and projects. The faculty in Costa Rica will provide, usually by correspondence, courses, advice, and academic
accreditation. If this program succeeds, it will be a major

contribution to the theological formation of the leaders of the
churches of Latin America, and it will provide unprecedented
validation for theological education by extension at all academic
levels.

5. Another intriguing question facing extension programs in
many places is, Will this training be recognized as valid for
ordination? The preparation of pastors is not the only concern
of the extension movement, and it may not be the most urgent
need in Latin America. In fact the most strategic contribution
of theological education by extension may be to bridge the chasm
that separates the clergy from the laity. But a crucial test in
the acceptance of extension, especially among the historic
denominations, is whether extension graduates are approved for
ordination. And the answer to that question will determine to a
considerable degree the seriousness with which the churches,
institutions, students, and teachers view their programs.

August 28, 1975 was an historic occasion for the Extension
Theological Seminary of the Southeast and for the National
Presbyterian Church of Mexico, for on that day 21 men received
their diplomas after completing 30 courses by extension over a
period of six years. That program, which had begun in the late
60's with very limited resources, had grown to almost 400
students in 13 centers scattered widely over three states of the
Yucatan Peninsula and down into Belice. Many of these students
had initiated and/or were in charge of congregations; a new
presbytery had been inaugurated largely through their efforts;
the churches were growing. Now the first ones were to be
graduated. But the big, remaining question was, Would the
presbyteries ordain them? This was vital to the program and to
the students and to their congregations, and it was a challenge
to the presbyteries. Up until that time the four prebyteries in
the area had very few pastors. This one group of graduates could
double the number of pastors in some presbyteries, and it would
open the way for many more local leaders who followed in their
footsteps. After some hesitation these men have been accepted
for ordination. The program has recently been linked to the
denomination's main seminary in the capital city 1500 kilometers
away. And additional centers are now functioning in the
Federal District and in other states. The breakthrough was a
success.

The Baptist Extension Institute for Theological Education by
Extension in Sao Paulo is probably the largest extension program
in Brazil, and it is based at the Baptist Seminary in Sao Paulo.
The staff has prepared and published an impressive series of
self-study texts covering the curriculum, which appears to be
like any other seminary or Bible institute curriculum. Officially,
this program is for the training of laymen and lay preachers—not

for ordained pastors. Candidates for ordination are supposed to attend the residential program in Sao Paulo. On the other hand the directors of the extension program candidly admit that many of their students are the ones who are raising up and leading the congregations throughout the State of Sao Paulo and that they may break open the door to ordination by their effective extension programs in Latin America.

6. Another final dimension of the extension movement is the ideological and practical concern for human development in all its dimensions. Are all these extension programs concerned only with the preparation of religious functionaries of the institutional church? Or are they concerned with the everyday problems and on-going struggle of the people they serve? The following examples indicate that some attempts are being made, but far more needs to be done.

The Northwest Presbytery of Colombia serves a remote, poor, rural area where the church is expanding and growing rapidly. Their program includes theological education by extension, church planting, health services, and agricultural development. The congregations are scattered, transportation is very difficult (on foot or horseback) or costly (plane), and resources are limited. It is still not clear how these obstacles can be overcome and the different aspects of the program integrated effectively.

Nelson Castro, a participant in ALISTE Group II and now the International Coordinator of ALISTE, has developed an approach to leadership training for the Covenant Church in Ecuador which is based on Pablo Freire's psycho-social methodology. In each congregation interested members meet to make a study which may involve Biblical and theological studies, community projects, and other kinds of action and reflection.

The Baptist Seminary of Mexico has for some time been engaged in research and action among the poor classes of Mexican society in an attempt to work out a relevant understanding and model for ministry and a basis for theological reflection on liberation. Now they have developed with the Center of Ecumenical Studies a decentralized theological education program for laymen applying these same concerns.

IV. CONTINUING CONCERNS

Latin America is certainly one of the most exciting and tragic regions of the world. Her vast human and natural resources have long been subjugated to foreign and oligarchical interests, but there are signs of massive unrest and a potential for far reaching liberation. Similarly the Christian movement

in Latin America has long been used to support and gloss over
the established structures of privilege and exploitation, but
there is a tremendous movement of faith and self-discovery among
the people, especially the poor. In this context the concern
for alternatives in theological education, especially for the
extension movement, takes on significant proportions. The
currents and developments that we have considered in this paper
leave us with many questions, unfinished tasks, and areas for
urgent research. We shall look at some of these matters in this
final section.

A. *Fundamental Questions*

1. Will the process of change, the search for more effective
approaches to theological education, continue? Over the past 10
years the extension movement has grown so fast and caused such
sweeping changes that it is difficult at this time to see its
full implications or predict how far it will go. On the one
hand the excitement has stimulated much activity and reflection;
on the other hand it has precipitated enormous problems and
created urgent demands. On the one hand it has challenged many,
many institutions and organizations and individuals to new
endeavors; on the other hand it runs the risk of becoming a
hollow fad or another poorly grounded institution. At this
early stage it is still relatively easy to be innovative and
open to new ideas. In time it may become more difficult, or
change itself may become so normative as to weaken the very
foundations on which it is based. One of our basic needs is to
develop an understanding of the dynamics of change in theological
education and the ministry in order to use wisely the opportunities presented by the present moment of history.

2. What will be the shape of the ministry in the future?
Our interest in alternatives in theological education is not
primarily for our own programs and institutions but rather for
the ministry and the church and its mission in the world. We
have noted that theological education is a vital link in this
chain and that it can have disastrous effects on the other
elements in the chain. Insofar as we are now embarked on the
uncertain seas of change in theological education we look toward
the formation of new patterns and styles of ministry. Our
experience in Guatemala indicates that the first generation of
new leaders is pretty well absorbed by the older generation and
forced into many of the traditional molds. Our hope is that the
continuing, unending waves of new blood and the open door to the
ministry itself will make an increasing impact on the structures
of the past so that the ministry will become an ever more
Christ-like service in the church and society.

3. This leads us to the third question. Will the new
alternatives in theological education help the church to keep

on reforming itself (*ecclesia semper reformanda*) through a constant challenge to action and reflection upon the Gospel, to
renew itself through the recognition and nurture of all its
gifts, and through the mobilization of all its members for
mission? The possibilities are unlimited; the needs are self-
evident. We have only begun to look for and work toward these
goals through Him "who by the power at work within us is able
to do far more abundantly than all that we ask or think."

4. And finally will these changes in the church and its
ministry cause major breakthroughs in the church's mission, i.e.
God's mission, in the world? We have said that the churches in
Latin America are vital and growing rapidly. We have dared to
affirm that no other political or ideological force in Latin
America has greater potential for true revolution and liberation
among the people, especially the poor, who are the vast majority.
We have intimated that changes in theological education can
place the churches' leadership in the hands of the members so
that the ministry will reflect the needs and the potential of
the people. But we have still to see the outworking of a fully
Christian ministry--both prophetic and pastoral, in community
and service as well as proclamation, among the whole people of
God.

B. *Unfinished Tasks*

1. Although we have talked a lot about changes in the
structures of theological education, we still need to develop
more careful and more appropriate models for training and
ministry for the many varied situations and needs of the
churches of Latin America. How can you build an effective
decentralized program to reach sparcely scattered congregations
over thousands of square miles? How can you develop an extension program for Indian leaders whose ability to read and
inclination to study and home environment are so limited? How
can local leaders not only study by extension and other means
but also run these programs? The ALISTE materials (mentioned
in Section III, C above) provide a detailed guide to the
analysis of the components of ministerial training programs.
But we need more case studies, workshops, and training programs
to show how these procedures can be applied to widely divergent
situations.

2. We have mentioned the urgent need for more and better
self-instructional materials. Our problem is not merely to
organize a project and sign up a list of writers. We need to
work out in our own minds and with our colleagues and with the
people we serve the necessary issues of curriculum design and
course content and educational technology. We must develop
procedures for on-going evaluation and revision. We need to

develop alternatives to printed materials and also audio-visual
aids to complement written materials. We need to utilize
indigenous, non-formal approaches to learning. It is time to
go beyond the "stop gap" materials that were perhaps justified
at the beginning of the extension movement. No doubt many more
sample materials, workshops, and training programs are required
in this area, too.

3. In the extension movement we have insisted on the
strategic importance of the teachers and at the same time on a
radical transformation of the teacher's role. But, probably
because of the preoccupation with structures and the urgent need
for self-study materials, this whole dimension has been given
little attention. In the future we shall have to do a great
deal more for teachers in alternative programs through the
preparation of manuals and other aids, workshops, seminars and
other training programs. We shall need to provide much more
guidance and supervision in the field. In fact each program
should design an integral approach to the continual formation
of its own personnel.

4. Another aspect of theological education which needs
almost total reworking is evaluation and accreditation. Up to
now we have tried in some ways to resist the evils of traditional
patterns of examinations, grades, and diplomas, but in the
absence of effective alternatives we tend to fall back into the
old ways. We have fought to gain acceptance for extension,
saying that the old accreditation criteria are not at all
adequate, but we have failed to provide new criteria. Obviously
we need urgently to develop tools and procedures for evaluation
and accreditation, and we must involve not only program directors
but also students and teachers, church leaders and institutional
boards, and the associations of theological schools in these
developments.

C. *Areas for Research and Development*

1. One of the curious realities of theological education
around the world has been the lack of serious research into the
nature of theological education itself. Our seminaries are
staffed by the most capable biblical, theological, and
historical scholars, but apparently they have not taken the
initiative to question the programs that they themselves are
involved in. In recent years much use has been made of
Ephesians 4:11-16 to explain the biblical basis for rejecting
the Western, professional model of ministry, but many more
studies are needed to undergird the development of alternative
approaches to theological education and ministry. In some parts
of the world theological commissions have spent many years discussing the ministry and the sacraments, but in Latin America

very little has been written even in the extension movement on
this dimension. In this paper we have referred to Ronald Frase's
analysis of the effects of an imported concept and pattern of
ministerial preparation in Brazil; every church and theological
institution should do this kind of historical research.

2. In recent years the human sciences have developed research
techniques, concepts, and skills that can be invaluable for
theological education. In the past much useful material has been
drawn from the field of psychology for the preparation of pastors
for counseling ministries. We need now to utilize widely the
insights of sociology and anthropology, psychology, and economics
in the formation of theological education for the ministry of
the church as a body. We need to learn a great deal more about
how leadership is formed and selected, how groups function and
solve their own problems, what are effective modes of communication in different cultures, what are the dynamics of dependency,
etc. In Latin America, as Orlando Costas (Latin American Center
for Pastoral Studies) has pointed out, we need to develop a
pastoral sociology far more than we need the North American type
of pastoral psychology.

3. More than ever before we are today aware that theological
education has to do with education, and never before have
educators in other fields offered so much to theological education. This is another vast area for research, reading, and
application. In the extension movement we have been forced into
the field of educational technology in our desperate need of
self-study materials. We have discovered the enormous contribution of Pablo Freire and Ivan Illich, but we have made little
progress in applying their insights. We recognize the importance
of cognitive anthropology, non-formal education, and values
education, but we need to carry out field research and experiments in order to understand and utilize these contributions.
Some have begun to explore the concepts of "total language" of
Francisco Gutiérrez, and there are other educational developments
that can illuminate the task of theological education.

4. Finally we urgently need to find out more about what is
actually happening in the extension movement in Latin America.
We need to know not only how many extension students there are
but who are they, what are they actually learning, how does this
affect their ministries, and what are the results in their congregations and ministries. We know that self-evaluation is
always prejudiced and short-sighted, but we have been afraid that
outside evaluators will be unfair or uncomprehending. Perhaps
now the extension movement has gained sufficient self-confidence
so that it can cooperate in far-reaching analysis and evaluation
schemes. We need to develop tools and procedures for evaluation
in every aspect of our extension programs. The results of these

investigations will no doubt prove to be of great significance
not only for the extension movement but for theological education and the ministry in general.

D. *Dialogue and Dialectics*

1. As we conclude this paper, we do well to reflect upon the
dynamics in which we are involved in theological education in
Latin America today. The extension movement, as a movement, is
barely ten years old; it has swept throughout the region; and
it has challenged the traditional concepts and structures of
theological education and the ministry. This has caused considerable discussion in many circles. The process has been one
of *dialogue and dialectics*. As extension continues to confront
the residential approach to theological education, neither side
will surrender or be destroyed but rather both will be challenged
in an on-going search for better alternatives. In many cases, as
we have seen already, the confrontation will lead to combinations
and adaptations that will strengthen both.

2. Within this search for alternatives we have explored
simultaneously two very important avenues of educational innovation which seem to be contradictory. On the one hand we have
gained valuable insights and methods from programmed instruction
and other educational technologies that facilitate independent,
individualized study, which is so important for extension
students. On the other hand we have discovered in open education that motivation and integration can best be encouraged by
allowing the students to identify and pursue their own needs
and interests. This fundamental conflict should not be abandoned
but rather stimulate further developments in both directions in
tension and dialogue with each other.

3. Another tension has developed between formal, institutional education on the one hand and non-institutional, non-
formal education on the other. In this case most extension
programs would have to be included along with residential
schools as formal, institutional education. And at the other
extreme we may put those who would eliminate theological education as a separate entity. A strong case can be made for
removing all academic apparatus and letting the churches form
their own leadership in the regular activities of the local
congregations. It is well for all theological educators to
remember that their institutions and programs are secondary to
the life and mission of the church. And, as we have noted in
this paper, their contribution can be--and has often been--
negative as well as positive for the health of the church.

4. Finally there is an unending dialogue and an ever incon-
clusive dialectic between our traditions and the work of God's

Spirit in each time and place. Whatever our approach to theological education, whatever our understanding of the ministry,
whatever our ecclesiastical and theological position, we are
challenged by God's Word and by His Living Spirit to renewal
and reformation in the carrying out His Mission in the world.

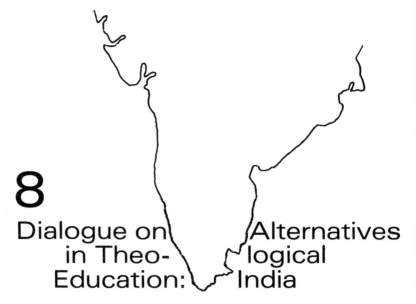

8
Dialogue on Alternatives in Theo- logical Education: India

The Board of Theological Education of the National Council of Churches of India extended the invitation to spend five or six weeks in India to visit theological schools and extension programs and participate in consultations and workshops. I agreed to stay four weeks in India, not wishing to be away from Guatemala too long. But since India is exactly half way around the world, it was evident that I could make the complete circuit within the cheapest air fare and that I should take in a couple of stops in Europe and several in Asia. The Theological Education Fund, which financed the project, proposed visits to some of these places and helped to arrange the contacts. The result: a unique 7-week trip around the world, October 7 to November 23, 1974, centering on an intensive one-month encounter with India.

The purpose for this trip cannot be stated in one sentence or precise objectives. Neither the B.T.E. of India, nor the T.E.F., not I had the direct intention of promoting theological education by extension, although this is what some people supposed. (1) Rather I was to see first-hand what is happening in extension in India: how widely it is being used; who is using it; whether it is simple imitation or genuine adaptation to meet local needs; what problems have arisen; what criticism and evaluation are being made; what has been achieved to date. (2) I wanted to pick up new ideas regarding theological education and even in the broader range of education in general: what are the needs; what critiques are being made of traditional forms; what new or non-traditional modes are being used; how are innovations introduced and adopted; what teaching methods and learning experiences are being tried. (3) I was to meet and talk with

church leaders as well as theological educators to discuss their
concerns for the mission of the church and the renewal of the
ministry and their concept of the role of theological education
in this context. (4) I was expected to share our concerns,
ideas, and experiences in Guatemala and in Latin America in
general, especially from the perspective of the extension movement. (5) The overall purpose was, I feel, to stimulate further
the deepening, broadening process of contextualization in
theological education in India. There is throughout the world
today a broad awareness of the inadequacy of traditional ways of
doing theological education; the extension movement is a working
alternative mode, a new perspective, an instrument for change.
And the extension movement itself is now becoming aware of the
possibilities and the demands of this process of contextual
development.

This report is an attempt to capture and pass on some of the
data, insights, and challenges of this unforgettable adventure.
It should not be taken for more than it is, just one person's
interpretation of seven weeks of exposure to many different
situations, facts, experiments, and issues. Rather than attempt
a synthesis, I shall relate as concisely as possible my
experiences and reflections. I hope those notes will serve to
further the process in which we all find ourselves.

I. PRELUDE: NEW YORK, AMSTERDAM, GENEVA

A. *New York*

During a brief visit with my parents the crisis of the
ministry in the U.S. was focussed in a startling way. My
father, Francis Kinsler, is pastor of the United Presbyterian
Church of Center Moriches, New York. At a recent meeting of the
Presbytery of Long Island a specialist indicated that soon only
congregations of 300 members or more will be able to support a
pastor and program due to rising costs. It happens that at
present 50% of the 8,000 United Presbyterian Congregations in
the U.S. have 200 members or less, and the same is true of the
Anglican Church and others. Already there is an over-supply of
professional pastors in our denomination, and our membership has
been dropping at the rate of 100,000 per year, yet our seminaries
continue to produce hundreds of graduates each spring. It seems
as if the present professional ministry is not capable of meeting
the needs of the historic denominations in the U.S. and that the
whole theological education enterprise is misdirected. And this
is not simply a practical, economic problem; it concerns the
nature of the ministry, the vitality of the church, and the
dynamics of mission. Moreover, this is the pattern of ministry
and theological education which has been imposed all around the
world, first through the missionary expansion of the church and

later through the hegemony of western theology and ecclesiology.
The implications for India (and elsewhere) are disastrous, as we
shall see.

At the headquarters of the Program Agency of the United
Presbyterian Church U.S.A. I talked with our regional liaison
officers about theological education in different parts of the
world. Paul Hopkins, secretary for Africa, made a comment on
the extension movement there which is perhaps over-simplified
but incisive and applicable elsewhere as well. Where extension
is brought in and run by expatriates, he said, it is a failure,
but where it grows out of the local situation in response to
local needs and is run by Africans, it is a success. This seems
to confirm some of our major concerns. Extension has been
largely introduced and run by expatriates in many parts of the
world; it has been presented too often as the answer to all our
problems in every situation; and it has been imposed as a fixed
formula. What is needed, on the contrary, in Africa, Asia, the
U.S., or anywhere else is a process of analysis and innovation
so that each church can freely design its own system of leadership development and training.

While at the New York offices one of our education secretaries
handed me a copy of the final report of the Native American
Consulting Committee's Indian Career Project. This report
presents the peculiar crisis of leadership among the minority
group churches in the U.S. and proposes a shift to theological
education by extension. It states flatly that the American
Indian churches (United Presbyterian, R.C.A., American Baptist,
Episcopal, U.C.C., United Methodist, and Christian Reformed)
"will be virtually without ordained Indian clergy within a
decade unless the present methods of church career development
are changed, and soon." In 1974 these denominations had only 65
pastors for 452 churches—and only four Indian students in all
their seminaries. The traditional way of sending promising
young men to college and then seminary would cost an estimated
$26,000,000 for 100 new pastors; but even then it is doubtful
whether the majority of the candidates would ever return to
serve in their own communities or whether the churches would be
able to support them at their new educational level. The alternative proposal is called "Indian Satellite Theological
Seminaries: Theological Education by Extension." One Hundred
local Indian leaders could be trained in four years at a cost of
$552,000; they would not be cut off from their communities; and
they should have no difficulty being supported by their churches
or communities when they finish.

B. *Amsterdam*

The purpose of my one-night stop-over in Amsterdam was to
talk over proposals for development projects in theological

education in Latin America with Orlando Costas, Secretary for
Studies and Publications of Evangelism-in-Depth, who is doing
doctoral studies at the Free University. Costas plans to set up
a Latin American Center for Pastoral Studies, and he is proposing
that we establish a similar Center for Studies in Theological
Education. Both of these could be modeled on our present ALISTE
Project for training extension specialists in Latin America, and
they could be based in Guatemala and linked to the new School of
Theology of Mariano Gálvez University. The former center would
work with pastors, the latter with theological educators, bringing them together locally and regionally for workshops and
intensive study periods and enabling them to expand their own
ministries through field research and innovation projects.

At the same time (October 9-11) the Latin American Biblical
Seminary in Costa Rica was holding a consultation on "New
Educational Perspectives in Theological Education." James Emery
of Guatemala presented a paper on "Non-Formal Education and the
Seminaries;" Ruben Lores presented "New Trends in University
Education" and "Proposals for the Latin American Biblical
Seminary;" and my paper on "Open Theological Education" was also
discussed. Lores has spent a year in the U.S. doing research on
non-traditional forms of education and will return to Costa Rica
in 1975 to take the lead in this process at the L.A.B.S. Because
of its size, prestige, and resources, this seminary could make a
major contribution to changes in theological education throughout
Latin America. They should, it seems to me, develop a center for
studies in theological education as an alternative to or complement of the proposal mentioned above.

C. *Geneva*

Shortly before I began this trip, Herbert Schaefer, Education
Secretary of the Lutheran World Federation, was in Guatemala, and,
after discussing at some length the possibilities and problems of
theological education by extension, he suggested I make a brief
stop-off in Geneva on my way to India. He arranged interviews
with several people at the L.W.F. and W.C.C. offices. It turned
out that many of these people are aware of the extension movement; some are vitally interested; no one has experience or
direct contact with the movement; most are too busy to give it
much attention. Schaefer himself has made a study of the extension concept, and he is involved in projects for development in
Christian education all over the world. It became evident in
our conversations that we who are involved in T.E.E. need to
establish contact with and benefit from other movements and
resource people. At all of these places--New York, Amsterdam,
Geneva--I received helpful suggestions for my itinerary through
India and East Asia.

II.   INDIA: BOMBAY, NAGERCOIL, TRIVANDRUM, MADURAI,
     MADRAS, BANGALORE, HYDERABAD, YEOTMAL, CALCUTTA

A. *Bombay*

This major city was only scheduled as point of arrival and
orientation for the month in India. Saphir Athyal, Secretary of
the Board of Theological Education of the N.C.C.I. and Principal
of Union Biblical Seminary at Yeotmal, came to meet me, and we
discussed the entire project. Naturally, I wanted to learn as
much as possible about India, about the churches in India, about
theological education in India, about the people and institutions
I would be visiting, and about the specific activities that had
been planned. (Athyal is a personal friend and was a classmate
at Princeton Seminary.)

What do we in the West, in Latin America, in the rest of the
world know about India? We have a vague idea of its enormous
population, its political history, its poverty, its religions.
We have met a few sophisticated, highly educated Indians at our
universities. We have tremendous admiration for Mahatma Ghandi
and Jawaharlal Nehru. But it is another thing to see India, for
India is a whole world in itself. Her present population of 585
million will reach 1162 million in 30 years at the present growth
rate--an inconceivable size and an economic impossibility.
Independent, modern India is just 25 years old, and one wonders
what makes it a nation at all--with 14 major languages and many
other tribal tongues, with many different scripts, with massive
illiteracy (perhaps 75%), massive unemployment and underemploy-
ment, unbelievable poverty. You read all kinds of statistics:
30% of the people don't eat even one square meal a day, 80% are
below the poverty line, etc. When you realize that these
figures represent hundreds of millions of people and you see
these people on the crowded streets of India's cities, they
become morally and existentially overwhelming.

Among India's religions Christianity stands third, with just
2.6% of the population, which comes to 14 million, about equivalent to the yearly national population increase. 82.7% are
Hindus, 11.27% Moslems, 1.9% Sikhs, .77% Buddhists, .47% Jains.
And what do we know about India's Christians? The Surian Churches
probably go back 1900 years to Saint Thomas, the disciple of
Jesus; the Roman Catholics to Francis Xavier (1541); and the
Protestant churches to Ziegenbalg and Plutschau (1706), the more
famous William Carey (1793), and the major Western missionary
societies. I visited the supposed burial place of Saint Thomas
in Madras, the southern coast of India where Xavier evangelized
the fishing villages, and Serampore College, founded by Carey
and his colleagues. I witnessed a Marthoma service, with its
sung Malayalam liturgy; I talked with half a dozen bishops of the

Church of South India about the work in their diocese. I was deeply moved by the hymns sung to the old folk tunes of the Tamil people and shared urgent concerns as I lived those days with Christian brothers whose experience is so different, yet basically our own, whose context is so different, yet so similar, whose mission is so different, yet one and the same.

3. *Nagercoil*

This is a major town, but not a major city, near the southern tip of India. My host was the Church of South India's Bishop Selvamony, and I stayed on the campus of Concordia Seminary. I was impressed by the ecumenical spirit here and elsewhere. The first evening I was at the Home Church of the C.S.I., the next morning at the Lutheran seminary, in the afternoon at the Salvation Army Headquarters, and the following day at the Roman Catholic Bishop's House. At two of these meetings all four groups were represented.

I was also strongly impressed--at Nagercoil and elsewhere--by the number and size of the Christian institutions in South India. There are numerous large and impressive church buildings, and there seem to be many large schools and colleges. Someone stated that there are 180 Christian colleges and universities in India. One of the most prestigious, which I visited later, is the Madras Christian College, which has three undergraduate and ten graduate schools located on 370 acres of land at Tambaram, outside of Madras. In India education is very important for employment and prestige, and Christian missions have invested heavily in educational work. I soon began to wonder to what extent the churches and the ministry are bound by an institutional mentality and structures.

The statistics I picked up in Nagercoil demonstrate that there is a crisis in the ministry in South India. The Kenyekumeri Diocese of the C.S.I. has approximately 160,000 members, 339 congregations, 110 parishes, 85 theologically trained pastors, plus about 260 paid church workers. The Kottar Diocese of the R.C. Church has about 300,000 members, 350 congregations, 78 parishes, 125 priests, and 250 catequists. The Indian Evangelical Lutheran Church has 10,000 members, 50 parishes, 18 pastors. This pattern, which I found throughout South India, is a serious deformation of the ministry and a tremendous challenge to the seminaries. Obviously there are far too few theologically trained leaders, and the vast majority of the churches' leaders receive little or no theological training.

C. *Trivandrum*

The next stop was Trivandrum, the capital city of the state of Kerala, where over 20% of the dense, largely rural population

is Christian. I stayed for two days at the Kerala United
Theological College, which serves primarily the three Malayalam-
speaking diocese of the Church of South India in Kerala. Concerned about the statistics I had discovered in Nagercoil, I
wanted to see what this seminary and the church leaders were
doing. The seminary has 22 full-time students, young men who
are candidates for the professional pastoral ministry. I asked
Principal V. T. Kurien why they have so few students, and he
said they take only those who are sent by the bishops. I asked
the local bishop why he doesn't send more students and he said
his diocese can't support more pastors. So what they have is
the Western pattern of highly trained, professional pastors, in
a situation where simple economics dictates that few men shall
be trained, that each pastor must serve many congregations, and
that the believers shall have little or no trained leadership.

There is another aspect of the ministry in Kerala and
throughout India, but it is just as disturbing. The South
Kerala Diocese has 103,000 members, 271 congregations, and only
76 ordained pastors, but it also has 118 full-time evangelists
and catequists. The latter are very poorly trained, receive
very low salaries, and have little authority or prestige. The
professional pattern of the West has been carried one step
further. Since it is not possible to support more trained,
ordained pastors, they hire a low class pseudo-clergy to work at
the level of the people. Many times while in India I raised the
question, Why not provide adequate training for these church
workers (e.g. by extension) and allow them to become fully
recognized ministers? I never received a satisfactory answer.

It is interesting to note that the work of the C.S.I. in the
Trivandrum area goes back to the London Missionary Society,
which was congregational in polity. The present ecclesiastical
structure is surprisingly hierarchical, with power, prestige,
and salary levels descending from bishop to ordained clergy to
unordained, full-time, paid church workers, to the laymen. This
is what Bergquist and Manickam (*Crisis of Dependency in Third
World Ministries*, Madras: C.S.I., 1974) call the "standard
missionary model" in South Asia.

The Kerala United Theological College has recently initiated
(in 1974) an extension program. There are three centers with 80
students studying simple courses: "Know your Bible," "Know your
Faith," and "Know your Church." One professor is in charge of
each course, and they rotate centers after each short term.
This program is not an attempt to change the pattern of ministry
or even to provide serious theological training for lay leaders.
But as the professors see the enthusiastic response of local
church leaders, they may discover a much broader, deeper
potential for decentralized training throughout Kerala. On the

other hand the traditional program may continue to absorb their
energy and attention; next year they plan to add a B.D. level
for residence students.

D. *Madurai*

One of the most stimulating experiences in India was my three-
day visit to the Tamil Nadu Theological Seminary in Madurai.
This is a large (166 students) institution formed in 1961 to
serve six C.S.I. diocese and three Lutheran churches among Tamil-
speaking people in South India, Sri Lanka, and Malaysia. The
26-member faculty, under the leadership of Samuel Amirtham, is
aware of the dangers inherent in present patterns of the ministry
and ministerial training, and they are involved in some exciting
experiments. The practical program now includes two weeks of
intensive exposure and reflection experiences each year: in
agriculture, evangelism, industrial problems, and Hinduism.
Having seen the value of studying theology in the context of
real life situations, next year they plan to restructure the
entire four-year program. The students will live on the campus
the first year, then off campus the second year, return to
campus the third year, and spend six months of the final year
entirely separated from the seminary. Classwork will relate to
these experiences, and some courses will be interdisciplinary
seminars, apparently a new thing in Indian education. These
changes are not merely structural but existential; the principal
himself plans to spend his next sabbatical in a rural parish
involved in popular education instead of doing research in some
German graduate school.

The seminary has started in 1974 an extension program called
Theological Education for Christian Commitment and Action. They
have about 150 extension students in six centers in different
parts of the state. They plan to take the students through five
brief courses per year for a total of ten in two years, covering
five areas: "The Word of God Today," "The People of God at
Prayer," "The People of God in Community," "The People of God
as Neighbors," and "The People of God in the World of God."
Each course consists of one weekend encounter between a faculty
team and the students in a center with lectures, Bible study,
workshops, and readings. Students carry on with readings and
assignments during the two-month interval between faculty
visits. Experience shows already that they are reaching capable
lay leaders in the churches, that these students are able to do
serious study, and that their experience and concern and daily
problems bring new vitality to the study program. But the program is definitely limited to "laymen" and does not challenge
the basic structure of the ministry or meet the basic pastoral
needs of the congregations.

E. *Madras*

The Community Service Center was in charge of my visit to
Madras, and they organized a two-day consultation on Laity Work
Retrospective and Prospective. A wide variety of groups were
represented, including the YWCA and Youth for Christ, the
Salvation Army and the Moderator of the C.S.I., a deaconness
training school and a Christian-Hindu dialogue center, and
several agencies concerned with urban problems. At first it
seemed that such a hodge-podge of programs, interests, and
issues would not permit meaningful dialogue and could not lead
to any consensus, but it was a significant event simply because
many of these agencies have sprung up in the last 10 years and
they had never met together before. I was asked to speak on
"Theological Education for the Laity" and challenged the basic
laity-clergy dichotomy, an issue which caused heated discussion
and remained unresolved throughout the consultation.

Since there seem to be in many parts of the world increasing
numbers of agencies--within and outside the ecclesiastical
structures--dedicated to specific causes and involved in varied
kinds of training, I shall repeat here some basic concerns that
occurred to me during that Madras consultation. (1) We must
define our missiological bases. It is not enough to express a
vague concern, to attempt to do good, to carry on an established
program. (2) We must clarify our relationship to the churches.
The effectiveness of these agencies may be endangered by
ecclesiastical bureaucracy on the one hand or by irresponsible
isolation on the other. They must show how they relate to the
mission of the church and seek to mobilize the whole people of
God for mission. (3) We should consider the possibilities of
pooling our resources. It may not be possible or helpful to
form a joint organization, but we could make available to the
people in our churches a whole range of experiences in study and
service. In fact the theological seminaries could provide an
integrative structure for those who desire recognized theological
preparation for ministry, and seminary students in turn should be
given the opportunity to choose varied experiences with these
agencies as part of their study program.

While in Madras I made a brief visit to Gurukul, a former
Lutheran seminary and at present an interdenominational center
for extension studies. The regular residence program was closed
several years ago, and faculty and students were integrated into
other seminaries. Gurukul was to be made into a center for lay
theological training and continuing education for pastors.
Unfortunately the power and prestige and most of the resources
departed with the residence program. But the present staff
operates two centers for the TAFTEE (see below) extension program
and brief institutes for pastors. The question in my mind is,

Could not a seminary like this, once freed from the demands of a
nine or ten-month residence program, expand its vision and its
outreach ten-fold by developing training programs for local
church leaders?

F. *Bangalore*

During my five-day visit to Bangalore I was the guest of Ian
McCleary, the New-Zealander who has directed and now serves as
advisor for the Association for Theological Extension Education.
Now in its fourth year, TAFTEE has faced enormous obstacles, and
apparently it is achieving very significant results. The program
was organized by representatives of conservative groups, and
their bias is drawn in the doctrinal statement. This has made
some denominational leaders and theological institutions wary or
antagonistic, but the majority of the students come from those
same churches, and the leaders themselves are increasingly open
and respectful of TAFTEE. Indifference and inertia have limited
the contribution of even the conservative theological schools to
the program, but TAFTEE has been able to produce an impressive
array of instructional materials, a tiny but efficient administrative organization, and an enthusiastic, largely voluntary
teaching staff. With unbelievably small economic resources
TAFTEE now maintains about 20 extension centers scattered far
and wide over much of India. And its student body of 350
includes many capable, disciplined men and women whose commitment, gifts, leadership qualities, and theological formation are
in some very significant ways superior to those of the more
prestigious seminary student bodies. During my stay in Bangalore
I participated in a service of recognition in which a number of
students of the local TAFTEE center received their certificates
for successfully completing 12 or 18 courses out of a total of
30.

What is the significance of TAFTEE with regard to the present
crisis in the ministry of the Indian churches? At this point it
is hard to tell. Many, perhaps a large majority, of the students
are "laymen" as in the other extension programs mentioned above,
but they are grappling with a serious theological program, not
just with "courses for laymen." The structures of the ministry
and theological training are not being challenged head-on,
perhaps for strategic reasons, but a growing number of men and
women are gaining a full ministerial training outside the
establishment and becoming equipped and conscientized in such a
way that they may one day challenge it. For obvious practical
reasons the program has so far functioned primarily at the
university level using the common medium of English, but already
advanced TAFTEE students have begun teaching sub-centers of
extension students at lower academic levels--as part of their
academic program! As materials become available (in the

immediate future) in the major Indian languages, TAFTEE will
begin to tap the enormous pools of local church leaders desirous
of theological education, especially those poorly paid unordained
church workers who have up until now been disenfranchized by the
elitist structures of the ministry and the seminaries. Then the
basic issues of the call, ordination, the gifts, leadership,
church polity, and the nature of the ministry will have to be
faced.

On the other hand TAFTEE's major contribution may be simply
to open the way so that the seminaries and ecclesiastical bodies
will take seriously the weaknesses in their own structures and
begin to make fundamental changes. While I was in Bangalore the
C.S.I. bishop there invited us to present the TAFTEE program to
a gathering of his church workers, and he himself encouraged
them to take TAFTEE courses as part of their ministerial preparation. We were also invited to meet several times with staff
members of the United Theological College in Bangalore (one of
the largest and perhaps the most prestigious Protestant seminary
in India) to help them develop a more adequate program for their
external B.D. students. Russell Chandran, Principal of U.T.C.
and President of the Serampore Senate, even recommended that
TAFTEE or some broader extension organization seek recognition
within the national accrediting association.

G. *Hyderabad*

Probably the most promising institution I visited in India
was the Andhra Christian Theological College in Hyderabad, which
like T.N.T.S. at Madurai is a regional seminary serving a
specific region and language (Telegu). Principal Victor
Premasagar had arranged about 14 hours of meetings for the 48
hours I was there--with faculty, regular students, evening
students, churchmen, and a local TAFTEE group. Far more important than any of the present programs at A.C.T.C. is the process
which they and their constituent churches (primarily Lutheran,
C.S.I., and Baptist) are involved in. Early in 1974 they held
a consultation to think through the whole problematic of
ministerial and theological training structures and the results
have been published in *Renewal of the Ministry in Andhra Pradeah*
(already out of print). Both theological educators and
ecclesiastical authorities recognize that the patterns of the
past are inadequate, and they are taking radical steps to change
them. Faculty teams are now holding consultations in different
sectors of the state in order to involve local leaders in the
process and with them develop new patterns of training and
ministry. In other words they are not simply trying to improve
or extend or change their institutional program but bring about
a renewal of the ministry and of the life of the church itself
for mission.

Research has revealed that the Western, professional model of ministry has virtually miscarried in Andhra Pradesh (as elsewhere in India). In the first place the clergy are given an inordinate status of authority because of the powers conferred to them at ordination--the sole right to administer the sacraments and a monopoly of administrative functions. In the second place the seminaries are unable to supply and/or the churches to support enough pastors. Some rural congregations have not had a pastoral visit with the Lord's Supper for five years. In the third place the teaching function has been widely neglected, making foolhardy the attempts of the seminaries to form theologians of their students. Rural pastors are unable to teach local leaders because they are expected to attend the sacramental and administrative needs of 5 to 25 congregations over a broad area. City pastors often have more than one congregation also, and their schedules are filled with committee meetings and administrative duties so that they rarely spend adequate time even preparing their sermons, much less training others to minister.

The new, developing plan for renewal proposes a broadening and diversification and multiplication of the ministry and of theological training throughout the state. A.C.T.C. will continue to provide extensive theological training for a core of full-time men who will be set aside for a preaching-teaching ministry, i.e., to equip local leaders for their ministries. Another former seminary will focus on the training of local church leaders for a voluntary pastoral-sacramental ministry, with the understanding that A.C.T.C. graduates will carry on indefinitely a program of continuing education with these men. Another seminary will help to form a third ministry concerned with development of social service. And the fourth kind of ministry is the general calling of all the members, a concept and practice which have been extremely weak.

The vision and extent of the Andhra movement are exciting, but major questions remain. Will the existing clergy be willing to turn over their sacramental authority and pastoral duties to local, less-trained, non-professional men? Will A.C.T.C. draw the kind of students who will be able to develop a preaching-teaching ministry among local church leaders? Will the latter feel the need for on-going theological training once they are authorized to celebrate the sacraments? In fact what will ordination do to these men and what will result from the breaking down of the professional rule of the ministry? Apparently A.C.T.C. is still locked into the self-defeating cycle of attracting young, unproven, and unoccupied men for the ministerial profession and sending them out to preempt the ministry of local leaders. Rajamundry seems to be making a very slow start, preparing only 50 or so local men at their campus during

two annual two-month terms for the sacramental-pastoral ministry
--when they should be providing a decentralized program (to
reach the most capable, most occupied people) for thousands of
local leaders for the thousands of congregations in the state.
Apparently relatively little thought or resources or action has
been given to ministry types three and four. And it is still
uncertain whether the four kinds of ministers will become four
classes in a new hierarchy, whether there will be free access
to all the categories and their respective training programs,
whether the whole church will discover its calling and participate in a genuine, dynamizing renewal of the ministry.

Just before leaving Hyderabad I met with the local TAFTEE
group, and we had an open discussion to bring out their evaluation of the program as well as suggestions for improvement.
Vinay Moses, the National Director of TAFTEE, was present, but
this did not inhibit the students. It should be mentioned that
the TAFTEE curriculum consists of programmed courses, each with
its respective workbook covering fourteen weeks of four lessons
per week for home study plus the weekly center meeting (quiz
and discussion). Some feel that the program is too confining
and would like to be allowed to do extra courses, perhaps
independently. Some recommended the formation of seminar-type
courses in which the students could investigate and present
different topics instead of all following a single predeter-
mined path of learning. Another idea was to design a program
of library research which individual extension students could
follow during their vacation periods at some nearby (or distant)
seminary. Another suggestion was to make some of the courses
optional or open, allowing a local group to plan and direct
their own plan of study, perhaps in response to some special
problem or need that they face. Some would like to have the
TAFTEE program related to the theological seminaries with a free
exchange of courses and credits. Some feel that the program is
long and demanding, since it takes at least five years to com-
plate. One additional suggestion was that TAFTEE groups take
time periodically to discuss what they are doing to determine
the future course of their own program, and to recommend changes
to the central administration. Finally it must be said that all
those TAFTEE students (10 or 12) are convinced of the program's
value to them personally and of its significance for the churches.

H. *Yeotmal*

The most important event during the month I spent in India
was the five-day National Study Consultation on Theological
Training of the Whole Church and New Patterns of Training,
sponsored by the Board of Theological Education of the N.C.C.I.
and held at Yeotmal November 1-5, 1974. About 30 delegates
attended, representing most of the major theological seminaries

in India, the churches, and other agencies. Eight or ten major
papers were quickly presented and discussed during the first two
days; then the participants formed three working groups to
develop concepts and proposals coming out of the opening
sessions; and after hearing and discussing these reports a small
commission put together a series of recommendations for final
approval and distribution to the seminaries, churches, and other
agencies. (The report of the consultation, which includes
resumes of the papers and committee reports as well as the final
recommendations, can be obtained from Saphir P. Athyal, Union
Biblical Seminary, Yeotmal, Maharashtra 445001, India.)

The three areas of concern expressed in the papers, analyzed
by the working groups, and defined by the final recommendations
are: the ministry of the whole church, the role of the theological seminaries, and new patterns of training. Ian McCleary
presented a paper on the TAFTEE experience. Victor Premasagar
described the Andhra Pradesh movement. I spoke on "New Patterns
of Theological Training: Lessons from Latin America." From the
beginning the delegates unanimously called for renewal and change
in the existing modes of ministry and training. As the consultation progressed, the extension concept and approach to the
problem became increasingly dominant. The first section of the
final recommendations emphasizes the fact that all members are
called and gifted for ministry, that local leaders should be
recognized and authorized for the pastoral-sacramental ministry,
and that highly trained preacher-teachers should give priority
to the equipping of local leaders in every congregation. The
longest section of the recommendations deals with the seminaries,
calling upon them to initiate a process of consultation with the
churches, recommending a reorientation of their curricula toward
the actual ministries needed, setting forth some specific
suggestions for the external degree programs, proposing up to
one year of field-based training for all residence students, and
encouraging these institutions to involve their faculties and
students in extension programs. The section on new patterns of
training recommends the formation of an all-India committee for
theological education by extension under the B.T.E. and Serampore
Senate.

Encouraging as these recommendations sound to an outsider,
there is little assurance that this consultation will lead to
fundamental changes. Institutions usually develop massive
inertia, and seminaries are no exception. Ecclesiastical traditions and structures are often dominated by vested interests.
And inherited concepts of education and religion are almost
immutable. The consultation itself had no legislative authority;
it could only recommend. But many who were there are caught up
in a process of change, are committed to renewal, and are capable
of moving others to reflection and action. This process will go

forward in varying degrees and in diverse ways, I am convinced, at the seminaries, in the churches, and through agencies such as TAFTEE.

About fifteen men and women, some of whom had attended the national consultation, participated in an extension workshop at Yeotmal for the following five days. Several of these people were already involved with TAFTEE, others came from other extension programs. Some were extension tutors (teachers), one a student, others administrators and writers of course materials. Although there was some confusion on this point, we decided that this should not be a writers' workshop or a workshop on programmed instruction but a workshop covering several basic elements of theological education by extension: structure, curriculum, objectives, principles of learning, programming, and center sessions. The wide diversity of the participants led us to divide up into three groups and even several sub-groups for much of the time. As each became involved in his area of concern at his own level, real progress was made. Almost all of the participants were able to design and present for group discussion samples or proposals for his own work before the workshop was concluded.

Harold England attended the workshop and reported on the extension program of the Santal Theological Seminary, of which he is the Director. The overall goal of that program is "to provide training and teaching to local, unpaid elders or leaders for the teaching, pastoral, sacramental ministry in every congregation and/or unit thereof throughout the whole church." The Santal Seminary served the Northern Evangelical Lutheran Church, which has approximately 300 congregations with 50,000 members among three linguistic groups (Santals, Bengalis, Boros) in the state of Bihar. England estimates that they will need to reach a minimum of 500 extension students, and their strategy is a relay teaching plan based on 2 Timothy 2:2 (from the seminary to a core of paid pastor supervisors to local leaders to the whole church to the world). During 1974, the first year of the extension program, they had 73 students for the first 12-week term and 56 students for the second term (during the rainy season). Prospects for the future include expansion across the border into Bangladesh, where their sister church is growing rapidly. This is one of the most significant extension programs in India because the seminary is throwing in its basic resources, has the full support of its constituency, is depending almost entirely on local personnel for writing course materials and teaching, is attempting to reach the varied linguistic and academic (primary to university) groups, and has an overall vision of the task before it.

I. *Calcutta*

My last stop in India was Calcutta, where I stayed with the
family of Saral Chatterji, visited Serampore College (of which
he is principal) and Bishops College (which is a major seminary
of the recently organized Church of North India), and took time
out for sight-seeing and shopping. During those last four days
a number of thoughts took shape or gained urgency in my mind.

1. Walking the streets of Calcutta, you can probably feel
the weight of massive poverty as well as any place else in the
world. The crowds are overwhelming. Beggers are everywhere.
Children and adults (and the ubiquitous sacred cows) pick over
garbage heaps in major thoroughfares. And families actually
dwell on the sidewalks with their bundles of rags and household
implements. The World Food Conference in Rome concluded at
about that time and demonstrated the incredible complacency and
preoccupation of the wealthy nations. The U.S. delegate, for
example, belatedly wired home suggesting an offer of an additional million tons of grain, when the actual need is for seven
or eleven or twenty million tons of grain. The *New York Times
Review* (Tokyo) for November 17 commented: "The World Food
Conference in Rome has ended without completing plans on how to
save 500 million people from threatened starvation in the next
year...."

How is this relevant to theological education or to my visit
to India? This very question reveals the irrelevance of theological education and of all our work in the church. It is high
time that we awake to the world's crying needs and re-study our
missionary calling.

2. While in Calcutta I read part of *Poverty and Development*,
a book by C. T. Kurien, a noted Indian Christian economist
(Madras: C.L.S.). His analysis of India's condition, which is
basically Marxist, may provide a useful analogy for theological
education. He points out that the economists are past masters
at describing (disguising) the economy's ills and proposing
solutions and designing five-year plans, but the most significant (and obvious) fact is that the masses are still poor and
getting poorer and only a few gain from the plans for development. They seem to be unwilling to face the basic problem,
which is the concentration of wealth, the means of production,
and power in the hands of a few--which inevitably gears production and consumption to benefit those few. Obviously the masses
must gain control of the means of production in order to participate meaningfully in production and be able to consume and
thus shape the economy to meet their needs. In a similar way
the clergy and the ecclesiastical structures and the seminaries
have been dominated by an elite class, who have prescribed all

kinds of programs and preached innumerable sermons to get the
congregations moving. But until the members themselves have
access to power and privilege, we shall not see a lasting
renewal of the church. This is, I believe, what theological
education by extension is trying to deal with.

3. The crisis of theological education in India is not at
all surprising in the light of the broader picture of the
national educational scene. While in Yeotmal I came across this
newspaper headline: "Varsity Degrees May Be De-Linked from
Central Gov't Jobs." India has an enormous civil service
bureaucracy, and these jobs are based on school results, so
literally millions of Indians are pushing for more and more
schooling. Government officials are now concerned about the
"haphazard expansion of secondary schools" and the "mad rush to
universities." As in many other Third World countries, it has
been assumed that huge investments in traditional education
programs will bring about development. The system has largely
failed. On the day I left Calcutta I read in the papers that
226,000 scientists (university graduates) are queued up at
government employment agencies all over India waiting for jobs.
What schooling achieves may in fact be counterdevelopmental.
People are schooled up to an economic and social expectancy
which makes them unemployable. And this swells the frustrated,
turbulent urban population.

Theological education likewise attracts promising young
church people, makes a relatively large investment in them, and
creates a professional expectation. Up to now there has not
been a large unemployment problem among seminary graduates in
India (as there is in Latin America), but this may simply be
because so few students are admitted and because so few employment alternatives are open to graduates. In any case the vast
majority of the congregations find it impossible to employ
seminary graduates, and very little is being invested in the
preparation of leaders who can serve (and are serving) in all
those congregations.

4. Attempts to change the ministry and theological education
inevitably face resistance in the established structures. A
seminary principal explained to me that the whole of Indian
society is based on the politics of vested interests. Any new
move becomes a matter of conflict between those who want to get
a new post and those who are defending the old posts. Job
security is the primary concern in the churches as well as in
the secular realm. Positions are gained and maintained by
pleasing others,making promises, getting votes. Any change is
difficult because it is a threat to those who hold positions of
power and privilege.

Along with this I was told several times that the seminaries project a false model among their students. Their ideal is to become like their professors, not pastors in the churches. They naturally want to go on studying in order to gain that kind of status, not return to the villages and work long hours for low pay and little recognition. So the need is not merely to take theological education to local leaders but also to take theological professors back to the real situation of the churches.

5. The established degree system of India is unique and enigmatic--and it is too complicated to explain here. As elsewhere in the world the seminaries jealously guard their accreditation in the name of quality, yet the way that quality is defined is highly questionable, and the validity of the whole system must be challenged. This system was imported directly from England, where interestingly enough it has been altered radically in the last four years with the introduction of the Open University. Fortunately the Serampore system includes external degrees, by which any candidate can earn his B.Th. or B.D. simply by "sitting" the prescribed examinations. These examinations follow traditional content areas, encourage rote memorization, and reveal little about a student's capability for ministry. But this enormous loop-hole in the theological education establishment should permit and even foster the development of new patterns of training.

The deeper issue here is the validity of any degree system at all. In India the seminaries find themselves caught up in the escalation process of all education. Just a few years back most seminaries functioned at the high school level and offered a L.Th. degree. Now the majority are at the university level and offer the B.Th. degree. Most are now pushing to reach or add the graduate, B.D. level. And some already offer a M.A. or M.Th. This tendency, coupled with factors mentioned previously, could be disastrous. More and more resources will be invested to supply fewer and fewer leaders for the churches at higher and higher support levels. Certainly there is a strategic need for theologically qualified leaders, but there is no assurance that this system will produce them. In fact, I was told that India's most outstanding theologians are not theologically trained at all (in the formal sense).

6. In this report I have said little about the vitality of the churches and their concept of mission, which are prior questions. I have focussed upon the existing patterns of ministry and theological education, which are only a part, though a very strategic part, of the larger picture. It seems to me that in India (and elsewhere) the churches must challenge the hegemony of the professional clergy in order to release the dynamics of the whole body of Christ. This can happen through

the formation of a new concept of ministry and of a new, open
structure of theological education. Only then will the churches
begin to understand and respond to their missionary calling in
today's convulsive world.

Apparently the major Christian denominations in India are
largely static, experiencing little numerical or missiological
growth. Congregational life centers wholly on the routine of
worship services, and ministry is almost entirely the function
of paid church workers and the ordained clergy. The extension
movement now taking hold through TAFTEE and some of the seminaries is beginning to take theological training to local church
leaders and to open up the ministry to the whole people of God.
This should contribute significantly to the churches' understanding of their nature and participation in mission.

7. All these impressions and ideas related to theological
education in India seem to reinforce a general proposal that I
have been formulating in recent months. It is evident that
theological institutions have in the past been founded and maintained in blissful ignorance of the many factors (biblical,
historical, theological, sociological, cultural, pedagogical)
that determine their effectiveness. It is evident that a large
part of the churches' resources is invested in the training of
leaders and that this investment is often misdirected or even
detrimental to the formation of the ministry of the whole body.
Therefore I would like to recommend the formation of Centers
for Studies in Theological Education and Ministry. With little
or no financing, interested churchmen and seminary faculties
could and should take up the responsibility to investigate facts
and issues such as we have commented upon here, to discuss the
many new educational insights and models being circulated today,
and to initiate new experiments and adaptations in their own
regions. As more and more people become involved in this process
and share their experiences, we should all discover many new,
more effective ways to serve our Servant Lord and His ministering
people. (See Chapter 14 of this book.)

III. POSTLUDE: SINGAPORE, MANILA, HONG KONG, SEOUL, TOKYO, LOS ANGELES, GUATEMALA

A. *Singapore*

On the way home from India I made several brief stop-overs,
most of them for just one night. The first was at Singapore. I
stayed at the Discipleship Training Center, which is a two-year
residential training center directed by David Adeney. James Wong
is the prime mover of extension in the area, and he described for
me what the Anglicans (his own denomination), Baptists, and
Lutherans are doing in Singapore and Malaysia. His own program

is four-pronged. There is theological training by extension for
older men who will form an unpaid, auxiliary ministry in the
parishes (ordained and unordained). A second program prepares
candidates for accredited external degree examinations in
theology under the Australian College of Theology. These are
younger men and women; they are the nucleus for the development
of house churches throughout the city; they may in the future be
paid or unpaid, ordained or not ordained. A third group is
studying the Bethel Series, a two-year intensive Bible study
program developed in the U.S. some years ago. And the fourth
program, slated to start in 1975, is a night school for church
leaders.

B. *Manila*

I was met in Manila by Emerito Nacpil, the Executive Secretary of the Association of Theological Schools of Southeast Asia
(ATSSEA) and President of Union Theological Semianry. He and his
colleagues at the seminary have many questions about extension
because they are already embarked on a program for numerous
church workers and other leaders scattered all over the
Philippine Islands. The geographical and linguistic problems
are monumental, but the potential for extension training is also
enormous. There are several other extension programs in the
country, and there is a Philippines Association for Theological
Education by Extension (PAFTEE).

An item that appeared in the Philippine Daily Express the day
I was there (November 16, 1974) deserves mention. The government's Department of Education and Culture announced that credit
will now be given for knowledge and skills or experience acquired
by out-of-school youth "as part of the formal school work."
Their concern is to minimize the effects of increasing drop-outs
due to poverty, e.g., those who must work on the farms. They
cited the UNESCO conference in Paris, which discussed the
adoption of validation schemes for non-formal education. This
trend should encourage theological educators to take increasing
cognizance of those many functional pastors (laymen and paid
church workers) who have generally been excluded or discouraged
by the academic "standard" of their institutions.

C. *Hong Kong*

One of the most significant papers I picked up on the whole
journey is an article on "Accreditation of Non-Traditional
Programs of Study," written by Manfred Berndt for the Association of Theological Schools of Southeast Asia. Berndt heads an
ATSSEA commission which is exploring this whole area of non-
traditional study, and he is the President of Concordia Lutheran
Seminary in Hong Kong. I spent one afternoon and evening with

him and heard a bit about his seminary's program. Their students
now are all employed, study by extension, and are involved in a
church growth scheme aimed at initiating Christian groups
throughout the city.

It seems to me that every association of theological schools,
if not every seminary, should follow ATSSEA's example and
investigate what is happening in the area of non-traditional
and non-formal study. Berndt cites especially three major
resources: (1) The Faure Commission (UNESCO) report, *Learning
to be*; (2) The findings of the Newman Panel, *Report on Higher
Education*; (3) The Carnegie Commission on Non-Traditional
Study's three volumes, *Explorations in Non-Traditional Study,
Diversity by Design,* and *The External Degree*. Many major
educational innovations are now in the planning, experimental,
and operational stages in different parts of the world, and they
should be an invaluable boost for theological educators who are
seeking change or who are trying to convince their constituencies
that such change is valid.

D. *Seoul*

Admittedly my main interest in making a three-day stop-off in
Seoul was to visit my brother and his family and to see what had
happened to the country where I had lived as a child of missionary parents. Theological education by extension is practically
non-existent in Korea, probably because the traditional seminaries are so "successful." The Presbyterian Church of Korea
(one of 14 Presbyterian groups), for example, has about 600,000
members, 2,700 churches, 1,300 ordained pastors, and 1,100
theological students. These statistics are just one indication
that Korean Christianity is unique among Third World countries.
with so many traditional seminary students and graduates, it is
unlikely that extension ministerial training will gain much
support in the immediate future. On the other hand the Korean
Christians have a continuing thirst for Bible study, and the
churches have unusual resources for popular study programs.
Radio HLKY has a tremendous audience all over the country, an
outstanding staff, and an annual budget of $900,000. One corres-
pondence course of basic orientation to the Christian faith,
which is promoted over HLKY, has 400,000 students enrolled.

E. *Tokyo*

Japan is another unusual situation and a sharp contrast to
Korea with only .5% of the population Christian. I spent one
night in Tokyo, attended a meeting of the Kyodon's Commission on
Theological Education, talked at length with James Phillips, and
walked through the adjoining campuses of Tokyo Union Seminary,
Concordia Seminary, and International Christian University.

Japanese pastors are generally highly trained (university or post-graduate level), but they serve small congregations and generally supplement their income by teaching, directing kinder-gartens, etc. The seminaries have been going through serious ideological struggles in recent years; student strikes and barricades are not uncommon; three major seminaries are still closed. Education is very important in Japanese culture (as in Korea) and very stereotyped; seminary classes are mostly lectures, and the teacher is kept on a pedestal; extension and other non-traditional forms are not given much place. On the other hand plans are now being laid for a University of the Air (radio and TV) in Japan (and something similar in Korea), so basic changes may be more feasible in the future.

F. *Los Angeles*

The stop-off in L.A. was to see Ralph Winter, Peter Wagner, and Fred Holland and talk over recent developments and new projects for theological education. Courses related to extension and programmed instruction are a high priority for students at the School of World Mission of Fuller Seminary, who are largely furloughed missionaries and national leaders. Fuller has also developed a serious extension program during the last two years with faculty members traveling as far as Seattle, Washington (1500 kilometers away) for bi-weekly seminars. These courses are now accredited and transferable.

G. *Guatemala*

I arrived, as planned, on November 23, the day of our semin-ary's graduation. But unfortunately I had picked up a virus somehwere along the way and was unable to make the three-hour drive to the scene of that event. That evening the Presbyterian Seminary of Guatemala held its 10th graduation since the initia-tion of the extension plan, the pilot program which has influenced so many others around the world. All ten of the 1974 graduates are men of experience and proven gifts in the work of the church. One is an ordained pastor and the director of a Bible institute, another is the coordinator of evangelism for his denomination, and eight are full-time church workers on their way to becoming ordained pastors. These are the local church leaders who in Guatemala and throughout the Third World are proving that extension is a valid and urgently needed alterna-tive model for theological education.

9
Dialogue on Alternatives in Theological Education:
Southern Africa

Theological education by extension programs have been springing
up in different parts of Africa over the past four or five years;
more recently the historic churches and major theological institutions have been involved in extension plans and proposals. For
some time Desmond Tutu, Assistant Director of the Theological
Education Fund for Africa and Madagascar, has been interested in
these developments, and he has arranged for contact and consultation with the extension movement in Latin America. I was asked
to visit South Africa, Botswana, and Rhodesia at this time; James
Emery was to visit East and West Africa in April of this year.
The purpose of these trips is to observe what is happening in
theological education in these countries, to discuss with local
leaders the needs, possibilities, and problems of their extension
programs, to share ideas, concerns, and experiences we have had
in Latin America, and to formulate some tentative recommendations
about the future. Experiences like these offer an extraordinary
opportunity to learn and to share in the process of evaluation,
innovation, contextualization, and renewal which is deepening and
broadening around the world today.

This report is part of that process, another way in which
others are invited to reflect with us about theological education
and the ministry. These notes go far beyond the specific matters
of theological education; indeed, theological education must be
analyzed in the widest context if it is to be relevant and
effective. On the other hand these are merely the observations
of an outsider on the basis of just 15 days in Southern Africa,
January 14 to February 1, 1975, and should be read with that in
mind.

I. CHALLENGING EXPERIENCES

The visit to Southern Africa was timed to include the annual meeting of the Association of Southern African Theological Institutions, which was followed by a special consultation between ASATI and church leaders from the region. It was a unique opportunity to discover both what is happening in theological education and what are the concerns of the churches. Representatives came to both meetings from South Africa, Lesotho, Swaziland, Namibia, Rhodesia, Mozambique, and Botswana.

A. *South Africa*

ASATI met in Johannesburg from January 16-20, for two days of lectures and two days of business (with Sunday off). Association membership is by institution and individual, and all professors of member institutions are invited to attend. About 60 people came to these meetings, which began with a rather heavy diet of academic papers and discussion. Several presentations dealt with the race problem and Black theology, however, and this is quite obviously the burning issue in Southern Africa today--for government, for society, for the churches, and for the seminaries. The crisis was faced squarely during the business session when the Association adopted a strong resolution regarding the expropriation of Federal Theological Seminary's campus. This institution was founded just 12 years ago by bringing together several theological schools of different denominations, some of which had been persecuted previously by the government because of their interracial policies. Apparently in South Africa it is illegal to prepare Christian ministers of different colors under the same roof.

Alternative types of theological education came up for discussion at the meetings and in private. I was asked to give a paper on the extension movement, philosophy, and methodology, which was received with much interest. Two major projects were discussed at the business session; one of these dealt with in-service training and the other was on theological education by extension.

While in Southern Africa I wanted to make contact with the Independent African Churches and to see what changes are taking place in non-theological education. I was able to explore both these areas on my first weekend in Johannesburg and found them to be most significant. Bishop Isaac Mokoena, head of St. John's Mission Church and President of the Independent Churches Association of South Africa (which represents 600 to 700 denominations with three or four million believers), arranged for me to visit three congregations, two homes, and a hospital on Sunday. I had no permit to go into the Black townships, but I got by with a

clerical collar. As I had expected, I found in these Independent
Churches deep devotion, spontaneous, emotional participation, and
indigenous leadership.

The visit to Turret Correspondence College was also challenging. There are many correspondence programs in Southern Africa,
espcially at the secondary level, but most of them are commercial
enterprises. Turret is concerned about development, especially
of the non-White population, and it is innovative. I met with
the staff and learned that they have been interested in theological education by extension for some tiem. They are experimenting with secondary correspondence courses (600 students),
study centers (for varied purposes), upgrading Black teachers
(500), scholarship aid for university level correspondence
students, and the use of regular newspapers (to help students
prepare for public school exams and also to provide advice on
such matters as how to get a license). They are trying to find
ways for non-Whites to overcome the tremendous disadvantages of
South African society and education. (P. O. Box 11350,
Johannesburg, South Africa.)

On January 21-23 the theologicans were joined by about 40
church leaders of the major denominations. The Dutch Reformed
Church, which is the largest among the White Afrikaaner population, was absent; it doesn't even belong to the South African
Council of Churches. But the Moderator of the Dutch Reformed
Mission (which means "Colored") Church did attend. There is a
third D.R.C. for Blacks, but I don't believe it was represented.
There were Anglicans, Methodists, Presbyterians, Congregationals,
Lutherans, Moravians, Roman Catholics, and Independents. It was
a very significant event. Apparently there had been a long-
standing separation between the churches and theological schools;
the goal of this consultation was to come together to share concerns and concepts of theological education and the ministry.
New patterns of training are being developed throughout the
region; the purpose of the consultation was to discuss together
the needs, possibilities, and implications of these innovations.

The consultation got off to a rather shaky start. Several
papers had been assigned previously, but the steering committee
wanted to make sure that the participants took the initiative
and developed their own agenda and came to their own conclusions.
So we began with group discussions and panel presentations,
fitting in the speakers along the way. The topics, which were
set day by day, followed a logical progression from "What is the
ministry?" to "What kinds of experiences does a person need to
equip himself for ministry?" to a discussion of the alternative
patterns of theological education. I felt that the discussions
were very general, indefinite, avoiding some very basic issues.
So, when I was asked to speak halfway through the consultation,

I made a radical challenge to the traditional patterns of training and ministry with a presentation called "Bases for Change in
Theological Education." This apparently offended some people,
and it especially irritated some Black leaders (for reasons I
shall discuss later), but I believe it helped to bring the discussions down to earth and to demonstrate the urgency of our
task. By the final day the participants had reached a general
consensus and agreed to prepare a summary statement covering
the issues that had been discussed. This statement was prepared
first by the theologians and churchmen separately, then together,
and it was adopted unanimously.

The Johannesburg statement begins by affirming that ministry
is the concern of the whole church, that the purpose of theological education is to develop the ministry of the whole church,
that training methods should be designed in terms of the nature
of the church and the objectives of the ministry, and that the
churches should be more flexible with regard to types of programs
to train people for ministry. It goes on to recommend guidelines for the setting up of internship and extension programs in
the immediate future on an ecumenical, interracial basis. It
also recommends a "radical evaluation" of residential training
programs and further investigation of such matters as ordination,
ministry and ministries, the position, status, role, and remuner-
ation of ministers in the church, and the relationship between
all this and theological education. (The full report of the
consultation may be obtained from Dr. Axel Ivar Berglund,
Director of Theological Education, South African Council of
Churches, P. O. Box 31190, Braamfontain, Johannesburg, South
Africa.)

On the day after the consultation the Committee on Theological
Education by Extension met to consider what steps to take. This
committee was apparently set up by the Joint Board of the
seminaries, and it will probably become attached to the National
Council for Theological Education of the S.A.C.C. The chairman
is Rev. Louis Peters, O.P., who has been directing a New
Theology Correspondence Course (university level) for the last
three years and who will give full-time to the planning and
introduction of the new extension scheme over the coming months.
(P. O. Box 5902, Johannesburg, South Africa.)

B. *Botswana*

The two-day visit to Gaborone, Botswana was reduced to one
due to unfavorable flying conditions, but I discovered much
interesting information in that short time. Botswana is a large
(the size of France) but sparsely populated (750,000), largely
desert country which became fully independent in 1966. The
churches are small, and there tends to be one major denomination

in each tribal area. Practically nothing has been done in theological education; candidates for the ministry were previously
trained in South Africa. It is now very difficult for Blacks to
enter South Africa for study, so there is urgent need of a
ministerial training program in Botswana. The Congregational
Church, for example, has 60 pastors for about 12,000 members,
but only ten are trained and ordained, and 45 or 50 of the 60
are over 60 years old.

A two-man team, Dick Sales and Escort Mbale, was to initiate
a major extension program the following week with six centers
along the major railroad line plus two other centers at distant
points led by two volunteers. Self-instructional materials have
been prepared in English at the mid-secondary level with feedback for the objective questions and discussion questions for
the center meetings. A test group experimented last year, and
40 students were expected to start this year. Funds came from
student fees, cooperating churches, and major donations from two
denominations. In a country like this extension is probably the
only way to do theological education; few traditional seminary
graduates would survive long on local support. (P. O. Box 237,
Gaborane, Botswana.)

Some very interesting educational programs have begun in
Botswana over the last year or two. The Botswana Extension
College, with the help of the International Extension College
(England) and the Ford Foundation, offers formal correspondence
courses at the junior-high school and high school levels utilizing radio and study centers as well as printed materials. Their
non-formal education programs include young farmers' clubs,
village development committees, housewives, agricultural demon-
strators, etc. The Department of Extra-Mural Studies of the
University of Botswana, Lesotho, and Swaziland has carried out
a massive educational program in connection with the Botswana
government's current five-year national development plan.
Printed materials and radio programs were prepared first; then
leaders were prepared for 1400 community groups through 14 2½ day
workshops; and 28,000 people participated in these groups during
the five weeks of the program, led by these local leaders and
listening in on ten broadcasts. The plan, the materials, and an
evaluation are being published in three large volumes.

C. *Rhodesia*

I flew up to Salisbury for three days, stayed at Epworth
Theological College, and learned about a number of programs of
theological and non-theological education. Epworth itself is
the main protestant seminary in Rhodesia with eight full-time
faculty (only two Black professors), 29 students in residence
(for four years), and five denominations supporting it. Several

of these same denominations and the Epworth faculty realize that this program is not sufficient to meet the needs of the country. It is even questionable whether this kind of training is appropriate, whether such an enormous investment in so few students is justifiable, whether the churches can support many professional pastors who graduate at this level (first degree university). Epworth is trying to add a number of extension activities in order to respond to the needs of the churches. (Rev. Michael Appleyard, Principal, Box H97, Hatfield, Salisbury, Rhodesia.)

The Anglicans recognize that in order to be self-supporting they must depend increasingly on a self-supporting, "supplementary clergy." Fourteen men have been trained already for this kind of ministry; 23 more are now being trained (four times as many as are in traditional seminaries); by 1980 there will be more supplementary than traditional clergy in the Anglican church in Rhodesia, Botswana, Zambia, and Malawi. These candidates study correspondence courses over a period of four years with three weekend encounters per year. Standard texts and essay questions have been used until now; they are beginning to move toward programmed instruction.

The Methodist Church of Rhodesia (English origin) has a total membership of about 65,000, with 399 churches, 607 other meeting places, and only 71 ministers plus 20 evangelists. The United Methodist Church of Rhodesia (U.S. origin) has a similar number of members and a similar crisis in its ministry. Apparently these two churches are unable either to prepare or to support an adequate number of pastors in the Western pattern. And they are in the process of designing some kind of extension training to provide for some kind of local congregational ministry. At present it is common for one pastor to look after the needs of 30 congregations.

The Lutherans face the same problem. They cannot train and support more professional pastors, but the existing supply of pastors is unable to care for all the congregations. They meet twice yearly with their pastors for continuing education, and they have two institutes which train laymen. This could become the basis for an extension program.

The Roman Catholics are beginning to make more use of married, ordained deacons, and they have to depend increasingly on catequists for pastoral work in the congregations. A Franciscan priest has already developed an extension training program for catequists. In that area each priest has ten parishes.

Unfortunately I was unable to make contact with a man by the name of Daneel, who runs an extension program for leaders of the Independent churches in Rhodesia.

One of the most exciting programs of non-theological education
which I came across in Southern Africa is Ranche House College
in Salisbury. Ken Mew, the Principal, gave me a good rundown of
their philosophy and activities. Apparently Ranche House is
similar to Turret Correspondence College in its emphasis on education for development and its efforts in adult education. They
offer regular secondary classes and probably graduate more than
any public school each year. They offer non-formal study programs
for adults, and they hold many different kinds of short conferences and meetings throughout the year. They hope to improve
human relations and human dignity through these programs. (P. O.
Box 1880, Salisbury, Rhodesia.)

D. *South Africa*

Before returning to Guatemala I made another brief stop back
In Johannesburg in order to visit two more very significant
programs, the University of South Africa in Pretoria and the All
Africa School of Theology at Whitbank. Since 1946 the University
of South Africa (UNISA) has operated entirely by correspondence.
In 1974 they had 34,421 students studying under six faculties.
Although almost 80% of the students are White, UNISA has more
non-Whites enrolled than any other university in South Africa.
The program's headquarters is an enormous, modern building over-
looking Pretoria, the capital city of South Africa. There the
500 to 600 academic staff and a similar number of non-academic
staff give full-time to the preparation of home-study materials
and the administration of this massive program. Up until now
there has been a relatively small number of candidates for degrees
in theology, but the faculty of theology is attempting a major
curriculum revision and trying to provide face-to-face contact
with the students. They could easily handle more students than
all the residence seminaries put together, with or without their
help, because the latter are trying to compete at more or less
the same level without secular accreditation. (P. O. Box 392,
Pretoria, South Africa.)

The All Africa School of Theology, based in Whitbank, is a
Bible correspondence program designed especially for pastors of
the African Independent Churches. Rev. F. H. Burke, a missionary
of the Assemblies of God in South Africa since 1921, founded and
directs the program; he has written almost all of the materials
(in English, with some translated into African languages); and
it continues as a family operation.

About 500 students are currently taking the ministerial
course, which costs $30 and is made up of about 20 individual
courses or units, each with an examination to be sent in and
graded by the staff, and normally takes three years to complete.
A number of churches have asked Burke to train their pastors in

this way, and most of his students are already church leaders.
A recent graduate is the charismatic overseer of a 500,000
member sect. (F. H. Burke, Box 263, Whitbank, Transvaal, South
Africa.)

There are, of course, other interesting programs in South
Africa, and several of them can be called theological education
by extension. Several Anglican diocese are preparing supplementary clergy through home study, periodic meetings, and supervised practical work. The Methodists are trying out a major
scheme of ministerial, in-service training. The Moravians have
a night-school seminary in Capetown, which permits the students
to be employed and the employed to study theology. An Anglican
missionary couple in Swaziland has been asked to set up an
extension program, which should serve all the churches there.
The Lesotho Evangelical Church has tried to set up an extension
program. In conclusion there are already numerous non-residential
theological training programs in Southern Africa, and there is
evidently a tremendous need for further development in this
direction.

II. GENERAL IMPRESSIONS AND BASIC CONCERNS

A. *The Needs of the Churches*

Probably the greatest overall concern that comes to mind as I
reflect on my brief visit to Southern Africa is the fundamental
conformism about theological education in light of the vast
unmet leadership needs of the churches and the tremendous new
possibilities of meeting those needs. There are notable exceptions, and there is much interest in new patterns of training,
but there doesn't seem to be a grand vision or a driving sense
of mission either in the seminaries or in the churches.

Institutions have a way of closing in on themselves, and
theological seminaries naturally tend to define the rationale
for their own existence. The importance of theology and the
complexity of the academic task and the absence of external
evaluation make it extremely difficult to look at the seminaries
objectively. Theological jargon, religious idealism, and
academic erudition prevent us from seeing and dealing with the
most obvious practical problems. For example none of the many
seminary professors and churchmen I asked could give me the
statistics regarding the number of members, congregations, and
ordained pastors in their churches in South Africa. I did
discover that eight of the major seminaries together produce
only 92 graduates per year, and it is evident that there are
thousands of congregations without trained pastors in South
Africa. The President of Lesotho Evangelical Church indicated
that they have 38 ordained pastors for a constituency of 220,000.

The seminaries seem to be content to carry on business as usual, investing their resources in the formation of small groups of mostly young, unproven men for the professional ministry. It is common for five to ten full-time staff members to train 15 to 30 full-time students for three or four years of largely theoretical theology.

Equally alarming is the pattern of ministry that has evolved in the churches. The relatively high level of theological training plus the relatively low economic and academic level of the membership produces a situation in which only a few full-time pastors can be supported. Their position is guarded through the rite of ordination, and the many unordained church workers continue to be deprived of full theological training and full recognition of their ministries. This problem is especially serious in the churches which have a common fund from which pastors are paid. This generally means that there is a common salary scale. And if White and Black congregations belong to same denomination, there is a natural drive toward equlization of salaries. This means that it will become increasingly difficult (largely impossible) for Black congregations to support a pastor, or for the denomination to support pastors in all the Black congregations. Thus it is common throughout Southern Africa for a pastor to serve (oversee) 5 to 35 congregations.

In contrast to this Western, White pattern of training and ministry, the African Independent Churches (Black) are able not only to survive but to respond to their people's needs and to grow remarkably through charismatic, largely untrained leadership. Neither the historic churches nor the Independent Churches themselves seem to realize the significance of this phenomenon. (Compare the fantastic growth of Pentecostal churches in Latin America.) There were two or three representatives of the Independent Churches at the Johannesburg consultation, but they were not asked to speak--and they didn't. I was anxious to take the first opportunity to see these churches in action, but I suspect that few of the people at the consultation ever visit these congregations, certainly not to learn how to develop effective leadership for their own churches. When the matter did come up at the consultation, however, the representatives of the historic churches had to admit that large numbers of their members attend prayer meetings and worship services with these Independent congregations.

B. *Changes in Educational Outlook*

The conformism and inertia of the churches and seminaries, which I have mentioned, are probably responsible for their lag behind recent, revolutionary developments in educational

philosophy, systems, and methods. As elsewhere throughout the
world the Western concept of education as schooling has been
adopted uncritically in Southern Africa. And, as Ivan Illich
has pointed out, this mentality is as difficult to change as is
religious ritual. Of course I, as a White North American, was
in an embivalent position as I tried to challenge this perspective and point toward new alternatives.

The "school mentality" affirms that people learn only when
they are taught, that schools have a monopoly on education, that
the more time spent in school the more the students are bound to
learn. Most churchmen and seminary professors assume, in like
fashion, that the best way to "form" or "produce" good pastors
is to send them off to school for three or four or more years--
the longer the better, the higher the academic level the better,
the tougher the requirements the better. So it sounds naive, if
not sacrilegious, to question the whole system, which is what I
tried to do. There are, of course, many bases from which to
challenge the traditional point of view: theological, historical,
sociological, economic, missiological, as well as educational.
But people do not easily abandon the foundations of their own
position in life and in the church.

Just take a look at the steep educational pyramid among Black
South Africans. Only .4% ever reach the universities. Therefore
it would be suicidal to limit "legitimate" theological education
to residential training at that level. The Black churches will
not be able to finance that level of training, nor will they be
able to pay pastors' salaries at that level for generations.
Yet the strongest opposition to my suggestions (to decentralize
training and offer it at several levels) came from Black churchmen and seminary professors--and understandably so. They have
had to struggle against enormous odds to make it through to the
top, and they are not likely to let anyone underestimate what
they have achieved. They rightly stand on a par with the White
Man, and their students and graduates and even the members of
their churches will strive to maintain their status in a social
order which tries to deprive them of equal education and equal
status.

I tried to meet this challenge head-on. I told them they are
simply trying to produce a White kind of pastor through a White
kind of training at the White level for a White kind of church.
I hope that some, at least, will see that what they need is to
develop their own way, a Black training at Black levels for
Black churches. And I firmly believe that they could develop a
far more effective system of training and ministry than the
Whites are able to produce even for their own churches. That is
why I emphasize so strongly the lesson of the African Independent
Churches. I don't believe the Western, professional model of

training and ministry is really effective anywhere in the Third
World--and I don't believe it is effective even in North America
or Europe! But unfortunately the last to accept this critique
and challenge are liable to be those who, like my Black
opponents in Johannesburg, have struggled so hard to reach that
shaky pinnacle of success in a foreign system.

So theological education by extension and other alternatives
may be rejected in Southern Africa, not directly, because some
have already been accepted in principle, but by denying them the
resources and moral support so necessary for them to prove themselves. And those most able to make a success of extension
are those most likely to reject it--at great cost to their
churches and to their people. Neither the evidence of the
extension movement elsewhere nor the growing evidence of secular
Southern African institutions like UNISA, Turret, Ranche House,
and many others is likely to convince them.

C. *The Race Problem*

Everyone knows that Apartheid is a terrible enigma, but it is
another matter to be in South Africa even for just a few days.
What does it mean in terms of daily life, in terms of human
dignity, in terms of the mission of the church, in terms of
theological education? We lived and mixed together, Blacks and
Whites, at the conference center in Johannesburg, but there was
some question whether this was legal. After a long day of
meetings I inadvertantly suggested to a Black theological professor that we go to a movie, but he wouldn't be allowed in a
White theater...and we couldn't ride the same bus downtown...
and he had forgotten to bring along his "pass," which meant that
he could be locked up by any policeman. Johannesburg is a very
impressive, large, clean, modern city built on a gold reef. I
was impressed by the number of swimming pools in the White
residential areas as I flew into the city and later by the
numerous luxurious mansions as I drove about. Then on Sunday I
went through the enormous "townships" of tiny, identical houses
built by the government and rented to the non-White population
(75% of the total). A Black man cannot own land in Johannesburg
and therefore is unlikely to build a house there. He is an
alien, classified by ethnic group and tied arbitrarily to some
"homeland." The extremes to which Apartheid is taken would be
laughable if they were not so tragic and inhuman.

Coming from Latin America, I expected to see signs of
rebellion and hear talk of revolution, but South Africa is not
Latin America. The 20% White population has tight control of
the country, and the non-Whites have learned patience and submission for centuries. I assumed that the rapid coming of Black
rule to most of Africa, the recent changes in Angola and

Mozambique (South Africa's neighbors), and current rumors of
changes in Rhodesia (South Africa's partner in Apartheid) must
make both Whites and Blacks realize that Black rule is inevitable in South Africa too. But I was told again and again that
the future is by no means certain. White South Africa probably
has more wealth (including 78% of the world's gold supply and a
monopoly on diamonds) and military power than most of Black
Africa.

The primary lesson that came home to me as I contemplated
this dilemma was that sin is corporate and structural, not just
individual and personal. In South Africa the blame could be
placed on the Afrikaaners, who are of Dutch descent. But in
Rhodesia the English descendants are responsible, in Angola and
Mozambique the Portuguese, and in Southwest Africa the Germans.
In parts of Africa Black rule has led to atrocities and genocide
among Blacks of different tribes. Racism is just one of the
forms that evil takes when one group of people obtains a
position of power and privilege. And the Christian churches are
implicated in this evil. The most powerful church in South
Africa is the Dutch Reformed Church, and it is apparently com-
promised in Apartheid. The South African Council of Churches,
on the other hand, has made a public stand against Apartheid,
but most of the member churches' congregations are de facto
segregated. If all Christians in South Africa were to oppose
Apartheid, they could obviously transform society, for 72% consider themselves Christians.

The Theological Education Fund has in recent years popularized
the concept of "contextuality" or "contextualization." Some in
Southern Africa and elsewhere have interpreted this term to mean
indigenous, adapted to local custom. And they have promoted
theological education by extension because it takes place in the
normal settings of the culture. This aspect is indeed significant. But the T.E.F. makes clear that contextualization is not
merely an identification with local culture but a challenge to
that culture from within on the basis of theological reflection.
It is in this sense that theological education by extension can
be so vitally significant. Sending a few Blacks off to Federal
Theological Seminary or Epworth or Cambridge or Princeton to
become spokesmen for Black Theology is not enough; it isn't even
the primary task. The critical tools of theological reflection
must be placed in the hands of local leaders throughout the
Black population. They are the ones who will be able not only
to proclaim the Gospel of liberation but lead their people and
their countries to a new way of life, a new humanity, through
reconciliation with God and among men.

III.   TENTATIVE RECOMMENDATIONS

A. *General*

1.   In order for changes in theological education to be meaningful and effective they should be set forth in terms of mission.
Our concern is not merely to manipulate our structures and change
our methods to get more students or to teach them more efficiently. We seek the renewal of the ministry. As we develop new
patterns of training, we should challenge our churches and our
institutions with a new sense of mission and a new vision of the
possibilities for service.

2.   Similarly, we should face squarely the needs of our
churches and the limitations of present programs of training and
patterns of ministry. Extensive research would be helpful, but
even a cursory glance at the statistics of our denominations
reveals tremendous deficiencies. This should be another basic
step in introducing change, i.e., to find out what our needs are
and then design programs that will meet those needs.

3.   Sometimes innovation comes in opposition to the established institutions or inspite of their indifference. It seems
as if there is sufficient concern in the seminaries of Southern
Africa to enlist their cooperation. The seminaries hold msot of
the resources for theological education; they could benefit
greatly from new educational insights and methods; and they
could play a creative role in the development of new patterns
of training and ministry.

4.   Similarly, every effort should be made to involve the
churches in the process of research and change—at all levels
and at each stage. The churches, after all, must provide the
resources, the candidates, the context, and the drive for theological education. The Johannesburg consultation was an
excellent start in this direction. More consultations, workshops, seminars, and other means should be used to take the
vision down to the grassroots and out to the whole field of the
church.

5.   There seems to be in South Africa a desire to develop
one all-embracing extension program and to get all the churches
and the ponderous ecumenical organizations behind it. This
procedure does of course have some big advantages. On the
other hand room should be left for experimentation, adaptation,
and independent growth. F. H. Burke of Whitbank proves that one
man can achieve almost single-handed more than a dozen seminaries.

6.   The process of change and the search for new patterns of
theological education are moving rapidly ahead not only in

Southern Africa but in many parts of the world. Therefore we can gain much by keeping in touch with others and exchanging insights and experiences.

7. It is also evident that other fields of education are going through a tremendous process of change all around the world. We can learn much from the numerous experiments and the sea of publications that come out of this process.

8. Probably a special effort should be made to discourage the African Independent Churches from trying to immitate and compete with the White, Western pattern of theological education. The fact that they have no seminaries and such limited resources could in fact make it easier for them to develop new, more effective patterns of theological education. If, on the contrary, they follow the traditional pattern, they will only be able to train a tiny fraction of the leaders they need, and they will probably train them away from their people.

9. Those who become involved in the new programs must decide, sooner or later, whether those programs can be given a fair chance with the meager resources that are left over after the needs of the established institutions have been met. They may in fact have to challenge the seminaries and the churches to take the new programs seriously and provide substantial funds and personnel. The reward can be very great. If even one seminary were to redirect its entire resources into some kind of decentralized theological education, its service to the churches could be multiplied ten-fold or more.

10. All of these general recommendations point to a process. There is no simple solution, no easy formula for theological education or for the ministry, for today or for the future. But as more and more people in the churches and in the seminaries enter into this process of reflection and change, they shall no doubt discover new and better ways to develop the gifts for ministry and mission.

B. *Specific*

1. One important first step following the Johannesburg consultation will be the visits which the Director of Theological Education and the Chairman of the Extension Committee will be making to different parts of the country in the coming months. They will be sharing with seminary staffs and churchmen the concerns and plans expressed at that consultation, finding out what others feel about them, and laying the groundwork for the new programs. This kind of personal contact and involvement should continue, and it can be directed by others, not just by the official promoters of these programs. There is an urgent

need for consultations in Swaziland, Lesotho, Southwest Africa, Botswana, and Rhodesia, as well as in South Africa.

2.   It would be helpful to move on rapidly from consultations, where people talk about the nature of the ministry and new patterns of theological training, to workshops, where they begin to experience and experiment with the new concepts and methods. Workshops can be very helpful among theologians and churchmen at all levels, and the ones who are carrying on consultations can also direct the workshops. In order to extend this process, they can prepare workshop materials and procedures to help others carry on workshops without the need of someone to direct them.

3.   A very useful way of keeping people interested and informed of new developments is to publish a regular bulletin. It can be simple and inexpensive, yet reach many churchmen and seminary professors and local leaders as well as those who are involved directly in new patterns of training. It can include news of consultations and workshops, descriptions of new educational approaches and experiments both in theological and non-theological education, analyses of the leadership needs of the churches and ways to meet those needs, and other related articles. There should be no problem finding an abundant supply of material to keep the concerns and the challenge of theological education before the readers.

4.   The person in charge of the bulletin is probably the one who should begin to collect materials and set up files on theological education and ministry. It can be very helpful to have a central deposit with copies of seminary catalogues, samples of syllabi and course materials, reports of consultations and workshops, and the kinds of materials mentioned above. Some of this can be used in the bulletin; some will be useful for workshops and consultations; some can be circulated to interested individuals; all of it can be made available to persons who want to look through it for their own use.

5.   Along with the previous points it should be very useful to maintain contact with people involved in theological and non-theological educational renewal in Southern Africa and around the world. I have mentioned Turret Correspondence College, the Botswana Extension College, the Department of Extra-Mural Studies of the University of Botswana, Lesotho, and Swaziland, and Ranche House College as examples of innovative non-theological programs; each one has produced provocative materials and challenging models for us to study. Ranche House, for example, has prepared a Directory of Adult Education Agencies in Rhodesia (1974), with 100 pages describing the purposes and activities of those agencies. The Botswana Extension College

recommends the Broadsheets on Distance Learning of the International Extension College (131 Hills Road, Cambridge CB2 2BP, England). The number and quality of decentralized school and university programs and instructional materials has grown enormously in recent years in North America and Europe. In theological education similarly there is a growing interest in non-traditional forms of study. There are several extension bulletins produced in Guatemala, Colombia, Brazil, India, the Philippines, etc. The faculty of theology of UNISA will probably be producing better printed materials and also visual and aural aids in the near future. The Association of Theological Schools of Southeast Asia has produced a valuable paper on "Accreditation of Non-Traditional Programs of Study." The materials prepared by Louis Peters, Dick Sales, and others in Southern Africa can serve as examples and inspiration for others who will be called upon to prepare course materials for new programs. There is an enormous wealth of material, but it will not be used unless someone collects it, sorts it out and interprets it, and makes it available to the right people.

6. The Extension Committee is now considering what levels of study should be offered. It seems as if the initial plan of diploma-level studies should be upgraded to a first-university-degree level. A Junior Certificate level and a primary school level should be added. Most non-European church leaders are probably at this third level. But great care should be made to affirm and defend the functional parity of all three levels. All three should be considered as basic ministerial training and valid for ordination--for those who are candidates for the pastoral ministry.

7. It is important to establish the validity of theological education by extension and the credibility of this particular plan. An intriguing possibility would be to link the university level with UNISA, i.e., to offer the UNISA B.Theol. degree by extension. There seems to be considerable opposition to this idea from the seminary professors on the grounds of theological perspective, educational methods, etc. But the UNISA faculty of theology seems to be genuinely open to criticism and desirous of cooperation from the seminaries and interested in forming something like an extension network. They might even incorporate some of the seminary staff members as adjunct professors for extension teaching and as guest professors invited to prepare some of the study guides. Neither the extension program nor the seminaries will probably ever have as many resources (staff, finances, technical advice, publishing equipment, etc.) as the UNISA faculty of theology has at its disposal. And the Joint Diploma Board and the seminaries cannot compete with UNISA's degree for credibility even in their residential programs.

There are, of course, other, non-academic dimensions of
theological education. And the Extension Committee should give
much thought to these dimensions. Seminary professors and churchmen rightly point to the development of the whole personality,
the practical aspects of ministry, the devotional life, and life
in community. Orientation should be given and experiences
planned so that the student can grow in these essential ways.
Extension centers can form a sense of teamwork and commitment.
Local pastors can encourage and counsel the students in their
practical work. Retreats and group learning experiences can be
held periodically. The students could plan and participate in a
daily discipline of prayer and Bible reading. In fact the entire
program could develop the esprit de corps of a mission order.

8. As more people become involved in new patterns of
theological education, the need will arise to train personnel--
to direct, to teach full-time or part-time, to write instructional materials, and even to design new programs. The most
common way to provide these kinds of training is to hold workshops either sporadically or according to some systematic
sequence. Those who work together in a particular program can
meet regularly for evaluation, discussion of problems, and
planning. It is also helpful to provide opportunities for new
people to visit programs already in operation and talk with
those who have had more experience. And visiting specialists
can provide insight and stimulation. Another possibility is for
the Extension Committee or one of the seminaries to design a
special training program for theological educators. (Cf. The
ALISTE Project for Training Extension Specialists in Latin
America, Chapter 13.)

9. The largest, most promising field for decentralized
theological education in Southern Africa is among the Independent
Churches. The South African Council of Churches and the Independent Churches Association of South Africa are working
together in the formation of a South African Theological College
for Independent Churches (SATCIC), which apparently is planned
along traditional lines but is still being formed. It may be
very important to enable SATCIC staff members to be exposed to
alternative patterns of education (both theological and non-
theological) at this stage before all their resources are
committed to the residential program. Perhaps resources can be
provided for some experimentation with decentralized programs.
Personal conversations, consultations, and workshops should be
planned especially among Independent Church leaders. And
special training could be provided for someone to work in this
area.

10. The final recommendation concerns a proposal which is
just now taking shape in Latin America. It is called "Centers

for Studies in Theological Education and Ministry," and its purpose is to stimulate people in different situations to take the
initiative in the development of plans and materials and personnel for theological education. With very little expense and
relatively little time to give, a small group of seminary professors or churchmen could begin to collect and analyze information and articles about new patterns of theological education,
discuss their own experiences and plans, and maintain contact
with others who are involved in the same process. An institution
such as Epworth Theological College might in fact make a much
greater contribution if, instead of trying to launch a major
extension program or a series of new programs, it would become a
center for the development of resources for decentralized training programs and thus help others to do the actual training of
local church leaders. The Centers for Studies in Theological
Education and Ministry could help greatly in the exchange and
mutual stimulation of people with similar concerns within
Southern Africa and with other parts of the world. This proposal
incorporates many of the recommendations listed above. (See
Chapter 14.)

As I conclude this report, it occurs to me that much of what
I have written reflects our experience in Latin America. The
extension movement has developed through much the same process
as I have recommended above. This can be a bad thing, if I am
merely projecting the ideas and plans of one region of the world
to another very different one. On the other hand this sharing
of insights and experiences can be a good thing if in fact the
problems and needs in Southern Africa are similar to those of
Latin America. It can be a good thing because the recommendations are not unrealistic ideals and impractical proposals but
workable suggestions, things which we have actually been doing--
within our many limitations.

10

Dialogue on Alternatives in Theological Education: U.S.A.

After several years' involvement in the movement called theological education by extension in the Third World, we have
discovered that similar developments are taking place in the
U.S. and that more changes in this direction are urgently needed.
The purpose of this paper is to explore these developments and
needs in the U.S., to bring to bear insights from the Third
World, and to share what is happening in the U.S. with colleagues
in other parts of the world.

For some time we have felt that the churches in the U.S. and
Europe have much to learn from their sister churches in the Third
World, particularly in terms of leadership and training patterns.
On the other hand we have been concerned about Third World
dependence on Western patterns of theological education and
ministry, especially among the historic denominations. This
paper is intended to stimulate further dialogue on alternatives
in theological education both in the U.S. and in the Third World.

The following observations and analyses are necessarily
limited in scope. They have taken shape during a visit to the
Western States during the summer of 1976. They owe a great deal
to conversations at the Cook Christian Training School in Tempe,
Arizona, Fuller Theological Seminary in Pasadena, California, and
San Francisco Theological Seminary in San Anselmo, California.
Most of the individual contacts were with Presbyterian pastors
and laymen, and many of the materials and specific problems
referred to are Presbyterian. Our purpose is to focus on the
present crises in the ministry and in theological education in
the U.S., utilizing these limited experiences and perspectives,

and to suggest possible changes and modifications that could bring renewal to the churches.

I.   CRISES IN THE MINISTRY AND IN THEOLOGICAL EDUCATION

Several serious crises demand immediate attention by the churches in the U.S., especially the historic denominations. We shall consider just four areas of the ministry and theological education at this point: minority leadership, the small congregations, the oversupply of professional pastors, and the struggle of the seminaries to survive.

A. *The Minority Churches*

After extensive research the Cook Christian Training School published the following data about the crisis in leadership among the Indian congregations of the major Protestant denominations throughout the U.S.

There were 68 Indian pastors for the 499 Native American churches surveyed.

The average age of these pastors was 52; about half of them will retire in this decade.

Only four Indian theological students were found among 28,000 students in the 202 Protestant seminaries surveyed.

Behind these statistics lie several fundamental problems. Cecil Corbett, the Executive Director of Cook School, states, "In most Indian communities the mantle of leadership is accorded by the community or parish, not an institution." He goes on to indicate, "Most non-Western cultures revere age as they select leaders more than does the majority culture." ("Reaching Out... Into Communities," *Indian Highways*, Tempe: Cook Christian Training School, No. 154, May 1975.)

The Western academic-professional model of the ministry and ministerial training is simply not meeting the needs of the Indian peoples in the U.S. Young Indian college graduates are not going to seminary, and they are not appropriate candidates for the ministry anyway. More mature leaders would not want to leave their communities for three years of seminary training; many of them would have to finish high school and college first; the cost would be prohibitive. So most of the Indian churches do not have pastors. The situation is so critical that radical change must take place immediately if these congregations are to survive at all.

The Association of Theological Schools in the U.S. and Canada has made similar surveys among the Hispanic churches, and they have discovered similar problems. The historic denominations have not grown at all like the independent and Pentecostal churches within the large Spanish-American population, and relatively few Spanish-Americans are going to the seminaries.

The reasons are quite clear. As in Latin America, the Hispanic-American people choose their leaders not primarily on the basis of academic credentials but for their personal gifts and experience and leadership qualities. The non-historic groups encourage leadership to form within congregational life and programs; those who become pastors often do not have a complete college education and would not be able to give up their jobs to go to seminary for three years; and most of the Hispanic congregations do not provide a salary comparable to that level of professionalization. If the historic denominations are to serve the Hispanic-American populations in the U.S., they will have to adapt their patterns of training and ministry to fit the needs, cultural style, and economic realities of these people.

Anyone who visits New York's Harlem, Chicago's West Side, or Los Angeles' Watts can observe the ubiquitous presence of Black protestant churches, their spontaneous and distinctive styles of worship, and the presence of capable indigenous leaders. Few of these congregations belong to the historic denominations, however, and very few of their pastors are seminary graduates.

Here again we find that traditional models of the ministry and of theological education have been ineffective. Black leadership, as well as Indian and Hispanic leadership, is selected and formed through a process of socialization and congregational experience, not by spending years in educational institutions. The major seminaries have tried to recruit Black students, and Black seminaries have tried to prepare candidates for ministry in the Black communities, but the basic needs of these communities will probably not be met by traditional seminaries at all. The Anglo style of professional ministry, which is instilled at both White and Black seminaries, will probably not be widely accepted or effective among Black people.

At least three important minority sectors of the U.S. population are not being served effectively by the historic denominations. One of the primary obstacles seems to be the traditional model of the professional ministry. And one of the basic keys to change is the process of leadership selection and formation.

B. *The Small Congregations*

Let's turn now to the majority population of main-line protestantism in the U.S. Here we find an even more urgent and

far-reaching crisis. There are now thousands of small congregations that may not long survive the rising cost of the professional ministry.

About two years ago a church executive from New York City told
a Presbytery that only congregations of 300 members or more would
be able to support a pastor and program in the near future. At
the present time more than half of the 8686 United Presbyterian
congregations have less than 200 members; two-thirds of all
United Presbyterian congregations have less than 300 members.
The other Protestant denominations probably show similar statistics.

What is going to happen to the 5791 United Presbyterian congregations that have less than 300 members or the 4343 congregation-
that have less than 200 members? Will they continue to serve the
many rural communities spread across the country? Will there
continue to be Presbyterian congregations in Alaska, in Appalachia,
and in the inner city? How can the churches maintain all their
small congregations and start new ones, even in the major towns
and suburbs, if they are unable to support fulltime professional
pastors?

Evidently something has gone wrong with the basic pattern of
ministry and theological training. The seminaries are doing
their best to train competent pastors and theologians. Seminary
graduates expect a job and a salary commensurate with their
training. The small congregations cannot easily offer either
the challenge or the salary necessary to get and hold these
professionals.

C. *The Oversupply of Professional Ministers, Especially Women*

Ironical as it may seem, just as the historic denominations
are facing large inadequacies in their ministry to the majority
and small congregations, they are building up a critical oversupply of seminary graduates who are seeking calls to churches.
The United Presbyterian Church, for example, reported a total of
13,842 ordained ministers in 1975, and the total number of
churches was 8,686. During the last five years this denomination
has been losing 50,000 to 100,000 members per year, and the
number of congregations has decreased a net of 347. Multiple
staffs are being reduced. Even the more successful pastors are
finding it difficult to move from one church to another.

Nevertheless the seminaries continue to produce hundreds of
graduates for each major denomination each year. One seminary
reported that 40% of this year's graduates had been located in
church vocations. What about the 60%? Another seminary was
able to find church-related jobs for just four of its 30 graduates

by commencement time. What about the rest? It almost seems as
if the most "successful" seminaries, such as Fuller, which had
1,394 students in 1975-76, are going to have the greatest
difficulty in justifying what they are doing.

Within this general picture we find a particularly serious
problem in the placement of women in the ministry. The United
Presbyterian Church, for example, has gone out of its way to
break down sexist practices in its liturgy and constitution,
and it has encouraged women to seek church vocations. Now
increasing numbers of women are attending the seminaries; in
one Presbyterian seminary almost 50% of the students are women.
But women seminary graduates are not being called to pastor the
congregations. And the general oversupply of professional
pastors makes it increasingly unlikely that these women will be
called.

D. *The Seminaries*

In the late sixties the Council on Theological Education of
the United Presbyterian Church commissioned an education consul-
tants agency to do an exhaustive study of all seven of their
seminaries to show whether they were equipped to serve through
the seventies. The Trout Report, which was presented to the
annual meeting of the Council in the Fall of 1970, gave a very
bleak picture. In their judgment the United Presbyterian
seminaries were not equipped to survive the present decade; all
of them were already on the verge of bankrupcy in the face of
fast-rising costs; and they were seriously out of touch with the
needs and concerns of the churches. The report noted particularly that the United Presbyterian Church did not need and could
ill afford to have seven seminaries all competing to do the same
basic tasks of professional training and advanced theological
research.

Six years have passed; these seminaries have in general
terms struggled to maintain their traditional programs; and for
several of them the future is still tenuous. Other denominations are facing similar crises. Many historic seminaries are
on the verge of collapse; some have already closed; a number
have survived by joining cluster complexes, which hides the
huge cutbacks in faculty, physical assets, and students.

At this critical moment in the life of the seminaries and
in the light of the impending oversupply of professional
ministers, the question of alternatives in theological education
becomes not only urgent but obvious, at least to the outside
observer. The churches can not afford more professionals trained
in the traditional pattern; they do need urgently to provide
training for local leaders, especially among the smaller congregations and among the minority groups.

II. FUNDAMENTAL ISSUES

The crises we have mentioned indicate that radical changes are needed and they suggest the direction which these changes should take. But they also bring out several fundamental issues that must provide the bases for genuine reform. There is no one cause for the crises in theological education and the ministry in the U.S. today; there is no simple solution. Rather, the whole matrix of candidate selection, seminary training, ordination, and employment in church vocations must be questioned. In this paper we can only enumerate hurridly some of these fundamental issues.

A. *Biblical and Theological Bases*

The Protestant tradition recognizes as one of its cornerstones Luther's doctrine of the universal priesthood of all believers. The Reformed Churches frequently refer to Calvin's concept of the radical vocation of every Christian. Many churches indicate at the top of their weekly bulletins that all the members of the congregation are ministers. Arnold Come, the President of San Francisco Theological Seminary, wrote sixteen years ago a book whose "central thesis is that the very distinction and even the terminology of 'clergy' and 'laity' should be completely eliminated from the thought and language of the contemporary church." (*Agents of Reconciliation*, Philadelphia: Westminster Press, 1960, p. 10.) Yet the historic denominations in the U.S. still seem to be incapable of breaking free from their pervasive dependence upon the clergy. The problem is not theoretical or theological in origin but practical and cultural. The old dichotomy between clergy and laity has made itself very much at home in contemporary, professionally-oriented U.S. culture.

The New Testament teaches that the ministry belongs to all the members of each congregation, that the diverse gifts of ministries should be shared among the members, and that the leaders in the congregations are called to equip others for ministry. (Ephesians 4:11-16.) As new churches were formed, the elders (mature, local leaders) were given full responsibility for guiding the congregations in all the ministries. The U.S. churches, on the contrary, ultimately place all the ministries in the hands of the ordained pastors, and the current system in effect limits selection, training, and ordination to young college graduates (unproven as leaders), who require a professional salary. Whatever may be said in theory about the ministry of the members is denied in practice, because each congregation must have at least one professional pastor; he is the only one who is really trained, fully ordained, and set apart with a salary to give his time to the work of the ministry; and he is himself an

outsider, hired or appointed for a certain period of time to
serve in that congregation.

The plight of the small congregations is symptomatic of a
basic fallacy in the entire system. If a congregation cannot
afford a professional pastor, it is expected to join with other
congregations or close. If the professional pastors were with-
drawn from the larger churches, they couldn't function either.
We might ask, in fact, whether the small congregations are not
perhaps the best suited for the formation of a genuine fellowship that could minister effectively to itself and to its
community. And we must also ask whether the dependence upon
professionals is not really a deterrant to responsible ministry
among the members in all the churches, both small and large. In
any case we must affirm unequivocally that the ability to hire a
professional pastor should never become, as it now is, essential
for the life of the congregations.

The basic issue here is not the legitimacy of paid professionals as such, but the dominance of and dependence upon paid
professionals. It has to do with the relationship between the
professionals and the members of the congregations, and this has
to do with the selection of candidates, the structure of
theological education, and ordination.

B. *Sociological and Psychological Factors*

The minority churches can teach us a fundamental lesson at
this point. They choose their pastors on the basis of maturity,
experience, dedication, and proven gifts. The same is true of
the fast-growing Pentecostal churches in Latin America. The
multitudinous independent churches of Africa, and indigenous
churches throughout the Third World. In most cases schooling,
both general and theological, is considered to be a valuable
asset, but it does not qualify a person to be a leader.

By contrast the White, Anglo-Saxon, Protestant churches in
the U.S. ignore the dynamics of leadership formation and choose
their pastors on the basis of academic credentials and a highly
subjective sense of call. Candidates for the pastoral ministry
are never chosen by their peers or by their congregations; they
never work their way up through the ranks of the deacons and
elders before going to seminary; they have no opportunity to
prove to the church or to themselves their gifts and ability to
lead. The assumption is that the ministry is a profession, that
candidates must make their vocational choice early in life in
order to get the proper schooling, and that success in the
ministry is a matter of professional competence.

The thesis of this writer is that the ministry is radically
different from the professions and that the Anglo churches should

learn from the minority and Third World churches how to select
leaders. Candidates for the pastoral ministry should normally
have experience in forming a family, earning a living, and
serving as "lay" leaders in the congregations before they are
even considered for the pastorate. They should be selected in
the context of congregational life and society. They should
demonstrate their gifts and ability to lead before they are set
apart for special ministries.

This process of leadership formation and selection is important not only for the leaders' understanding of their role but
also for the other members' understanding of their responsibility
for the ministry. It is essential for the dynamics of corporate
ministry. If the congregations begin to experience the emergence
of leaders (especially pastors) in their midst, they will realize
that the ministry is really their responsibility, whether they
hire professionals to help them carry out that ministry or not.
If the leaders are formed and selected by the congregation, they
are far more likely to have the gifts and abilities to lead and
also the confidence and genuine support of the members. The
vitality of any congregation is directly proportional to the
meaningful participation of its members in ministry--not the
competence of its professional pastors. And the vitality of
each member's faith is directly proportional to his or her
participation in ministry.

C. *Education*

This leads us to the question of training. We said earlier
that the seminaries no longer need to train so many young
college graduates for the professional ministry; there is an
oversupply. Now we are saying that there is a need to provide
training for mature leaders in the congregations--in the White
as well as the minority churches. If it is possible to provide
ministerial training for local leaders, we may find a genuine
solution for the small congregations that cannot afford a full
time professional. Moreover, as we have just intimated, the
seminaries could play a very significant role in the renewal of
the ministry in all the churches by providing training for
local leaders.

The educational world provides ample proof that education in
context is feasible. The colleges and universities in the U.S.
today offer all kinds of training--formal and non-formal,
professional and non-professional, under-graduate and graduate--
for people who cannot go off to school. They provide various
models and abundant resources for field-based or home-based
study programs that can provide credit all the way to a Ph.D.

The seminaries themselves are beginning to experiment with
alternative educational models, especially for the continuing

education of pastors. Eighty per cent of the students at San
Francisco Theological Seminary are now enrolled in their S.T.D.
and D.Min. programs, which utilize various forms of extension
education plus intensive short periods at the institution. Many
seminaries offer internship options as an integral part of their
M.Div. programs, and this is another form of field-based education. Fuller Theological Seminary offers beginning ministerial
students and laymen up to one year of basic theological training
through a network of extension centers scattered through the
Western States. The tools and models for providing the entire
spectrum of theological education for local congregational
leaders already exist.

And yet the question of quality will inevitably arise.
Middle class American congregations will never accept second-
rate training or mediocre leaders. Is it really possible to
provide competent theological education in context for the
American churches?

An educational analysis of the essential elements of ministerial training suggests that extension or contextual education
can perhaps be superior to traditional institutional training.
One factor is student selection, and the extension approach
broadens the scope of potential students to include the best
reservoir of capable people who attend our churches, including
rather than excluding those who have already excelled in other
professions. Another major factor is the maturity, seriousness,
and motivation of the students, and it is evident that local
congregational leaders are different from typical college
graduates. A third essential element is the relationship
between theory and practice, and extension offers the possibility
of direct integration of theology and ministry, because the
students are immersed in the daily problems of church and
society, not preparing for an unknown future ministry. Another
essential element is the teacher, and it is evident that practic-
ing ministers rather than research or classroom theologians are
the ideal mentors. It is perhaps questionable whether local
congregational leaders with jobs and families will be able to
set aside the time and maintain the discipline necessary for
serious theological studies; existing seminary extension programs
and rigorous Bible study programs such as the Bethel series
indicate that they can and will.

If basic theological education in the U.S. were carried out
by extension methods, it would of course change considerably.
It would be training in ministry rather than training for ministry. It could be spread over five or ten years rather than
three. If would probably be linked to the permanent, continuing
education programs that are now taking shape. It could be
adapted for different cultural contexts and academic levels--for

minority pastors, for potential rural and inner city pastors, for leaders of large and small urban and suburban churches, for people whose educational background runs all the way from high school to professional degrees in other fields. It would facilitate the formation of plural, diverse, or specialized ministries as well as all-around pastors. And it would help to break down the wall that separates the clergy from the non-clergy.

D. *Polity and Economics*

We are now involved in a whole series of inter-related issues and must focus briefly on two important aspects, organization or polity and economics. The changes in the ministry and in theological education that we have proposed have economic implications, and they require certain changes in the organizational structure of the churches.

At a recent meeting of the Navajo Episcopal Council Bishop Otis Charles made a simple but striking proposal that could transform the organization of that diocese and dynamize the ministry of those congregations. He enumerated the ministries in the church, then stated forthrightly that none of these positions, not even the priest or bishop, has to be fulltime or paid, but went on to leave open the possibility of paying certain people for special tasks such as administration, training the members for ministry, etc. He said that even if the church had no money at all it could still live and grow.

Several years ago the General Assembly of the United Presbyterian Church in the U.S.A. formed a special Committee to Study the Theology of the Call. This committee came up with some promising theological insights and practical recommendations. It stated that there is one basic call to ministry, which pertains to all communicant members. It recommended that the clergy no longer be referred to exclusively as ministers, and it proposed constitutional changes that would allow ordinary members to administrate the sacraments if authorized by the local session and presbytery. After several preliminary hearings those recommendations were dropped.

At the present time the entire matrix of ecclesiastical structures, seminaries, and ordination seems to be organized in such a way as to produce, support, and protect the professional pastors. And now the oversupply of professionals is beginning to tighten up the clergyman's union in order to limit the number of new candidates. If the churches are to develop a more dynamic, indigenous ministry, they will have to break out of the present structures. The various ministries must be ordered in some way, but no ministry should necessarily require a salary. Training for ministry is essential, but it should not be

limited to the professional pastors. The doors to training,
ordination, and ministry should always be kept open.

E. *Mission*

The whole purpose of the church--its ministry, its organization, and its resources--is to carry out God's mission in the
world. And the purpose of this paper has been to explore ways
in which the churches in the U.S. could activate their tremendous potential for service and witness.

The churches need well-trained leaders who can equip the
members for ministry. This requires adequate theological education, and it requires leaders who can lead the congregations.
The seminaries can help provide the tools for training, but the
congregations must develop and select the leaders.

The churches are called to serve people of every socio-
economic level, every sub-culture, every minority group, every
place. If there is any bias in the Bible, it is in favor of
the poor and the oppressed. In order to identify themselves
with these diverse peoples the churches must design patterns of
ministerial training that will stimulate the emergence of
indigenous leaders. They must adapt their requirements and
structures to respond to these diverse realities.

The historic churches in the U.S. need to learn once more
how to grow, within and without, in maturity and in outreach.
The basic human needs are the same as ever, but they are also as
complex as contemporary life. The current crises of U.S.
culture and the complicity of U.S. Christians in the tragedies
of today's world demand serious theological reflection and
missionary involvement by a broad spectrum of the churches'
leadership.

III. AREAS FOR EXPLORATION AND INNOVATION

Having surveyed four areas of crisis in the ministry and in
theological education and having enumerated some of the underlying issues, we are ready to consider specific areas for
exploration and innovation. First we shall refer again to the
minority churches and the smaller congregations. Then we shall
suggest possibilities for the middle-sized and larger churches.
Finally we shall touch upon three specific sectors of church
leadership potential: women, youth, and older people.

A. *The Minority Churches*

The Cook Christian Training School has already initiated
radical changes in response to the leadership crisis among the

Indian churches and is setting an example for others to follow.
It is now developing extension programs to train congregational
leaders in their local contexts in several different parts of
the country. Instead of spending all its time and resources
teaching a handful of inexperienced young people at the Tempe,
Arizona campus, the staff invests much of its time and resources
in the preparation of instructional materials, the orientation
and training of adjunct faculty, and the design of new programs
that will permit many mature leaders who are serving their congregations as "laymen" to become responsible for all the
ministries in those congregations.

Fuller Theological Seminary is experimenting with a theological studies program for Black pastors. Those who are not
college graduates enter as special students for the first twelve
courses, until they have demonstrated their ability to do
seminary level work, then they are admitted into the M.A. degree
program, which requires an additional twelve courses. Students
must be at least 35 years old and have a minimum of five years'
experience as pastors. They are expected to spend 21-26 hours
per week for three or four years to complete the program. They
may choose any of the 200 courses offered at the seminary, or
they may concentrate on Black studies.

New York Theological Seminary has a similar, though much more
extensive program for Hispanic and Black pastors in its
metropolitan area. In New York there are several thousand
indigenous pastors, mostly Hispanic or Black, who generally
support themselves in secular employment, who have relatively
little education, and who are far beyond the reach of the traditional seminaries. They want to obtain educational legitimization, theological understanding, professional competence, and
secular skills. With the help of Adelphi and Empire State
College the Seminary has developed accredited college degree
programs which enable them to reach these goals, give them up
to 60 hours of credit for life experience, language, and trans-
fers, and allow them to continue their employment and congregational responsibilities.

These examples may seem to indicate that alternative approaches
to theological education are already meeting the leadership needs
of the principal minority groups in the U.S. Certainly the
potential is there. But the task has only begun; only minimal,
marginal resources have so far been invested in these programs;
only small numbers of minority leaders are being reached. And
there is a danger that the theological education establishment
will continue to restrict or withhold accreditation and full
acceptance of alternative forms as it absorbs the bulk of the
resources available in maintaining traditional programs.

B. *The Small Congregations*

It seems evident that the developing leadership crisis among
the smaller congregations could be met by following the example
of the minority churches. Local leaders should be encouraged
to take increasing responsibility for their own ministry,
preferably in a collegiate, sharing fashion, not just one per
congregation. Training programs could be designed especially
for them by the seminaries or by regional ecclesiastical bodies,
utilizing the materials and models that the seminaries have
already developed for continuing education of pastors. Extension
networks such as Fuller is now forming could reach out to any
and all parts of the country.

The students in each area would meet regularly, perhaps once
a week, for class seminars and peer group sessions. They would
carry on systematic study at home: readings, papers, projects,
etc. And they would be involved continuously in the practice
of ministry in their local congregations. Intensive seminars
could be held for weekend and vacation periods locally,
regionally, and at the seminaries to provide special educational
experiences. Pastors with advanced training and special
orientation could serve as local faculty; seminary professors
could participate in the other activities and help in the
preparation of course syllabi and study materials. Other educational institutions and people from other professions could
provide additional resources.

In time this open door to theological training and the
ministry should generate tremendous growth in the leaders themselves and in their congregations. It should provide an on-
going challenge for renewal and service, especially in those
remote and difficult areas where professional pastors do not
like to serve and are too expensive to support.

C. *The Middle-Sized and Large Churches*

The problem of the larger congregations is not so obvious,
but is just as serious and may be more difficult to handle
because the members can continue confidently to depend on professional pastors to do the work of the ministry. What first
strikes the visitor from the Third World is the fact that U.S.
congregations meet just once a week and the members need to wear
name-tags in order to be able to greet each other. The Sunday
morning worship services are certainly impressive, but participation in ministry is not encouraged by being a spectator at
those services.

On the other hand creative things can and do happen in some
of these churches, and dynamic, corporate ministry can be

encouraged. The First Presbyterian Church of Fresno, California, for example, has a whole series of programs involving scores of people in active, responsible ministry. The pastors and leading "laymen" have been developing their concept of a "caring, sharing, training" church for years. One group is responsible for the evangelism program; the participants are now in training and will in turn train others. Each semester a new group goes through a period of training in Christian education and takes over the Sunday school program for the following semester, using their own, not prepared, materials. During the summer some forty people are involved in training a group of about fifteen young people from Fresno and from other parts of the country in an intensive, multifaceted leadership formation program that is tremendously meaningful for all who are directly involved and for the whole congregation. Additional groups of young people are sent out on summer training "cruises" that take them to different parts of the world. The senior pastor of this church is himself a former seminary professor and an ardent supporter of theological education by extension. The former pastor now heads Fuller's extension program, which set up its first extension center in Fresno.

A growing, dynamic church such as this provides a much more effective setting for training leaders of growing, dynamic churches than any seminary. The seminaries can offer certain resources which these churches cannot offer. To develop their full potential the churches and the seminaries should explore the many possibilities for working together to build up the ministry of the whole people of God.

Many more pastors could become adjunct professors of the seminaries, especially those who are effective participants in dynamic ministry in their own churches and those who are involved in or have completed the D.Min. and S.T.D. programs. The larger churches should give high priority to this aspect of ministry as they call their pastors. Multiple staffs could include theological educators. Dynamic churches could help form leaders in the small congregations and in other larger churches, and they could be challenged to initiate new congregations.

D. *Women*

The present system of church vocations offers very poor prospects for women who want to study theology and serve in the ministry, because, as we noted earlier, most churches prefer to hire men as their pastors. In contrast the perspectives presented in this paper open up new possibilities for training, service, and ordination for women on a par with men.

E. *Young People*

Although this paper seems to favor the selection of mature
leaders to guide the churches, special attention could and should
be directed toward young men and women. As in the case of women,
the alternative approach to ministry and theological education
proposed in this paper could open up much wider possibilities
for young people.

Under the present system very few young men and women can or
should be encouraged to go to seminary or consider a church
vocation because of the oversupply of professional ministers.
Those who take that route must renounce other possible vocations,
and those who choose other vocations *de facto* reject serious
involvement in the churches. Under a new system great numbers
of young people could be encouraged to become involved in intensive leadership training programs, dedicate a summer or a year
to some special ministry, and take theological studies by extension, even as they prepare for some other vocation. These
experiences would serve to discover early those who have special
gifts for leadership in the church and also to deepen the sense
of calling for all who participate, whatever their profession.
Young people who choose to go directly into church vocations
should take at least their first year of theological studies by
extension and serve as apprentices in congregations in order to
test their calling and gifts.

F. *Second Career and Retirement Service*

Special attention should also be given to the potential for
leadership among older people in the churches who may be called
to fulltime service at mid-career or after an early retirement
from other professions. Here again we find a great untapped
leadership pool that could be activated through locally based
training programs such as we have proposed in this paper. The
total number of highly capable, trained leaders could be multiplied several times over simply by reaching into this sector of
the churches' population. These men and women could play a
strategic role not only in their own churches, but also in
nearby smaller congregations and especially among the many
millions of older people throughout the country who need a
special ministry. Serious involvement in theological studies
and ministry could make these older leaders a vital force in the
renewal of the churches' ministry, and it would revitalize their
own lives.

IV. THE FUTURE SHAPE OF THEOLOGICAL EDUCATION AND MINISTRY

As a final step in this dialogue on alternatives in theological education and ministry, we shall take a tentative look at

the future shape of theological education in the U.S. These
projections are not just wishful thinking, for some significant
progress has already been made. On the other hand there may be
strong resistance to change. The very fact that the seminaries
and the professional clergy are in crisis may cause them to
welcome new alternatives, or it may cause them to hold even more
tightly to the old ways. Certainly it would be easier to maintain the status quo.

A. *The Seminaries*

Instead of being primarily classroom institutions the seminaries should become resource centers for studies in theological
education and ministry. Rather than centralize and monopolize
theological education they should encourage and enable others to
carry out many of the actual tasks of ministerial training by
designing educational models, preparing instructional media and
materials, and training personnel for a wide spectrum of programs
to meet the churches' leadership needs. Seminary staffs would
have to be theological educators and not just theologians as in
the past; they would have to learn a great deal about educational
technology. They would also have to become more closely related
to the life and mission of the church in today's world.

No doubt some will say that the seminaries already have
difficulty running their present programs and cannot be expected
to take on all these additional tasks and programs. Perhaps
some seminaries should get out of the business of residential
training; if they were free from the bondage of class schedules
and housekeeping, their ability to serve the churches might
increase many times over. The Association of Theological Schools
of the U.S. and Canada reports that member institutions now spend
an average of $25,000 to train one student; that investment
could easily train ten students using extension methods. On the
other hand some seminaries have discovered that most extension
students can bear the full cost of their training, in contrast
to young residential seminary students, who normally pay less
than 30% of institutional costs. If the new extension programs
were completely self-financing, they could expand indefinitely.

The fulfillment of the goals presented here does not require
any enlargement of our seminaries; all these programs could be
carried out through a redeployment of their present resources
and through the incorporation of other elements that are readily
available. We have already suggested that the most effective
teachers for basic ministerial training will probably be found
among the pastors, and one of the foremost tasks of the pastors
should be the training of others for ministry. Hundreds of
pastors are now engaged in advanced theological studies by extension; some of them should specialize in theological education;

all of them should be expected to participate in the training of
others as part of their own advanced preparation. With these
additional resources the seminaries could readily offer the complete spectrum of theological education by extension.

B. *Local and Regional Foci for Theological Studies*

The shape of theological education at the local and regional
levels will probably vary greatly according to the context and
the resources available. Every major urban center has an
abundance of resources; rural districts will have to pool their
resources over a large area or draw from the urban centers. The
churches in each place should begin to assess their needs, survey their resources, and build local and/or regional theological
education teams--denominationally, ecumenically, or both. From
this local and regional base they will be able to call upon the
seminaries for help in curriculum design, the training and
orientation of personnel, occasional direct participation in
intensive seminars and extension courses, evaluation, and
accreditation.

Communication and coordination between these local and
regional foci for theological studies and the seminaries may
require some sort of clearing house, association, or consortium,
which again could be handled denominationally or ecumenically or
both. At the very least each denomination will want to facilitate interchangeability of credits and experiences among its own
seminaries and set certain guidelines and standards for their
specific ministerial offices. In any case it is high time that
the seminaries gave up their isolation, individualism, and
competitive stance in order to respond to the churches' needs
more effectively.

C. *Centers for Advanced Theological Learning*

As many of the seminaries turn toward close cooperation with
the churches in training local leaders and building a more
dynamic ministry, some seminaries could dedicate their attention
to advanced research in the theological disciplines. Each
denomination would need few of such centers, and they could be
related to the overall network of theological education in very
significant ways. In most cases they would be closely linked
to a university and a cluster of theological seminaries.

The main components of these centers for advanced theological
learning would be people, libraries, and avenues of publication.
They would bring together long-term research fellows, theologians
in residence for definite periods, seminary faculty on sabbatical, outstanding pastors and other churchmen with advanced
degrees in their respective fields, and graduate students. They

would be engaged in the formation of primary materials for
theological research, the publication of periodicals and
articles for various constituencies, the preparation of course
materials and texts, dialogue on contemporary world issues, etc.

Whether the same institutions and staffs should be involved
in basic ministerial training and advanced theological research
at the same time is debatable. The important thing is to give
full attention to both fundamental tasks and to keep both of
them in close touch with the church and the world.

D. *Ministry in the Local Church*

It is difficult to say what might happen to the ministry of
the local church if such radical changes as we have contemplated
here should take place. Probably many different things would
happen, because there would be many new options for many more
people to study theology and to participate in every aspect of
the churches' ministry. To open up theological education is to
open up the churches' ministry to the whole membership. This
is bound to increase not only the number of trained leaders but
the quality of leadership. As the members participate in the
formation and selection of their leaders, they will perceive
their own responsibility for ministry. The ministry will become
increasingly an expression of the whole congregation and not
primarily the function of paid professionals.

The shape of the ministry in the local church should become
much more varied and flexible. There could well be as many
paid, fulltime staff as we now have; in fact there may be an
increase; but the assignments given to professional church
workers and their relationships within the congregations would
be fundamentally changed; and some congregations could choose
to carry out their ministry without any paid staff. A church
which now is required to have a professional pastor and a certain number of unpaid elders could decide to have half a dozen
ordained pastors and a score of elders, with perhaps two
pastors on parttime salary and an elder as fulltime administra-
tor. A large church could experiment in the formation of small
sub-congregations, each with its own ordained, voluntary
ministry but sharing the resources of a professional counselor
and a theological educator.

The most exciting aspect of this new perspective of theological education and ministry is its potential for on-going
renewal and growth. The internal structure of the local congregation would be open to constant renewal as new people entered
theological studies and took their place as responsible leaders.
The outreach of local congregations and the formation of new
congregations would not be limited to outside subsidies,

professional people, or denominational projects; any church or group could initiate a new work; and this would be a challenging experience for all concerned.

> We are to grow up in every way into him
> who is the head, into Christ, from whom
> the whole body, joined and knit together
> by every joint with which it is supplied,
> when each part is working properly, makes
> bodily growth and upbuilds itself in love.
>
>   --- Ephesians 4:15-16

PART
III

Tools for Change
and Development in the
Extension Movement

11

Materials for Workshops on Theological Education by Extension

Over the past ten years workshops on theological education by extension have been held in many different places, and the demand for workshops increases as the extension movement continues to spread. This set of materials has been drawn together from workshop experiences; all of them have been used--in one form or another--many times. They have been prepared in order that others may benefit from these experiences and join in exciting process of reflection and innovation that is sweeping the world of theological education.

In 1973 we prepared a first set of materials called "Self-Study Workshop on Theological Education" with a similar purpose, but at that time we did not focus our attention specifically on the extension philosophy and methodology. The present set of materials is more directly related to extension, but our basic concerns continue to be much broader and deeper than any specific system of theological training. It is our conviction that the extension movement can and should challenge the church at large-- ecclesiastical leaders, theological educators, and the whole people of God--to a new understanding of and participation in ministry and mission. We hope these materials will be useful not only for those who are, or expect to be, involved in theological education by extension but also for others who are attempting to face the complex, vital issues related to ministerial formation and are continuing the search for more effective alternatives in theological education.

The topics for study are:

I.   BASES FOR CHANGE IN THEOLOGICAL EDUCATION
II.   A WORKING DEFINITION OF THEOLOGICAL EDUCATION BY EXTENSION
III.   THE LOGISTICS OF THEOLOGICAL EDUCATION BY EXTENSION
IV.   DEMONSTRATION OF AN EXTENSION CENTER MEETING
V.   SELF-STUDY MATERIALS FOR EXTENSION STUDENTS

The topics may be used as a sequence of exercises for an extension workshop, or they may be used separately in varied circumstances. Each topic is presented with general and specific suggestions and should be adapted to meet local needs and to fit scheduling requirements. The first topic, for example, could be dealt with in two hours or in two days, depending on the interests of the group and the time available and the procedure which they choose to follow.

The leaders of each extension workshop should make clear to all the participants that it is, as the word itself indicates, a work experience. In a workshop we meet together not primarily to listen to and discuss papers as in a consultation, not only to exchange ideas on certain topics as in a seminar, but primarily to carry out work projects. The materials included in this packet are intended to help the participants to:

A.   Ennumerate several basic issues related to ministerial formation and work out their own analysis or philosophy of theological education.

B.   Consider various essential aspects of theological education by extension and formulate a definition which they can use to explain the concept to others and to evaluate their own programs.

C.   Work through a simple procedure to identify the resources and limitations for theological education which they can apply in any situation with a view to setting up new training programs or adapting old ones.

D.   Observe and participate in demonstrations of extension center meetings in order to bring out the nature and functions of these meetings and describe the role of the teacher and the role of the student.

E.   Discuss the essential elements of self-study materials for extension students, evaluate available course materials, and list alternative types and media.

On completion of these experiences the participants should be able to lead others through similar exercises, share with them the insights they have gained, and thus continue the process of reflexion and innovation.

I. BASES FOR CHANGE IN THEOLOGICAL EDUCATION

Perhaps the most significant aspect of the extension movement is that it is bringing to the attention of church leaders and theological educators of all kinds a number of basic issues that may well determine not only the effectiveness of our training programs but also the very nature of the ministry, the vitality of our churches, and the fulfillment of our mission in today's world. It is important for extension educators to reflect upon these issues again and again, and it is our obligation to set them clearly before our colleagues and the church at large.

This exercise is planned to put forth some of these basic issues for discussion. It is intended to stimulate debate, whether the group includes extension educators, traditional theological educators, or both. Our purpose is not to elienate those who are outside the extension movement, nor to impose our criteria, but to insist that these issues be faced squarely and realistically. Of equal importance, we must insist that extension theological educators work through these issues and not simply carry on their programs with triumphalistic optimism. The extension movement not only raises basic issues; it challenges us to make radical changes; it can be an invaluable vehicle for change.

This study can be used by faculties, at workshops and consultations, and in many different settings. It may be best to circulate the study paper well in advance so that the participants can read it, mark the points they wish to clarify or discuss, and prepare their response. Or someone could give a general presentation of the paper with the help of visual aids and local illustrations. A third possibility is for one or more people to present the study section by section, leaving time for group discussion after each point. Whichever the method of introducing the material, the most important aspects of this exercise are the group discussion and the individual conclusions. If there are more than 15 participants, they should probably divide into smaller groups and then report back to the plenary session. In conclusion each participant should be encouraged to write down his own analysis, summary, and remaining questions. The entire process may well take several hours.

A brief outline of discussion questions is provided in the following pages. The content paper, which is not copyrighted and may be reproduced and circulated to the participants, is presented under the same title in Chapter 1 of this book.

BASES FOR CHANGE IN THEOLOGICAL EDUCATION

DISCUSSION QUESTIONS

INTRODUCTION

1. What are the most important reasons for change in theological education?

2. What are the major weaknesses of traditional ministerial training programs?

I. THEOLOGICAL BASES FOR CHANGE: *What is the Ministry?*

A. Is there a false dichotomy between clergy and laymen in our churches? How do different types of theological education affect this dichotomy?

B. What are the dynamics of ministry, as presented in Ephesians 4:11-16? How should theological education relate to this pattern and process?

C. How did Paul find and prepare leadership for the churches he founded? How can leaders be found and prepared for all the churches around the world today?

II. HISTORICAL BASES FOR CHANGE: *Can the People Participate Fully in Theological Study and Ministry?*

A. How did Wesley develop leadership for his growing movement? Can we do something similar today?

B. Compare the Presbyterian-Anglican-Congregational pattern of ministry with the Baptists and Methodists in the expansion of the U.S. frontier. What lesson does this case study provide?

C. How are pastors prepared and selected in the large Pentecostal movement in Latin America today? How could we follow their example?

III. SOCIOLOGICAL BASES FOR CHANGE: *Who Are the Leaders?*

A. What are the essential qualifications for leadership in our cultural settings? Are these qualifications taken into account by our theological institutions?

B. How are leaders formed? Do our institutions encourage or by-pass the normal processes of leadership formation in the church and society?

C. How are leaders selected, invested with authority, and supported? What effect do our training systems have upon the selection of genuine leaders for ministry in the churches?

IV. EDUCATIONAL BASES FOR CHANGE: *How Can the Leaders be Trained?*

A. Do our theological institutions follow the elitist trends of educational systems in general? How can we avoid this tendency?

B. Are we applying the new educational technologies? Can extension methods be as effective as traditional methods?

C. What is the essence of real learning? How do residence and extension systems foster real learning?

V. ECONOMIC BASES FOR CHANGE: *What Kind of Theological Education Can We Afford?*

A. What is the total cost of preparing one pastor in our theological institutions?

B. How much does it cost a congregation to support a professional pastor? Compare the different levels of training and professional support.

C. What is the relative cost of training pastors in residence and by extension? How can we best invest our limited resources for theological education?

VI. MISSIOLOGICAL BASES FOR CHANGE: *What Are the Goals of Our Theological Training Programs?*

A. What is the role of the pastor in leading the local church in mission? How can every congregation have at least one adequately trained pastor?

B. Consider the tremendous, complex, urgent needs of our world. Who can (and must) lead the churches in meeting these challenges? How can they be trained?

C. How can we build up the whole body of Christ in a dynamic process of ministry? What kinds of theological education will facilitate this process most effectively?

II. A WORKING DEFINITION OF THEOLOGICAL
EDUCATION BY EXTENSION

An important task for extension workshops and for other
groups interested in extension is to prepare a definition of
theological education by extension. The purpose of this exercise is first of all simply to help the participants to clarify
their own concept of extension and to formulate a definition
which they can use to explain the concept to others. But our
purpose goes much deeper than any simple definition. We want to
reflect on what the extension movement is trying to achieve, to
focus on some basic issues of theological education from the perspective of the extension movement, to stimulate extension
leaders to deepen their concerns and comprehension of their task,
to encourage others to take a more serious look at theological
education by extension, and to provide criteria for evaluating
extension programs.

The effectiveness of this exercise depends on the way it is
presented and the active participation of the group. The study
paper is found in Chapter 3 of this book and may be reproduced
without permission. At the end of the article there are some
general suggestions on procedures for group study. Following
this explanation there is an outline of the contents with discussion questions for each section. It may be helpful to use the
whole paper or just certain sections. Maximum use should be made
of extension programs represented by the participants or found in
the immediate region in order to bring the whole matter close to
home and to minimize the impression that this is an imported concept. If the majority of the participants are already involved
in extension and/or convinced of its value, this material can be
used primarily as an evaluation of existing programs, i.e. to
discover how effectively they are fulfilling their purposes, responding to the multiple dimensions of the extension process,
integrating the essential elements of their programs, etc. The
mutual exchange of ideas, criticism, encouragement, and searching
questions will probably be the most vital element in the entire
exercise.

Here are some specific suggestions for a sample procedure;
each group or leader will have to decide how best to plan the
experience. As a first step have the entire group meet together
for fifteen minutes and throw out some of the basic questions to
be considered: What is theological education by extension?
What is the purpose of theological education by extension? In
what ways should we extend theological education (not just
geographically)? What are the essential elements in any extension program? How does extension differ from residential training, correspondence courses, brief institutes, night Bible
schools? This will start the process of reflexion, bring out

what ideas the participants already have, and establish a basis
for investigation. Only three to five minutes should be allowed
for answers to each question at this stage; the major discussion
can be handled much more effectively in small groups.

Divide up into groups of five or six and allow two or three
hours for discussion of the paper. If the participants have not
yet read it, it will be necessary to read it now--together or
silently. Discuss each section using questions suggested in the
following outline or other questions and issues to be defined by
the group or leader. In these group discussions attention should
be focussed on how the programs represented are responding to the
issues raised. Section V of the article should probably be
omitted or replaced by examples to be presented by each group.
Finally each group should draw up their criticisms, changes, and
amendments of the concepts presented in the article. The
coordinator of this exercise should circulate among the groups
periodically to see that they advance more or less at the same
rate or according to the agreed schedule.

The entire group should meet for a final plenary session.
A panel may be formed of representatives of the groups who will
present their reports and lead the discussion. The participants
may want to prepare a revised or a new definition of theological
education by extension. In order to facilitate this process a
committee (perhaps the panel members) may be assigned. Their
definition may be presented to a later plenary session,
duplicated, and circulated.

A WORKING DEFINITION OF THEOLOGICAL
EDUCATION BY EXTENSION

DISCUSSION QUESTIONS

INTRODUCTION

1. What is theological education by extension?

2. What is the purpose of theological education by extension?

3. In what ways should theological education be extended (not just geographically)?

4. What are the essential elements of any extension program?

5. How does extension differ from residential training, correspondence courses, brief institutes, and night Bible schools?

6. What are our objectives for this study?

I. THE PURPOSE OF THEOLOGICAL EDUCATION BY EXTENSION

A. To whom should we extend our programs of theological education? To how many people?

B. Is extension a valid alternative system of theological education? What are some educational advantages of this approach?

C. What concept of the ministry does traditional theological education project? What concept of the ministry does theological education by extension project?

D. Traditional educational programs reinforce the hierarchical social, economic, and ecclesiastical structures. How can theological education by extension reverse these trends? Is it actually doing so?

E. How can theological education by extension contribute to the renewal of the ministry of the whole church for mission? To what degree is this really happening?

II. VARIOUS DIMENSIONS OF THEOLOGICAL EDUCATION BY EXTENSION

A. Is it possible to extend our extension programs to all the geographical areas where we have churches? What areas have we neglected?

B. Are our extension classes and home study assignments arranged so that most of our leaders can participate? How could they be made more accessible?

C. Is our curriculum being adapted culturally so that the various groups represented among our students can readily assimilate new concepts and skills and apply them in their ministry? In what ways should it be adapted?

D. What academic levels are prevalent in our churches? At what levels should we offer theological training? How can we maintain the functional parity of different academic levels?

E. Are we training leaders among the highest and lowest social and economic classes as well as the middle classes?

F. Do our training programs include elders and deacons and ordinary members as well as pastors, church workers, and candidates for the pastoral ministry? Where should we place our priorities?

G. Are all sectors of the churches' membership represented among our students? Is the whole body of Christ being challenged and trained and mobilized for ministry?

III. THREE ESSENTIAL ELEMENTS IN THEOLOGICAL EDUCATION BY EXTENSION

A. Why are self-study materials so essential to extension programs? Are adequate materials available--stating clear objectives, geared to the students' capabilities, and following carefully planned learning sequences? Are these materials being evaluated and revised constantly? What non-formal educational processes are included in the program? What kinds of printed and non-printed materials can be used other than programmed materials?

B. What should be the role of practical work in the formation of extension students? In what ways can their courses be applied directly and regularly in their ministry? How could the students' experience and needs become the basis for the curriculum itself?

C. How frequently should extension students meet together?
    What are the basic functions of the center meetings?
    What is the relationship between the center meetings,
    the self-study materials, and the students' practical
    work? What should be the role of the student and the
    role of the professor at the center meetings?

IV. EXTENSION AND OTHER TYPES OF THEOLOGICAL EDUCATION

A. What are the basic differences between extension and
    residential programs? What are the advantages of each?
    What are the disadvantages?

B. What are the basic differences between extension and
    correspondence courses? What are the advantages of
    each? What are the disadvantages?

C. What are the basic differences between extension pro-
    grams and brief institutes? What are the advantages of
    each? What are the disadvantages?

D. What are the basic differences between extension pro-
    grams and night Bible schools? What are the advantages
    of each? What are the disadvantages?

V. SOME EXAMPLES OR MODELS OF THEOLOGICAL EDUCATION BY
    EXTENSION

Present and discuss the different extension programs represented in the group. Look for significant differences
which could be analyzed and presented at the plenary
session.

Consider the many possible adaptations of theological education by extension: kinds of organization, combinations with
other types of theological education, use of different
media and means of transportation, etc. The group may
suggest different models for specific purposes and for
specific areas or needs.

III. THE LOGISTICS OF THEOLOGICAL EDUCATION BY EXTENSION

Logistics is "the branch of military science having to do
with moving, supplying, and quartering troops." The course of
many battles has been determined by logistics. And wars have
been lost when supply lines, movement, and care of the troops
broke down, as in the case of both Napoleon and Hitler when they
ventured too far into Russia.

What follows is an exercise in the logistics of theological
education by extension. It is high time that churchmen and
theological educators look around them and make a careful study
of the possibilities for training local leaders for the church's
ministry. We have lost many battles already because of our
shortsightedness and poor planning. And we are learning, along
with educators in other fields, that there are many experiences
and resources for leadership training that a sedentary institution cannot provide. The extension movement is in one sense an
attempt to set up new lines of communication and supply so that
the church's frontline troops can carry out their mission
effectively.

The purpose of this exercise is to develop a simple procedure
which the participants will be able to use to identify the
resources and limitations for theological education in any
situation and also to see the possibilities for setting up new
programs or adapting old ones.

The first step is to make an inventory of possible resources
for theological education. Some illustrations are given to
stimulate thinking in new directions. The person leading may
add other examples and ask for ideas from the group. Then the
participants will spend ten or fifteen minutes working out an
exhaustive list of potential resources in the areas they serve,
individually or in groups of two or three. *The second step* is
to analyze the limitations which should be considered before
setting up any training program. Here again it will be necessary
to give several illustrations in order to explain the importance
and nature of this analysis. Then the participants will be
asked to spend another ten or fifteen minutes preparing a list
of limitations or obstacles in the areas they serve. *The third
step* is to put together the resources and limitations that have
been listed and begin to set down plans for the development of
new or modified training programs. Once again illustrations
should be given in order to provoke creative ideas. Then the
participants, individually or in the same groups, will be asked
to design two or more alternative plans for theological education in their areas, using the resources and taking into account
the limitations which they have identified earlier. This may
take 30 to 45 minutes. *The final step* in this series is to hold

a plenary session and ask the participants to present the results of their investigations, i.e. the resources and development of training programs. The leader of this exercise should circulate among the participants during the work periods in order to offer suggestions and answer questions, and he will be able to find interesting case studies for the final report-back session. Also, he may want to ask some to share their findings at steps one and two so as to stimulate the others.

Following is an additional exercise for groups that want to continue this investigation in greater depth and detail. It will take an additional two or three hours. *The first step* is to select a limited number of projects from the preliminary plans developed in the previous exercise and to reorganize the participants in groups of five or six. These groups may be made up of persons representing different areas and programs so as to facilitate cross-fertilization of ideas and to give the participants experience in analyzing situations different from their own. But the leader of each group should be a representative of the area to be studied. At this first meeting of the groups the leaders should present their preliminary investigations, and the participants should help to formulate clear goals for the training programs being studied. *The second step* is a plenary session in which the leader of the exercise will present for discussion two aspects: the training system as a whole and the essential elements of any training system. Here again some examples are given; the leader should find further illustrations, preferably from the region represented, and the participants may offer additional examples. *The third step* is to go back into the groups and work out a careful plan for theological education that will respond to their goals, make the best use of their resources, take into account the limitations of the area, and integrate the essential elements into a complete training system. *The final step* is a plenary session, during which the groups will present the results of their studies, making use of maps and any other materials and methods they choose. These projects may be discussed and then written up and duplicated for circulation to the participants and to others.

The concepts and materials provided here are based on a more detailed study of the analysis of programs of theological education prepared by James H. Emery for the training of extension specialists under the *Asociación Latinoamericana de Institutos y Seminarios Teológicos de Extensión*. Although our focus here is upon the formation of extension programs, the same basic procedure can be used for the development of other types of theological education. Also, various systems may be combined to reach the desired goals more effectively. Copies of the following material may be circulated among the participants, but this is not absolutely necessary. All the participants will need paper or notebooks, however.

THE LOGISTICS OF THEOLOGICAL EDUCATION BY EXTENSION

PART I: RESOURCES AND LIMITATIONS

In this exercise each participant will make a list of all the
available resources for theological education in a specific
region, identify any limitations which should be taken into
account, and then begin to work out plans for the development
of a new or modified extension training program. At the end
of this process he should be prepared to present his analysis
to the group. And he should be able to lead others through a
similar process...in his own region or in any other situation.

A.   RESOURCES

The first step is to make a list of all the possible resources
for theological education in your own church and region. This
should cover much more than just traditional institutions,
although they are a logical starting point. If your church
has a seminary or Bible institute, list its physical resources
(buildings, course materials, equipment), budget, personnel
(how many teachers, staff, students), etc. But then go on to
other resources that do or could contribute to the formation
of leaders for the church's ministry.

We all tend to think in terms of our own experience and forget that there are many other ways of doing things.   In
Guatemala it just happens that the area where the Presbyterian
church is growing fastest has no formal training program
whatsoever.   In less than ten years fifteen congregations
with more than 1000 members have grown up entirely under
local initiative and leadership. And the leaders themselves,
except for one, have all been formed in that situation.
Evidently there are tremendously effective resources for
real theological education right there, although there is no
institution, no budget, and no personnel specifically
assigned for this task.

Consider the many resources in the ordinary life of the
church. Some of our church members have attended Sunday
school for ten, twenty, or more years; they could have been
trained for all of the church's ministries. The programs of
evangelism, worship, and service in the local church should
be the normal instruments of training in those areas. You
don't learn to evangelize or worship in a classroom, and
probably even preaching is best learned in a non-academic
setting. The gifts of ministry should probably be developed
and recognized through the processes of leadership selection
at the congregational level rather than the subjective and
artificial ways in which the historic churches choose and

train their pastors. In some denominations local pastors are
primarily considered to be teachers, called to train others
for ministry, but in most cases their time is used up doing
other things. The congregations themselves could provide the
primary resources of theological education.

There are many other possible resources for the training of
church leaders both within the church and outside it. Some
churches have youth, women's, and men's organizations, educational institutions, and conference centers. Government and
secular agencies offer adult education, training in group
dynamics and community development, workshops in diverse
skills, libraries, etc. There are increasing numbers of
publications and other mass media programs that can be useful
for theological education. Educators are constantly developing new materials and methods for group and individual study.

As you make out your inventory of resources you may consider
the ideas presented here, but you should go on in your own
thinking. Be as specific and as complete as possible. And
be prepared to share and explain your list to others.

B. LIMITATIONS

Before setting up specific plans for any training program you
should take into account the factors that may prevent its
formation or limit its effectiveness. Some of the obstacles
may be eliminated or circumvented; others may determine the
kind of program you develop.

Some factors are quite obvious, such as the economic question.
It is futile to think of establishing a traditional, high
level seminary unless your church is very large and can
obtain large quantities of funds to build and support it.
Similarly, though less obvious, it is useless to send young
candidates for the pastoral ministry to that kind of institution unless there are churches which can offer salaries
somewhat commensurate with that kind of training.

Other factors can pose enormous problems and yet find solutions. Some churches are spread over vast geographical areas
and need extension training for their leaders. One such
program is maintained through voluntary, local tutors;
another makes use of small airplanes; still another depends
on local and regional staff teamwork. The feasibility study
for any extension program should consider geographical
distances, means of transportation, quantity and quality and
distribution of potential teaching staff.

There are other, more subtle factors. Many traditional institutions have only young, unmarried students for obvious practical reasons, but they may serve indigenous societies in which the young and unmarried are not accepted as leaders. On the other hand some institutions have tried to decentralize in order to reach the natural leaders only to discover that their constituencies reject extension because they think it is not adequate or proper training. Both residence and extension programs, but especially the former, find themselves contributing to the massive migration of people from rural communities to the urban slums, even though their express purpose is to train leaders for the village churches.

In the formation of new extension programs the following limitations may be very important. There may be no self-study materials available and no one trained to prepare them. The personnel and funds available for extension work may be too limited because so much is being invested in residential training. Some potential students may not have the basic skills necessary to begin theological studies; others may find it too difficult to take up disciplined study after many years away from school; and some outstanding church leaders may simply be too busy to participate.

These and other problems or limitations should be listed carefully and analyzed for possible solutions. Then you are ready to go on to the third step in your study of the logistics of theological education by extension.

C. DEVELOPMENT PLAN

Having investigated the possible resources and the limitations of your region, you can now begin to work out some tentative plans for a program of theological education by extension. There may be many different ways of training local leaders in your region, some of them completely new. Each participant should draw up at least two alternative plans which he will submit to the group for discussion and perhaps later to his own church or institution. Probably no plan developed at this moment will be readily applicable, but this exercise can be very stimulating for our own thinking and for others also.

In any given case it may seem as if the resources available are woefully small and the limitations and obstacles very large, but this very situation may force us to take new and creative steps that will be far more effective in the long run. We may avoid the pitfalls that others have fallen into, and we may discover surprising solutions. The new

extension training program in Botswana, Africa, for example,
had resources to support only two teachers, was forced to
depend on volunteer tutors in some centers, and now apparently will be able to expand indefinitely because the students
themselves are offering to teach.

Each participant is asked to draw up at least two alternative
plans for several reasons. In the first place this will
widen his possibilities and open up more avenues of exploration. In the second place it should be useful to compare
the potentials of different kinds of investment. Also, it
will provide more practice in the kind of analysis that
each participant will have to go through with his own
colleagues and perhaps others in the future. To cite one
isolated example, the Presbyterian Church of Guatemala
invests $4000 of its budget each year in theological educa-
tion. This is the basis for the seminary's extension program
which serves approximately 250 students, most of whom are
married. If we were to send one married student to the
Theological Community in Mexico City or to the Evangelical
Seminary of Puerto Rico it would cost more than $4000 per
year. So it is that each church must study carefully its
leadership needs and utilize its resources in the most
effective way possible.

PART II: THE SYSTEM AS A WHOLE

This exercise is based on the previous investigation of
resources and limitations. First a small number of projects
should be selected from the preliminary plans developed in
the previous exercise--either by the leaders of the workshop
or by the participants themselves. It may be useful to
choose cases which represent widely different situations and
perhaps ones which are especially difficult. Then the
participants should divide up into groups of five or six.
These groups may be made up of persons who represent different areas and programs so as to facilitate cross-fertilization of ideas and to give the participants experience in
analyzing situations different from their own. The leader
of each group should be a representative of the area to be
studied.

A.   THE GENERAL GOALS

The first study session will be held in the *project groups*.
Each leader will present to his group his analysis of
resources and limitations and his preliminary alternative
plans for theological education by extension. Discussion
can at this point be limited to clarification of his information and ideas.

Then each group should formulate clear goals for their training program. This will require some discussion of the leadership needs of that church, its concept of the ministry,
the potential students, etc. Is the primary need for more
pastors or for trained leaders of several different kinds?
Should they be trained at one level or at several levels?
What should the pastors and other leaders be trained to do?
What are the major problems in the life of the church? How
can the ministry become a vital function of the whole congregation? What kind of theological education will renew
the church's ministry?

The groups should finalize their discussion of these and/or
other questions by setting down a list of general goals for
their theological training project.

B.   THE SYSTEM AS A WHOLE

The participants will then come together for a *plenary
session*, at which they will consider two main topics. The
First is a study of theological education as an integrated
system. The second topic is an analysis of the basic
elements that make up any system or program of theological
education. When these concepts have been clarified sufficiently, the participants may return to their groups and
work out their projects in detail.

It may be helpful to build your training system around the
students rather than the institution. The important thing
is to integrate the resources and experiences, information
and skills in the students' lives and ministry. An interesting example of this is the Open University of Great
Britain. It makes use of correspondence courses (text
books, manuals, and other materials), daily radio and television programs scheduled to complement the correspondence
materials, extension centers where the students can receive
additional help (tutors, libraries, equipment), and short
summer residence periods for intensive studies in each basic
course. In this way thousands of working people throughout
the country are earning regular university degrees without
leaving their jobs.

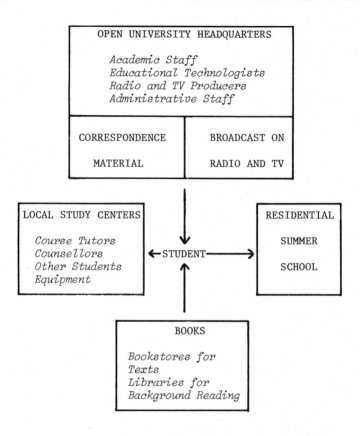

Of particular concern for theological education by extension
programs is the integration of theory and practice. In
designing your program be sure to specify how these two
essential dimensions of the curriculum are related in the
students' learning experience--at the weekly assignment
level, in terms of each course, and in terms of the program
as a whole. Their studies should find some direct application in their own personal lives, in their ministry to the
congregations, and in their communities. Without this kind
of integration learning becomes abstract, superficial, and
irrelevant.

Another matter of basic concern in building a theological
training system is contextualization. This means on the one
hand that the studies must be integrated into the students'
frame of reference, the church's needs, and the patterns of
the culture. On the other hand contextualization means that

the Gospel itself, when it is integrated into the local
situation, will work redemptively, making all things new--
in the life of the students, in their churches, and even in
their communities. The danger is that our training systems
may impose mental and cultural patterns that belong neither
to the Gospel nor to the local people, thus inhibiting the
growth of the church. Contextual integration includes not
only the contents of the courses but also the way they are
taught, the relationship of the program itself to the local
leadership selection process, the source of the texts and
other materials, in fact every aspect of the program. This
dimension of your program is probably far more important
than academic excellence, which is often a dominant force
against contextualization, producing theological egg-heads
rather than church leaders, professional clergy whom the
congregations cannot support, a ministry which is hierarchical and not democratic or dynamic.

C. THE BASIC ELEMENTS IN THE SYSTEM

Having discussed the importance of building an integrated
system, the *plenary session* should also consider the basic
elements that make up that system. The leader may ask the
participants to list the different elements that they consider to be necessary for their training systems. The list
should include the following: personnel, materials (and
equipment), experiences, organization, finances. They
should clarify the importance of each of these elements and
consider how they will work out their analysis of each one
in their project groups.

Only "experiences" will be mentioned here because this is an
aspect which is often overlooked and which can be especially
significant in extension programs. We have noted, for
example, that people learn to evangelize and to worship not
by reading books or listening to lectures primarily but by
the actual experience of evangelizing and worshipping. If
these are basic concerns of theological education, we
should plan specific experiences of evangelism and worship.
Similarly, some people have suggested that extension programs
lack important experiences that residential programs provide,
such as life in community and library research. If you
consider these experiences to be essential, see if you can
design experiences of these kinds for your extension students during their vacation periods, with the help of residential seminaries and institutes. Perhaps there are other
kinds of experiences that should be planned for your training program.

D. CONCLUSION

After discussing the previous two topics, the participants
should return to their *project groups* and work out their
plans in detail. They will probably need two or three
hours to do an adequate job. They may want to divide into
sub-groups to deal with specific aspects of their program or
to write up their final proposals. This is only an exercise,
but it may well produce workable plans. And it should be a
valuable experience in preparing the participants to
analyze their own programs and also to help others work
out their training systems. Each group should prepare a
report of their project for the final session, using visual
aids (maps, diagrams, etc.) and other methods.

At the final *plenary session* the groups will present their
projects for evaluation and possible referral to the
respective churches or institutions. The participants may
want to have these projects reproduced for wider circulation.

IV.   DEMONSTRATION OF AN EXTENSION CENTER MEETING

The heart of theological education by extension is the local
extension center. If the local centers meet regularly and carry
out their essential functions effectively, the program will be
healthy and lively even though the materials may be deficient
and the central administration is very inadequate. If on the
other hand the centers do not continue to beat regularly and
vigorously, the whole program will probably break down. For
this reason extension theological educators are giving increasing attention to the ingredients and dynamics of extension center
meetings, the role of teacher and student, and the use of various
kinds of instructional materials and teaching methods.

This exercise is built around a demonstration in order to
focus reflextion and discussion on the practical realities and
skills of extension work. It can be used to dramatize the
nature of theological education by extension and also to train
extension teachers. The procedures for this study should be
adapted to meet local needs and circumstances. The following
suggestions all require the use of self-study materials for two
small study units, which each workshop director must provide in
quantity as the basis for the demonstrations.

One procedure would be simply to demonstrate a center meeting
and then discuss with all the participants what they observed.
This would take only two or three hours. On the other hand the
same basic procedure could be amplified for a two, three, or
five-day training session for extension teachers. The course

materials that they are to use can be introduced, time given for study, and demonstration sessions led by the teachers themselves. The following procedure is more extensive than the first and shorter than the second and would take four to six hours. The suggestions and concepts provided here can be utilized in any of the procedures mentioned.

The first step is to choose the self-study material to be used in the demonstration, prepare copies, and distribute them to all the participants. Two small units of study will be necessary for the two demonstrations planned. This material should be circulated at least one day in advance of the exercise with clear instructions that all participants should complete the study before the period assigned for the demonstration, just as if they were extension students. If this is a training workshop for teachers of one institution, it may be best to choose lesson material from one of the courses they will be teaching. If the participants are from several different backgrounds and institutions, it may be helpful to choose a Bible study related to the concept of the ministry.

The second step, at the time appointed for the exercise, is to introduce the study with a brief discussion of the importance of the extension center meetings. The leader may ask the participants to share their experiences and ideas, and he may offer his own comments. Then he should instruct the participants as to the procedure to be followed.

The third step is the first demonstration of an extension center meeting. This can be arranged in several ways. One format is to select six or eight of the participants to form a small circle in the center of the room; they will form the demonstration class; and someone who has been successful as an extension teacher will be prepared to lead them. The other participants will form a larger circle around the center class; they will be instructed to remain silent during the demonstration; they should also take notes of their observations.

The fourth step, when the demonstration has finished, is to have a general discussion and evaluation of what went on in the demonstration class. The leader of this discussion may or may not be the person who led the class, and the members of the class group may remain in the inner circle or join the others in the outer circle. The discussion may go through three stages. First the leader may ask for general comments from the observers and from the participants. Then he may throw out specific questions to bring out certain issues and aspects. Finally he may make use of an evaluation sheet to get the general response of the group.

The fifth step, perhaps after a break, is for the participants to draw up a list of functions of the extension center
meetings, then a list of guidelines on the role of the teacher,
and also a list of guidelines on the role of the student.
These ideas may be written on a blackboard as they come out of
the discussion; they should be written down by the participants
also. A committee may be assigned the task of preparing copies
to be circulated later.

The sixth step is to hold a second demonstration of an
extension center meeting, utilizing the second unit of the self-
study material that has been circulated. This time all the
participants should be divided into groups of six or eight, and
leaders chosen to begin the class session. After 15 or 20
minutes the coordinator of the exercise may circulate among the
groups and ask a different person to become the teacher in each
one. If there is sufficient time, another change of leaders
can take place later. When the class has ended, the groups
should be instructed to carry out their own general discussion
and evaluation of the experience as students and teachers in
the demonstration class. The discussion may follow the same
procedure used in the larger group following the first demonstration, including the evaluation sheet, if at least one copy
can be provided for each group.

The seventh step, if time permits, can be a final plenary
session. The participants should report back from their experience in the groups so as to develop a general feeling as to the
learning that has been going on. Then the leader may ask the
participants to list the problems that have surfaced in the
demonstrations or that they have experienced in their extension
programs. If there are more than 25 participants, it may be
preferable to form a panel of experienced extension teachers to
respond to the questions and problems presented. Later the
panel and participants may want to make further suggestions
about activities that can be carried out in the weekly center
meetings or by the groups of extension students.

The following materials cover some of the points mentioned
above, but they are suggestive only. Each workshop leader should
select the materials and areas for discussion that seem most pertinent and urgent for his situation. Even more important, each
workshop should respond to the participants' concerns and
encourage them to develop their own solutions and guidelines.

A. OBSERVATION OF AN EXTENSION CENTER MEETING--QUESTIONS FOR
   DISCUSSION
B. EVALUATION OF AN EXTENSION CENTER MEETING--EVALUATION SHEET
C. FUNCTIONS OF AN EXTENSION CENTER MEETING--SOME AREAS FOR
   DISCUSSION
D. THE ROLE OF TEACHER AND STUDENT IN EXTENSION THEOLOGICAL EDUCATION

A. OBSERVATION OF AN EXTENSION CENTER MEETING

QUESTIONS FOR DISCUSSION

1. *What are your general observations?*

   a. What was good about the class?
   b. What was not so good?

2. *What was the role of the teacher?*

   a. What did he do?
   b. What should he have done?

3. *What was the role of the students?*

   a. What did they do?
   b. What should they have done?

4. *Was the class an effective learning experience?*

   a. Was there much active participation by all?
   b. Were they dealing with real problems and issues?

5. *What are the functions of the extension center meetings?*

   a. How do they contribute to the students' academic progress?
   b. What else should they contribute?

6. *What problems can arise in an extension class?*

   a. How can these problems be dealt with?
   b. How can they be avoided?

7. *What additional activities can help the students in their personal life and ministry?*

   a. How could they share personal needs and experiences?
   b. How could they deal with problems and concerns that arise in their congregations?

B.   EVALUATION OF AN EXTENSION CENTER MEETING

EVALUATION SHEET

1. *Interest, Participation, and Dynamics*

   a.   How many participated fully?_____How many little?_____
        How many did not participate?_____

   b.   How many took initiative--only the teacher?_____Just
        two or three?_____Several?_____

   c.   Did the discussion revolve around the teacher?_____
        Did the students exchange ideas among themselves?_____
        Who asked the questions?_____Who gave the conclusions?
        _____

   d.   Was the participation spontaneous and dynamic all the
        time?_____Half the class?_____Only for brief
        moments?_____

2. *Content and Learning*

   a.   Did the class deal with matters that are important for
        the students' life and ministry?_____Did it discuss
        academic topics with little significance for real
        life?_____Was much time wasted explaining confusing
        words and questions?_____

   b.   Were doubts cleared up?_____Were mistaken ideas and
        misinformation corrected?_____Did new ideas or plans
        take shape?_____

   c.   Were the students concerned primarily about the lesson
        itself?_____About satisfying or impressing the
        teacher?_____About improving their ministry and help-
        ing the church to grow?_____

   d.   Was there a feeling that everyone was learning something
        valuable?_____Were they deepening and broadening their
        understanding?_____Did they practice and improve their
        skills?_____

3. *Leadership Development*

    a. Did the students demonstrate their ability to express their ideas, reasoning, and questions?_____Did they relate what they are studying to the problems of their own communities and congregations?_____

    b. Did the participation in class contribute to the students' formation as members and leaders of groups?_____Are they conscious of their role and also of the needs of others in a group?_____

    c. Was there mutual pastoral care during the meeting?_____ Were personal problems and needs dealt with?_____How are negative feelings handled?_____

    d. Did the experience in the class deepen the students' concept of the ministry and their fellowship in the ministry?_____

C. FUNCTIONS OF AN EXTENSION CENTER MEETING

SOME AREAS FOR DISCUSSION

1. *Consider the needs that the students have in their personal lives and ministry as well as in their theological studies and the ways in which the center meetings might respond to those needs.*

   a. In what circumstances do the students live and work?

   b. What are their family responsibilities?

   c. What is their work in the local congregations and what problems do they face there?

2. *Think of the opportunities that the center meetings offer, just by bringing these groups of students and professors together regularly.*

   a. How can the students be encouraged in their personal lives and ministry?

   b. In what ways can they share their experiences and obtain help in solving their problems?

   c. What should the meetings do to help them in their ministerial formation?

3. *Discuss the significance of the center meetings for the students' progress in their theological studies.*

   a. What orientation, discipline, guidance, and clarification do they need in their courses?

   b. What should the discussion of the lesson content emphasize?

   c. How can the discussion of each lesson reinforce each student's understanding, integration, and application of the ideas and skills being studied?

4. *Mention other activities which could or should be included in the regular center meetings.*

   a. Should time be set aside for prayer, fellowship, and worship?

b. How can administrative needs, such as matriculation, collection of fees, attendance records, be handled efficiently?

c. Should there be a special time for the students to report on their work and problems in the congregations?

5. *Remember that the center meetings are important for the professors and for the development of the program itself.*

a. What orientation and inspiration should the professors gain from these meetings?

b. How should the center meetings contribute to the evaluation, revision and amplification of the course materials?

c. How could the center groups participate in the formation of the whole extension program?

D. THE ROLE OF TEACHER AND STUDENT IN EXTENSION THEOLOGICAL EDUCATION

POSSIBLE GUIDELINES

1. *The Role of the Teacher*

   a. Organize the center, find and incorporate local leaders as students, and coordinate the administration.

   b. Attend the center meetings regularly and punctually.

   c. Direct the study program: Provide materials, assign and review home study, supervise examinations.

   d. Stimulate the students through personal conversation, participation in class, encouragement.

   e. Prepare himself fully for each week's session.

   f. Coordinate the class discussion to insure wide participation, comprehension of vocabulary, concepts, and issues, and covering of material assigned.

   g. Help to clarify doubts, integrate ideas, and apply the material to the local situation.

   h. Facilitate integration of what is being learned through discussion, reviews, tests.

   i. Evaluate the student's progress and help them evaluate their own progress.

   j. Share his own ideas and experiences, convictions and doubts, successes and failures, needs and concerns.

   k. Be a learner among learners and a teacher among teachers.

   l. Demonstrate genuine interest in the students in class and out of class, as students and as church leaders and colleagues.

   m. Be a friend and counselor and help them develop their gifts as friends and counselors.

   n. Develop a pastoral relationship personally and in the group.

   o. Formulate questions and give answers that will lead the students on in their development.

   p. Help the students to learn to think for themselves.

   q. Help them find their own conclusions, solutions, answers.

   r. Help them to discover and develop their gifts.

    s. Keep in touch with what is happening in the congregations through the students' reports.

    t. Grow in his own understanding of the God's mission in the world through study and fellowship with the students.

2. *The Role of the Student*

    a. Fulfill the requirements of the program: Fees, recommendations, etc.

    b. Carry out the course assignments regularly and fully.

    c. Attend the center meetings regularly and punctually.

    d. Encourage fellow students and the teacher through personal conversation and participation in class.

    e. Help to guide the class discussion; encourage others to express their ideas; help clarify vocabulary, concept, issues; facilitate progress through the material to be covered.

    f. Provide concrete examples and practical applications of the lesson material from his own experience.

    g. Foment genuine fellowship and companionship in the group.

    h. Be concerned about the life and ministry of the others; help develop mutual pastoral care among the participants.

    i. Learn to be a participant-observer in the group and a leader of groups.

    j. Be a faithful steward of his time and talents, studies, and ministry.

    k. Be a learner among learners and a teacher among teachers.

    l. Formulate questions and answers that will stimulate the others in their own thinking and development.

    m. Share his own ideas, convictions, doubts, needs and concerns.

    n. Help the group formulate their conclusions, solutions, and answers.

    o. Help the members of the group to discover and develop their gifts.

    p. Learn from what is happening in the other students' lives and in their churches.

    q. Examine critically the material being studied and the ideas expressed in class.

    r. Seek to apply and test all that he is learning in his own life and ministry.

s. Offer criticisms and suggest changes in the study
materials and in the center meeting procedures.

t. Grow in his understanding of God's mission in the world.

(It is interesting, after making lists of guidelines on the role
of the teacher and the role of the student, to compare the two,
note the differences and similarities, and to discuss these concepts. This in turn may lead the participants to question their
own ideas and change their lists.)

V. SELF-STUDY MATERIALS FOR EXTENSION STUDENTS

Everyone recognizes that self-study materials play an essential role in theological education by extension. Because extension students meet with their professors only for brief periods, in most cases once a week, and do not live at or near the seminary campus, they must be given tools and procedures by which they can study on their own. For this reason people related to the extension movement everywhere have invested much of their time preparing self-instructional materials.

In some cases this urgent quest for adequate materials for extension students has actually produced effective tools for learning. But in most cases it has produced very limited, provisional results, often called preliminary editions or even stop-gap materials. It may be that inordinate importance was given to these self-study materials. It may be that inordinate importance was given to these self-study materials, and undue pressure was placed on unprepared, inexperienced writers. Nevertheless the fact that so many theological educators have begun to use new kinds of materials and methods of teaching and to investigate the educational dimension of their task is itself tremendously significant. Perhaps for the first time in history we are developing theological *educators* and not just theologians for the preparation of the church's ministry. And many theological educators in the extension movement are continuing to search for greater understanding of and more effective approaches to education for ministry.

In their quest for effective self-study materials, the promoters of theological education by extension soon turned to programmed instruction, which is the science or craft of planned, individualized, guided learning. This has produced considerable controversy, not so much at the practical level as at the ideological or philosophical level. Few people are willing to reduce human learning to stimulus-response sequences, and few theological educators are willing to accept the behaviorist presuppositions of Skinnerian programming. On thd other hand extension students do need guidance in their studies; planned sequences are more helpful than unorganized materials; and programming has taught us a great deal about how people learn.

Other educational concepts and trends have influenced the extension movement, and some of them form an anthithesis to programmed instruction. Paulo Freire conceives of genuine education as conscientization, problematization, and liberation--a process in which each person determines his own needs and works toward his own solutions in dialogue with others. The open classroom approach is based on the students' interests; the students themselves determine the content and sequence of learning

with the help of teacher-counselors. These concepts bring out
the essential factors of motivation, integration, and growth;
they help us to understand human nature as well as human learning

The following exercises draw upon the experience of extension
theological educators over the past ten years as they have dealt
with these issues in the search for adequate self-study materials. Our purpose in extension workshops is not to give pat
answers or set formulae but to involve others in this quest and
to share with them these insights and problems. The tension
between Skinner and Freire, programmed and open education, can
in fact be a very stimulating dialectic to keep us on the move,
to warn which incorporate the values of both tendencies.

These four exercises take at least an hour each. Obviously
the concerns expressed here could be expanded into a three to
five-day workshop for writers of extension materials. Several
aspects of the problem are introduced briefly in the following
outlines. Each workshop should select and adapt these ideas to
their own needs. Sample lessons and course materials should be
available to the participants as they discuss the principles and
methods presented here. And they should make their own experiments. Our purpose here is not so much to train writers of
extension materials as to deepen our understanding of self-study
materials, to form criteria for evaluation of prepared materials,
and perhaps to discover persons who should be encouraged to use
their gifts for this strategic task.

A.   DEFINING OBJECTIVES
B.   OBSERVATIONS ABOUT LEARNING
C.   CHARACTERISTICS OF PROGRAMMED INSTRUCTION
D.   PROBLEMATIZATION AND PROGRAMMING

A. DEFINING OBJECTIVES

This study will take at least an hour. Begin with a discussion of points one to four, using as many examples as possible. Then give the participants 15 or 20 minutes to try writing some objectives as suggested in point five. Then have them share their results for evaluation by the group. If time permits, give them another work period to refine their objectives or write new ones.

1. A New Approach to Curriculum Design

In the past academic programs have been worked out in terms of content categories. Seminaries and institutes generally had departments of Bible, church history, systematic theology or doctrine, and practical theology. The courses were further broken down into logical, cognitive, abstract units. It has become increasingly evident that this approach is not as effective as we had assumed. Church history and doctrine should be studied together. Biblical studies are relevant and meaningful only as they are related to history, doctrine, and contemporary issues. All our theological studies must be integrated and applied in terms of our ministry and mission in today's world.

Perhaps the most important and enduring contribution of recent educational technology is the place it gives to objectives in curriculum design Rather than waiting for the student to finish his theological course, we begin by setting down a careful description of the roles he will play as a minister or church leader. Then we try to identify all the skills and concepts and information that he needs to fill those roles effectively. Finally we set down specific objectives for units of study, experiences, and courses that will help him to prepare himself for his ministry. This approach has obvious advantages in terms of relevance, integration, application, and motivation.

The process of defining and using objectives has been compared to the making and use of maps. Before setting out on a trip the travelers decide on their destination. They they choose the route they wish to take, picking out the intermediate points along the way. Finally they can plan their trip step by step, with a clear picture of the objectives to be reached each day or even each hour. And each point on their itinerary is important because it marks their progress toward their final destination.

2. *The Importance of Objectives*

Defining objectives is important not only for the students
but also for the course writers and for the teachers and
administrators of the program and for the churches they
serve.

a. For the Students

It helps them to see at all times their destination, the
relevance of the material, and the importance of each
unit of study.

It enables them to distinguish the essential points in
their studies rather than simply memorize everything.

It gives them a clear idea of their own progress as they
advance through the material.

b. For the Course Writers

It helps them to plan the course, select the essential
information and skills, and organize the learning steps.

It gives them clear guidelines for evaluating their
materials step by step and at the end.

This in turn enables them to identify and revise weak
points and keep rewriting the materials until they fulfill their purposes.

c. For Teachers and Administrators

Defining objectives gives them a clear picture of what is
to be taught.

It provides guidelines for evaluating the students' progress, i.e. for examinations and grades.

It enables them to see the relationships between different
units and courses and the integration of the whole
curriculum.

d. For the Churches

It gives them a clearer understanding of the program.

It helps them to know what to expect of graduates.

It enables prospective students to know whether they
should enter the program and what they should expect
from it.

3. *A Crucial Issue: Who Defines the Objectives?*

This question is crucial and controversial because it deals with the basic philosophy of theological education. Traditionally it was assumed that the authorities of the church or the institution should define the contents and objectives of their training programs, based on the Bible and other secondary norms. On the other hand educators now point out that the students must participate meaningfully in the definition of goals and the selection of course contents and in the whole educational process.

In theological education by extension this issue is not as polarized as it might seem, because many of the students are the leaders in their congregations and in their churches' governing bodies; some are members of the seminaries' boards of directors. On the other hand the problem is more complex because extension institutions prepare their course materials in printed form.

Each program should struggle with this issue and search for ways in which the students can participate in the definition of objectives. This may mean that the curriculum will be more flexible, that the students will have a wider selection of courses or units or fields of specialization, and that the organization and order of study will change. But the concern for carefully defined objectives remains.

4. *The Characteristics of Good Objectives*

a. Good objectives *expresss the intent* of the lesson or course; they do not describe the contents. They should indicate clearly what the students should know or be able to do when they finish that unit of study, not what they are to study, to go through, or to do in the unit itself.

b. In order to specify what the students are to learn, state your objectives in terms of *what they are to do* to demonstrate the knowledge or skill that they have learned. Expressions like "to know," "to understand," and "to appreciate" are too vague and inexact; they must be replaced by words such as "to write," "to identify," "to list."

c. To avoid ambiguity for the students, for the teachers, and for evaluation purposes, good objectives are *explicit, measurable, and detailed.* They indicate exactly what the students should be able to do, under what circumstances, and all that is expected. If they are "to trace Paul's

missionary journeys," for example, the objectives should
specify whether they should do this with or without a
map, whether the map will have the place names on it
already, whether the students will be allowed to use
their Bibles or not, whether they must be able to respond
only in writing or also orally while teaching a class,
etc.

d. Finally, good objectives should usually indicate *the
    level of acceptable performance*. Using the previous
    example, we should specify whether the students need to
    recite all the place names or only certain ones, whether
    they should be able to work out their maps in one hour
    or in any specified length of time, whether their lines
    can be one centimeter off or more, etc.

For the beginner this process may seem tedious and pedantic;
to all of us it is a long and difficult process; few writers
have been able to follow through consistently and write all
their objectives in this way. But if we fail to write
specific objectives, our writers, our students, and our
teachers will not be able to see clearly where they are
going, how to get there, or even whether they have arrived.
The discipline of defining explicit objectives has helped
many writers to clarify in their own minds what they want
to teach and eliminate much irrelevant material.

5. *A Trial Assignment*

Having discussed the previous issues and guidelines, each
participant should try to write some specific objectives.
One topic may be used for all, or the participants may prefer to work in their own fields of specialization. In
either case they should work out objectives for a small unit
of study only, not for a whole course. After 15 or 20
minutes ask them to read their results and evaluate them as
a group or in small groups, referring back to point four
above. If time permits, give them another opportunity to
refine their objectives or write new ones, then discuss
them again.

Throughout this presentation the leader should refer to
objectives that have been prepared by others. Before asking
the participants to try writing some objectives--or after
they have done so--give them some samples to evaluate.

The defining of objectives is analyzed clearly and succinctly
by Robert F. Mager, *Preparing Instructional Objectives*
(Belmont, California: Fearon Publishers, 1962).

B. OBSERVATIONS ABOUT LEARNING

This study will take one or two hours. First discuss with the
group points one and two. Then let them look over any samples
of extension course materials that are available and evaluate
them in terms of the four principles presented under two. After
sharing their conclusions, they should go on to the second assignment listed below. It would be helpful to give each participant
a copy of the list of four observations about learning.

1. *How People Learn*

Programmed instruction is not mysterious or magical. It is
simply an attempt to apply systematically what we can all
observe about the way people learn. It makes use of a number
of very specific techniques, and the writing of good programmed materials requires considerable practice and exper-
tise. But the basic observations or principles underlying
these techniques are surprisingly simple. Even so, many
people jump right into the complex, technical aspects of
programming without really thinking through the basic principles.

The purpose of this unit is to identify four simple observations about learning, to use these principles to evaluate
extension course materials, and to explore ways of applying
them. These principles are taken from Ted and Margaret Ward,
Programmed Instruction for Theological Education by Extension
(U.S.A.: CAMEO, 1970). There are of course many different
ways of analyzing human learning, and these principles can be
stated differently. Our interest here is simply to stimulate
thinking about how people learn and about how we can prepare
materials that will help them to learn more effectively.

Read over the following observations or principles and discuss them as a group or in smaller groups. Give a number of
illustrations of each point, and ask the participants to add
their own examples. These illustrations and examples should
be taken from everyday experience and traditional academic
situations as well as from programmed courses. When these
observations have been discussed sufficiently, go on to the
assignments presented under three and four.

2. *Four Simple Observations*

a. *Learning proceeds best as the learner associates new
    information with information he already knows*. (This is
    the old and still valid proposition that learning proceeds
    from the known toward the unknown--for example, Jesus used
    parables to link new information to things his hearers

already understood: sowing seeds, fishing, investments, and caring for vineyards.)

b. *Learning (retention) depends on the use of newly acquired information very soon after it is acquired.* (This is the basis of the common tactic for better remembering a person's name--actually to say his name very soon after being introduced.)

c. *Learning depends on the perceived importance of information.* The importance of information must not only be indicated or demonstrated for the learner, but he must also experience a situation in which he finds that the information relates to his own purposes and goals. (A parent will often show a child an example of what happens if a certain teaching is ignored--for example, a drunken person will be pointed out as illustrating the consequences of abuses of alcohol.)

d. *Learning (retention and accuracy) is increased when the learner is informed very promptly whether or not his use of new information is appropriate.* (For example, Jesus gave Peter prompt and strong encouragement for announcing the deity he had recognized in Christ--according to Matthew.)

3. *Assignment #1*

The participants should now spend 20 or 30 minutes looking over extension course materials. They should try to find out how the writers have applied the four principles listed above. It may be that the samples available are very poor examples; some principles may have been used and others ignored. In any case this assignment should help the participants to see what is involved in preparing extension course materials and to evaluate materials that have been prepared. They may come up with suggestions on how to improve the materials they examine.

After analyzing one or more samples individually, the participants should come together and share their observations.

4. *Assignment #2*

Now divide the participants into interest area groups to discuss how they would begin to lay out a course for extension students. If the institutions or programs represented use traditional categories for their courses, one group could work on a Bible course, another in church history, etc. They should take 20 or 30 minutes to sketch out some preliminary plans based on the four simple observations about learning that are listed above. Then the groups should report back to a plenary session.

C.   CHARACTERISTICS OF PROGRAMMED INSTRUCTION

This exercise will take one or two hours. After a brief introduction the participants will discuss a list of seven criteria or
characteristics of programmed instruction. (Copies of this list
should be passed out, if possible.) Then they will look over
samples of programmed materials, either theological or secular
or both. Finally each person should prepare a series of frames.

1. *Introduction*

    The format of programmed instruction may be very simple. Pro-
    grammed material usually consists of small units of informa-
    tion, followed by a question or problem, space for student
    response. This description is, however, only a caricature,
    i.e. it does not explain the more important characteristics
    of programming. Unfortunately some writers have laid out
    their material mechanically, chopping up their lecture notes
    or a traditional text into small bits, without any thought of
    objectives or sequences. And this has given some seekers, as
    well as opponents of programming, a very negative impression.

    The following list of seven criteria of programmed instruc-
    tion is taken from *A Programmed Learning Practicum*, by
    Brethower, Markle, Rummler, Schrader, and Smith. Each point
    should be discussed and clarified with examples. Note that
    feedback is not explicitly mentioned, yet some kind of built-
    in confirmation is necessary if the students are to proceed
    on their own. Also, instead of small units the authors speak
    of increasingly complex steps as the students progress through
    the material. And the material is not acceptable until it has
    been tested and revised so that the students actually reach
    the objectives.

2. *Seven Criteria or Characteristics of Programmed Instruction*

    a. *It is instructional material. It is not a test or a
        series of questions.*

    b. *It has specific objectives which it aims to meet.*

    c. *It is developed empirically. Program structure--content,
        sequence, step size, and format--is a synthesis of the
        programmers' assumptions and feedback obtained from
        students.*

    d. *It is self-instructional. Its contents need not be
        explained, reviewed, or repeated by other instructional
        materials nor by an instructor.*

    e. *It is self-pacing. It need not be limited by time con-
        straints such as a 50-minute class period, by a group
        presentation device such as a movie, nor by student*

group characteristics, e.g. a "slow" student will not hold back the others.

f. *It requires students to solve problems or make discriminations as they proceed through the instructional material.*

g. *It requires increasingly complex behavior of the student as he progresses through it. Each step leads to and contributes to new behaviors in subsequent frames. Repetition and isolated "review" frames are not essential. "Review" is handled by gradual addition of complexity.*

3. *Assignment #1*

The participants should now be given 15 or 20 minutes to work through one or more short samples of programmed material either theological, secular, or both. It may be helpful to choose samples which are simple and complex, that demonstrate different types of programming, and that represent different fields of learning. After working through each sample they should refer back to the above list to see whether the material has applied these criteria adequately.

It may be helpful then to ask the participants to share their observations and to raise further questions about programming

4. *Assignment #2*

Now each participant should choose a specific objective for a small unit of a theological course and try to write a series of frames that would enable extension students to reach that objective. In order to save time and coordinate efforts it may be preferable to give the participants all the same objective, but each one should work individually. One or more advisors should circulate among the participants to answer questions and offer suggestions.

After 20 or 30 minutes the participants should share and evaluate their results.

D. PROBLEMATIZATION AND PROGRAMMING

This exercise will take one or two hours. It begins with a brief discussion of problematization and programming. The participants should examine a set of materials, such as those prepared by the Conservative Baptist Extension Bible Institute in Honduras, and discuss how these materials are made up. Then each participant should try to prepare a complete unit of study following this model.

1. *What is Problematization?*

Paulo Freire criticized severely traditional education, because it imposes prefabricated information on the students and requires them to memorize it and store it up for possible future application. It gives out gratuitously answers for which the students have not asked questions, solutions for problems which they do not face. It creates dependence on the teacher, books, the school, others in general rather than developing the students' ability and confidence in facing their real needs and problems. Genuine education takes place when the students begin to analyze their situation and take steps to overcome their needs, solve their problems, formulate and answer their own questions.

In theological education by extension it should be both wise and easy to use this approach, which is called problematization. Many of our students are leaders in their congregations; some of them are pastors and church workers; most of them are mature people with families and jobs. They are already facing all the problems of life and the ministry. Therefore we should be able to devise a way in which our curricula will respond to the students' needs and problems.

Many extension programs have developed more or less complete sets of self-study materials. Those who wrote these materials assumed that they would help the students in their ministry, but, since they are printed and take a great amount of time and money to prepare, they are not very flexible. They follow pre-defined sequences toward fixed objectives. They do not respond immediately to the diverse, changing problems the students face week by week. Yet these extension programs require some kind of self-study materials, and the materials should be prepared carefully so as to reach widely and deeply into the whole range of theological studies.

Discuss this apparent conflict of interests in a plenary session or in groups. Consider both concerns conscientiously. Suggest ways in which an extension program can use the problematization approach to curriculum design and also the programming approach to course writing. Then go on to the following point.

2. *Problematization and Programmed Materials*

One of the most interesting models of theological education by extension has been developed by George Patterson in Northern Honduras. This program combines problematization and programmed materials in a unique way. If possible, send for a set of his materials and his manual for extension teachers. (These materials are readily available in Spanish from him, Apartado 164, La Ceiba, Honduras. Some have been translated into English and may be requested from J. E. Hudspith, Chiengmai, Thailand.) If these materials are used, they should be passed among the participants so that they can analyze and discuss how they are put together. If they are not available, someone can describe them on the basis of the following paragraphs. (See also the article by Patterson in the *Extension Seminary* Quarterly Bulletin, No. 3, 1974.)

It should be noted, in the first place, that the Honduras program has a very definite goal and a very specific target population. It has been designed to train semi-literate, extremely poor, rural people to plant churches throughout their region. The extension centers form a chain; the "staff" consists of one person who trains three students who teach 20 more in eight sub-centers; and some of these train another 25 men in more remote villages. At each link in the chain the students are charged with the task not only of training others but also of raising up at least one new congregation. Each tiny group meets regularly to discuss their work in the villages and to get help in solving the problems that arise week by week. The lone institute professor meets only with the original three students, and his main task is to prepare miniature self-study materials for the whole program.

Since most of the students read very little and slowly, the language must be simple and the study units are very short. They are made up as one-week pamphlets, pocket-size, with simple drawings, cartoons, and figures. Each one was written originally in response to a specific need of a student. Gradually a large collection has been built up, and they are arranged more or less in the order in which the students face problems as they establish new congregations. They are now available in quantity so that the students can give them to their students as needed.

Each pamphlet has as its specific objective to provide a remedy for a particular problem in the students' ministry. For example, some early problems are: The believers do not witness; people do not respond to our witness; the new believers don't know how to pray; they don't request baptism. Later on the students receive help in pastoral counselling, organizing a new church, and even in training a new pastor. They draw directly and in an interdisciplinary fashion from the Bible, church history, and systematic theology, but they all focus on concrete issues and immediate needs. They are problem-centered.

These materials, which vary from 10 to 60 pages, are also programmed. In other words they are self-contained units which semi-literate people can follow without any help. Each pamphlet includes the following.

a. A specific problem in the students' life or ministry.

b. Biblical, historical, doctrinal, and/or practical information bearing on that problem.

c. Questions or some exercise to test the students' comprehension of the new information, followed by feedback to confirm and reinforce their understanding.

d. An assignment which will require them to put into practice what they have learned.

e. Drawings, figures, or cartoons to dramatize and enliven the presentation.

3. *Assignment: Prepare a Programmed, Problem-Centered Study Unit*

We have chosen the Honduras model as a basis for this exercise for several reasons. In the first place, it demonstrates that problematization and programmed instruction can both be used effectively in the same program. In the second place, these materials are brief and simple so that we can analyze them in a brief workshop exercise. And in the third place, the participants can work out an entire unit in just a few minutes and in this way gain considerable insight into the process of writing self-study materials. Also, some hidden talent may be discovered through this exercise, and some participants may become interested in giving their time to this important task.

Give the participants 20 or 30 minutes to prepare a programmed, problem-centered study unit. They should first choose
some specific problem that occurs frequently in their congregations, then follow the procedures and prepare the elements
mentioned above. Each participant should work out one
pamphlet, even though his information may be limited, the
programming superficial, and the art work very crude. When
they have finished, have them present and explain their work
to the group.

12
The Spanish Intertext Project

The movement called theological education by extension first
took root in Latin America. The Evangelical Presbyterian
Seminary of Guatemala began its pioneering experiment in 1963.
From the beginning one of the crucial elements in this movement
has been the self-study textbook, because extension students
must learn a great amount on their own. The men and women who
attended the first international extension workshop in Armenia,
Colombia in 1967 set up a committee for the orientation and
coordination of authors who would prepare extension study
materials in Spanish-speaking countries of Latin America (CATA).
The extension movement is now almost ten years old, and CATA
has had five years in which to carry out its mandate. So it is
time to report and reflect on these efforts to prepare extension
textbooks in Spanish. The CATA experience, both negative and
positive, may be helpful to those who are organizing similar
projects in other parts of the world. It should at least provide background information for those who will carry forward the
task in this part of the world.

This paper will present first a resume of CATA's experience
through four stages or periods. Then it will discuss the basic
problems CATA has faced. Finally it will mention several aids
for authors which CATA has used or proposed.

These pages include considerable self-criticism and may give
the impression that little has been accomplished. Certainly
few or no definitive Intertexts have been produced. On the
other hand all the men and women who have participated in this
project are volunteers, robbing time from heavy schedules in

order to launch out on unchartered waters. These people took on
a task which is greater than they first realized and perhaps
greater than their capabilities. They have opened the way for
others who will finish what they have only begun.

I. THE HISTORY OF CATA

A. *The first stage can be identified as PRE-CATA, and it can be
    characterized as ISOLATED, INDIVIDUAL EFFORTS.*

The extension concept created an immediate demand for textbooks which would not only provide the basic content of the
course material but also guide the student progressively in the
learning of that material. It was evident that most seminary
and Bible institute professors had given little attention to the
learning process and that self-study textbooks at this level did
not exist. Theological education in general has depended almost
entirely on traditional books and professor contact (classroom
or tutorial).

Therefore the people and institutions that began to experiment
with extension theological education had to produce their own
materials. Generally these programs started out with extremely
limited resources. They developed simple workbooks to accompany
the textbooks which the students were assigned. Often these were
questionaires written up hastily lesson by lesson late at night
to be passed out the next day to waiting students in scattered
extension centers. Many of the authors had little or no experience as theologians or as educators and could give only parttime to these experiments. The Guatemalan workbooks were the
first to take definite shape and sizeable proportions and were
used in several other countries. But generally each extension
program struggled independently with this tremendous task with
no coordination or orientation whatsoever.

B. *The second stage can be identified as ARMENIA TO BOGOTA, and
    it can be characterized as a POPULAR APPROACH.*

The workshop at Armenia, Colombia in September 1967 led to the
formation of the *Unión de Instituciones Bíblicas de la Gran
Colombia* (UNICO), the *Comité Asesor de Textos Autodidácticos*
(CATA), and the *Comité Latino-Americano de Textos Teológicos*
(CLATT). These organizations set in motion a number of activities which attempted to incorporate as many people as possible
in order to produce a complete set of intertexts in just two or
three years. Institutions in general and specific individuals
were invited to write and produce these books. Lists of format
and content advisors were drawn up. Publishers were contacted.
Workshops were held. Many authors began to write. And Pert
charts laid out in detail the steps for the completion of some
of the textbooks.

But the activist, popular approach did not produce the desired
results. Some authors got tied up in the mechanics and theory
of programmed instruction. Others discovered that they did not
have sufficient background in the subject matter. Many did not
have enough time to give to writing. Most of the advisors failed
to provide the necessary orientation and evaluation, which in the
case of some manuscripts would have required a huge investment
of time. The Pert charts became meaningless. And by the time
CATA met in Bogota in December 1969 not a single Intertext was
near publication.

C. *The third stage can be identified as BOGOTA TO GUATEMALA,*
    and it can be characterized as an ELITIST APPROACH.

At Bogota CATA met with representatives of UNICO, CLATT, and
AETTE (the Brazil counterpart of CATA) plus Ted Ward and Ralph
Winter. Every aspect of the Intertext project was discussed and
a more realistic strategy was defined. It is called an elitist
approach in contrast to the previous popular approach. Previously much time and energy had been invested in
large numbers of authors who had little probability of producing
outstanding textbooks. Now CATA decided to move more slowly and
concentrate its resources on a small number of authors. Instead
of inviting and encouraging many to write, important qualifications for potential authors were listed. Instead of trying to
get out the complete set of Intertexts rapidly, efforts were
focused on a few of the most promising authors and their manuscripts. Those who had major difficulties were allowed to drop
out or encouraged to work with others as teams. New writers
were largely left on their own. And the members of CATA were
encouraged to spend more of their time writing.

In this period, from December 1969 to February 1972, several
major manuscripts were produced and published. Only one went
through the complete process for approval as an official CLATT
Intertext. Another was in the process. And two came out in
English.

D. *The fourth stage can be identified as POST-GUATEMALA, and*
    its strategy is still to be defined.

The members of CATA met in Guatemala in February, 1972 and
laid the groundwork for this new stage in the development of
Spanish Intertexts. CATA was organized by a small Colombian
organization (UNICO); it has worked almost entirely on its own
initiative; and it has had the same personnel for almost five
years. It is time for a change.

The need for orientation and coordination of authors of
Spanish Intertexts is greater than ever. But the panorama has

changed. Extension theological education, which was little more
than a vision and a slogan five years ago, is now an established,
broadly based movement. Numerous Spanish didactic materials
have been written and tested and revised, and many authors are
now writing parttime or fulltime. Individuals, institutions,
churches, and mission organizations now consider that the preparation of extension textbooks is a high priority. Increasing
numbers of Latin Americans are involved in theological education
and they should take the leadership in the extension movement
and in writing Intertexts.

Therefore CATA has called for a consultation which will bring
together representatives of the major extension programs in
Spanish-speaking Latin America. This broad, grassroots gathering will meet in Colombia January 8-13, 1973 in order to discuss
their needs and set down the guidelines for future orientations
and coordination. CATA's final task is to find these people,
present them with the challenge, and bring them together so that
they can take over this responsibility. At the January consultation CATA will cease to exist. Those who meet in Colombia
will take the responsibility for future structures and programs.

II.   MAJOR PROBLEMS CATA FACED

A. *One of the basic problems from the beginning of the Spanish
     Intertext project has been the definition of CURRICULUM
     (function, content, structure, and levels).*

Originally it was felt that CATA should confine itself to
matters of style and format, but it was necessary to define the
content and structure of the curriculum. Each Intertext was to
be a link in a coordinated plan of study. Therefore someone had
to set down the whole curriculum and divide it up into course
units. There was no desire to impose a curriculum on any institution, and there was no desire to impose a particular doctrinal
position. But the curriculum had to be defined so that the
textbooks could be assigned and written and evaluated.

Seminary curricula have generally been defined in terms of
content which is broken up into traditional categories. The
curriculum developed by CATA begins with an analysis of the
ministry and is oriented toward the functions which the student
should learn to perform. Each course is defined in terms of
skills to be acquired as well as information to be assimilated.
In Biblical studies, for example, a minimum of course time is
spent on the historical background, introduction, and content
survey of the books of the Bible; major emphasis is placed on
learning to do inductive study. The relationship between content
and functions or skills in curriculum design is a matter of continuing debate.

A basic curriculum design was prepared; it was approved by
CATA and UNICO; and it was circulated to the members of CLATT.
CLATT contacted potential authors, and CATA served as the
editorial advisory committee. Although several academic levels
were contemplated CATA and CLATT have limited themselves to the
post-primary level. The preparation of texts in systematic
theology was left entirely to the individual institutions so as
to allow for greater freedom in this area and to avoid any
doctrinal alignment in the Intertext project.

The curriculum approved at the Mexico meeting of CATA and
UNICO in December 1968 is as follows:

BIBLICAL STUDIES

History and Composition of the
  O.T.
Inductive Study of Genesis,
  Exodus
Inductive Study of a Poetical
  Book
Inductive Study of Isaiah,
  Jeremiah

History and Composition of the
  N.T.
Inductive Study of Mark
Inductive Study of Romans,
  Galatians
Inductive Study of Revelation

HISTORY AND THEOLOGY

History of Christianity
Protestant Christianity
Latin America Church History
Roman Catholicism

Biblical Theology
Systematic Theology
Personal and Social Ethics
Sects

PRACTICAL THEOLOGY

Anthropology and Psychology
Homiletics
Pedagogy
Christian Education
Music

Church Administration
Evangelism
Church Growth
Christian Home
Pastoral Counseling

A matter of continuing concern is the length of this curriculum. Each institution is free to modify or shorten the list of
courses. And some have broken it into stages with corresponding
certificates.

B. *Another basic problem from the beginning of the Spanish
    Intertext project has been the definition of FORMAT
    (strategy, size, layout, pedagogical principles, and methods).*

Debate regarding format has focused on programmed instruction.
The members of CATA and others involved in extension have long

felt that the concept of programmed instruction would help enormously in the preparation of extension texts. But there has been
also resistance to it and misunderstanding of it. At one point a
superficial, mechanical pattern of objective and discussion
questions was recommended. The misleading term "semi-programmed"
was used. A sample programmed lesson was prepared and circulated
The value of non-programmed workbooks was discussed. The enormous
size of programmed textbooks was a concern. The possible combinations of workbooks and traditional textbooks were considered.
Some premature and rather simplistic materials were written.

No final decision has been made on all these matters concerning format, but general agreement has been reached with regard to
programmed instruction. First, programmed instruction is one of
the most costly forms of education, requiring a huge investment
in the preparation of materials. Second, writing programmed
material is not a mechanical, formal task; it requires a fundamental understanding of the content and of the learning principles. Third, it is not meaningful to speak of semi-programming;
if full programming is not possible, then parts of a course can
be programmed and other kinds of instruction used for the rest of
the course. Fourth, programmed instruction should not be
employed only for teaching simple information; rather it should
be employed to teach the most basic and the most difficult concepts of the course. Finally, the preparation of programmed
textbooks does not require extended, technical training in programming, but it does require an extended process of testing and
revision of the material.

The basic principles underlying programmed instruction are
essential for the preparation of Intertexts. Ted Ward has listed
four simple observations about how people learn:

1. Learning proceeds best as the learner associates new informa-
    tion with information he already knows.

2. Learning (retention) depends on the use of newly acquired
    information very soon after it is acquired.

3. Learning depends on the perceived importance of information.

4. Learning (retention and accuracy) is increased when the learner
    is informed very promptly whether or not his use of new infor-
    mation is appropriate.

Jim Emery has listed five principles or steps for preparing
programmed material.

1. As far as possible set down explicit and detailed objectives.
    The teacher and the student must know exactly what the end
    result is to be in terms of observable action.

2. Find out exactly what the student knows and can do before he begins the study. While the course objectives define the end point of the course, the student's previous knowledge defines the starting point.

3. Analyze and define the steps necessary to carry the student from where he is to where he should be at the end of the course. This is usually done by starting with the final objective and working backwards, specifying exactly all the information and skills needed to reach that final objective.

4. Require active response. What is essential in learning is that the mind of the student be kept actively in dialogue with the material he is studying.

5. Provide immediate feedback. If the student can immediately check his answer and know that he is on the right track, he continues with sure steps, and this provides a continuing source of positive motivation.

C. *A third fundamental problem in the Intertext project has been to find CAPABLE AUTHORS.*

At first a general call for authors went out from CATA and CLATT, and many enlisted. But it soon became evident that very few were qualified to write Intertexts. At the Bogota meeting in 1969 the following qualifications were suggested for Intertext authors.

1. They should be experts in the subject matter assigned.

2. They should have experience teaching the subject on the level for which they are to write.

3. They should be convinced of the importance of theological education by extension.

4. They should understand the principles of programmed instruction.

5. They should understand the culture(s) of Latin America.

6. They should have sufficient time and discipline to do the job.

7. They should have an understanding of the Intertext project and be willing to folow the recommendations of CATA and CLATT.

These guidelines were suggested in order to avoid complications and delays with incapable authors. But it has been almost impossible to find authors who meet these qualifications. The outstanding theological educators in Latin America are generally too busy to write anything, and they would not generally consider the writing of extension texts a high priority. The people who are involved in extension are perhaps even more busy, and often they are not experts in any field of theological studies.

Moreover, these Spanish Intertexts should be written by Latin Americans. At first it was stated that only Latin Americans could write the final Intertexts. Outstanding Latin Americans were approached. But it became evident that it was far more difficult to incorporate them into the project. Those who are capable are in greater demand than missionaries for seminary teaching and for other positions.

No solution has yet been found to this problem. But there are more possibilities now than previously. Extension theological education is now recognized as a major movement, and the preparation of extension textbooks is considered to be an important task. Professors at major seminaries and other outstanding leaders can be expected to give time to this project in the future.

D. *Another major problem facing CATA has been the EVALUATION of manuscripts.*

The problem of evaluation has been similar to the problem of finding capable authors. Those who were needed and asked to serve as advisors, including the members of CATA, did not have the time to carry out this responsibility. The analysis required for a complete reworking of a poor manuscript is almost equivalent to the writing of an original work. The Mexico meeting (1968) produced a list of advisors for content and format and an elaborate system of evaluation and revision of manuscripts. Then at Bogota (1969) it was decided that this was not realistic, and another system of evaluation was worked out.

The Bogota recommendations are more realistic suggestions for the evaluation of manuscripts based on the recognition that the authors, advisors, and CATA members are all volunteers who have relatively little time to give to the Intertext project.

1. The first suggestion was to depend on the members of CATA primarily to stimulate, orient, and evaluate the work of the authors in each region, because these are the men who most understand and are most committed to the project. Other advisors are less accessible and do not always respond.

2. In order not to invest a great amount of time on manuscripts which have less promise, CATA should work intensively with authors who are most qualified.

3. Although CATA should work primarily with a few, highly capable authors, others are encouraged to work out materials for their own institutions. As they gain experience and ability they can be included among the few capable authors and receive greater attention from CATA.

4. In order not to overload the members of CATA with long manuscripts to be evaluated, they should be asked to evaluate intensively small sections only and to discover in this way if the author is competent in his subject matter and presents it adequately.

5. The process of evaluation and revision of manuscripts can be summarized in two aspects. First, training programs and orientation materials should be provided for the authors. These include writers' workshops, books on programmed instruction, expositions of the extension concept and methodology, a detailed analysis of the curriculum, etc. Second, a series of check points should be worked out so that the authors can confirm or correct their work in various stages. These include evaluation by CATA members and other advisors if available, field testing by the author himself, and final evaluation by CLATT institutions.

6. Specific materials should be prepared for the evaluation process, including a list of suggestions to help each author evaluate his own work, a pre-test and post-test for each Intertext to be used in field testing, a guide to help CLATT institutions evaluate the preliminary editions.

CATA and CLATT have tried to incorporate the Bogota suggestions, though some of the materials mentioned here have not yet been prepared. Some manuscripts require more evaluation and revision than others. In any case each Intertext will have to go through several revisions. It is important to get some texts published and circulated so that extensive use can lead to more effective revisions.

E. *The last major problem to be considered here is the PUBLICA-TION of the Intertexts.*

This aspect of the Spanish Intertext project was left in the hands of CLATT. CLATT is simply a list of theological institutions in Spanish-speaking countries of Latin America coordinated by a secretary. The purpose of CLATT was to evaluate preliminary editions of Intertexts and recommend them to the publishers.

This arrangement was worked out so that the books would gain wide support and merit publication. It was assumed that the major evangelical publishers would be the best ones to handle printing, stocking, publicity, and distribution of these books.

Recently, serious questions about this set-up have been raised. These publishers take a long time to get books printed. The normal network of distribution requires huge mark-ups in the cost of the books and may place them out of reach of most extension students. The best channels for publicity and distribution are not in the hands of these publishers but in the hands of CLATT, CATA, and the institutions actually working in extension. The individual authors and institutions are required to put out and circulate and test the preliminary editions, and apparently they are expected to put up the capital for the final editions. The five publishers chosen by UNICO and CLATT are all based in the U.S.

These factors indicate that the whole matter of publication (printing, stocking, publicity, and distribution) should be restudied, and more satisfactory arrangements should be made. Two alternatives have been suggested. The final editions could be published by the sponsoring institutions through local commercial printing shops. Or off-set masters could be circulated to several strategic points for local printing.

III. AIDS FOR AUTHORS

A. *Perhaps the first aid that should be mentioned is the LIST OF QUALIFICATIONS.*

The list which was made up at Bogota is given at Point II, C above. This list is not intended to exclude others from entering the project. It is rather intended to focus attention upon authors with greater potential. And it should help new authors realize what is involved in this task and take seriously the challenge it represents.

B. *Another important aid is the growing BIBLIOGRAPHY of books and materials concerning different aspects of the Intertext project.*

Background information concerning extension theological education and the Intertext project is presented in *Theological Education by Extension*, ed. by Ralph D. Winter; *An Extension Seminary Primer*, by Ralph R. Covell and C. Peter Wagner.

Recommended for study of programmed instruction are: *Programmed Instruction for Theological Education by Extension*, by Ted and Margaret Ward; *Developing Programmed Instructional*

Materials, by James E. Espich and Bill Williams; *Preparing Instructional Objectives*, by Robert F. Mager; *Good Frames and Bad*, by Susan M. Markle; *Practical Programming*, by Peter Pipe; *A Guide to Programmed Instruction*, by Jerome D. Lysaught and Clarence M. Williams; *Developing Vocational Instruction*, by Robert F. Mager and Kenneth M. Beach.

Periodical bulletins which continue to give news and articles about extension and extension textbooks are: *Boletín Informativo de CLATT* (in Spanish); *Extension Seminary* (in English and Spanish); *Programming News*, and *Theological News*.

C. *One of the basic means of preparing and helping authors is through WORKSHOPS.*

Extension workshops have been held periodically in different parts of Latin America, and they are becoming increasingly common in all parts of the world. Some deal with the theory and methods of extension theological education. Others deal primarily with the writing of programmed textbooks.

D. *An important aid for authors is the CURRICULUM ANALYSIS.*

The basic curriculum design prepared for the Spanish Intertext project is widely circulated and gives a brief resume of each course. The more detailed layout of these courses which was proposed at Bogota has not yet been completed.

It is important for each author to know what his particular text should cover and how it relates to the other Intertexts in the general plan of the curriculum. Also, he should know the number and size of the units into which he should fit his material. The CATA specifications for each text are 15 week-long lessons made up of five hour-long units each. Some courses are planned for double this length.

E. *Also recommended as an aid for authors is the following CHECK POINT PROCEDURE.*

This procedure was set up at Bogota. It can easily be varied. The important thing is to provide guidance and evaluation at several stages in the preparation of each Intertext.

The first check point is on completion of the list of objectives and the outline of the content of the text. The author should then consult with the regional secretary of CATA and, if possible, with authorities in the field to see that he has demonstrated adequate comprehension of the subject and its purpose. The second check point is after writing sample units. The author should then test these units with an informant to

assure himself that the material actually teaches and the student
achieves the specific learning objectives. The third check point
is after completing several lessons. The author should then consult again with the regional secretary of CATA who will evaluate
the style and strategy of the course. Further check points are
recommended periodically as the author continues through the
book. He should test each new strategy and perhaps every fifth
lesson with individuals or groups of students. When he completes
the preliminary edition he should ask for the evaluation of CATA
and other specialists (format and content), test it in a normal
teaching situation, and present it to CLATT for evaluation and
testing.

F. *Another aid which has been proposed is a list of GUIDELINES
    FOR EVALUATION OF MANUSCRIPTS*

   Such a list would be helpful to the author himself, his
advisors, those who will test the manuscript, and the institutions that will evaluate and approve it for publication. It
should cover these matters: objectives, content, relationships
between Intertexts, coordination and sequence of the material,
strategy of the instructional program, system of evaluation and
grading, use of the book at the weekly center meetings, language
and style, attractiveness. These guidelines have not yet been
prepared.

G. *Also proposed was a FILE OF POTENTIAL AUTHORS AND ADVISORS*

   In order to find capable authors and advisors CATA recommended
the gathering of data about outstanding people who might someday
be encouraged and given time to write extension textbooks. Contact should be established with these people, and they should be
kept informed of developments with regard to extension theological education and the Intertext project. Perhaps resources
could be secured to help these people give time to writing.
This recommendation is especially important if key Latin American
leaders are to be integrated into the project.

13

The ALISTE Project for Training Extension Specialists

The theological education by extension movement is very young, and it is growing phenomenally. The leaders of the movement and many of the participants are convinced that it has great possibilities, but they are also conscious that it has serious shortcomings and tremendous needs. In January 1973 the *Asociación Latinoamericana de Institutos y Seminarios Teológicos de Extensión* was organized in order to overcome these shortcomings and respond to these needs. ALISTE now presents this project as a contribution toward the development of the extension movement on this continent.

A. *General Goals*

1. One of the most serious criticisms of the extension concept and movement is that it has been in large part the work of expatriates, although it was born in Latin America and is a creative response to the needs of this continent. One goal of this project is to facilitate the *formation of Latin American leaders* who will take over the leadership of the movement and guide its future development.

2. Another criticism is that extension programs have multiplied across the continent by simple imitation and by superficial transplanting of certain organizational structures and pedagogical techniques. One of the goals of this project is to provoke and stimulate *profound reflexion and serious evaluation* of theological education so that it will respond

increasingly to the biblical concept of the ministry and
incorporate new advances in educational theory and methodology.

3. The extension movement could be simply an extension of older
traditions and content, the imposition of one static form
instead of another. One of the general goals of this project
is to form a nucleous of leaders with sufficient understanding
and creativity to make *new experiments and adaptations* in
theological education by extension *so that it will be indigenous and contextualized in keeping with the multiple
realities and complex needs of this continent.*

4. The formation of this project was motivated by the widespread
demand for the training of teachers and writers for the many
extension programs in Latin America. This project proposes
to *train the people who will be able to carry out that task*
in their respective countries, counseling, directing workshops, participating in consultations, preparing materials,
and writing articles on the different aspects of theological
education by extension.

5. Finally, the purpose of this project is to form with this
group of leaders *a new base for the planning and coordinating
of the extension movement in Latin America.*

B. *Specific Objectives*

1. In order to reach these general goals it is important to
initiate a process of self-study and self-evaluation in the
different existing programs of theological education. ALISTE
will provoke such a process as one of the preliminary steps
of the project.

2. It is necessary to *find, train, and guide capable persons so
that they will take the leadership of the movement.* The
project includes a process of selection based on local programs and also a training program and a setting forth of new
leaders in the local, national, and international circles of
the movement.

3. The candidates should have *an intensive experience in an
existing program* to observe it and participate in it and to
evaluate it. In the second stage of the project the candidates will have the opportunity of participating in the
extension program of the Presbyterian Seminary of Guatemala
as observers, students, and professors.

4. The participants will *deepen their understanding of the basic
elements of theological education* through investigation of

their local situations, their experiences in Guatemala, and additional readings. They will develop their ability to explain and adapt these basic elements through seminars and workshops.

5. The candidates will have *to guide others in the writing of different kinds of self-study materials*. The project will give them the opportunity to write, use, and evaluate these materials.

6. These persons will have to *direct workshops and consultations on theological education by extension* and help others develop appropriate programs, personnel, and materials for diverse situations. Therefore the project includes preparation and planning and also experimentation, providing for the candidates to direct workshops and carry out consultations in different countries.

7. We propose to form *a nucleous of leaders for the extension movement in Latin America*. The project hopes to bring together the participants as a team, together with the directors of ALISTE and the members of the faculty of the Presbyterian Seminary of Guatemala, so that together they can plan the work, carry out the studies, and direct the workshops during and after their participation in the project.

C. *Conclusion*

It should be noted that this project has been planned with specific objectives in order to give it direction and content. But *the project itself is open-ended*. It is open-ended because new Latin American leaders will take the responsibility for the future of the movement. It is open-ended because it presents the challenge of extension not as a static formula but as a new horizon and a call to creativity. It is open-ended because it will stimulate the churches and local institutions to define their own necessities and discover their own models of theological education in order to train their own leaders for the ministry.

II. PROGRAM

This project is designed in a very special way in keeping with the objectives pursued. It is not simply a training program. The urgent need is to find, train, and channel new leaders for the extension movement in Latin America.

A. *Four Stages*

1. *The first stage* will take place in the local situation.
   ALISTE will circulate information about the project with
   guidelines for self-study and evaluation for theological
   institutions. Those that are interested in the ALISTE project will carry out this self-study in order to identify
   their needs, consider new possibilities and select a candidate to participate in other stages of the project. It is
   important that all the persons related to the institution,
   especially the members of the faculty, participate in this
   process of conscientization and commit themselves to the
   process of evaluation and change. In some cases the national
   association of seminaries or of extension will carry out this
   study and select the most capable person or persons. In
   other cases a denomination or a group of churches will do so.
   It is possible that one of the leaders of ALISTE will visit
   and participate in this process.

2. *The second stage* will be carried out in Guatemala under the
   guidance of the Presbyterian Seminary of Guatemala for a
   period of three months. There will be training workshops
   and practical experience in the extension program of that
   institution. The participants will do investigations and
   hold seminars on the philosophy of theological education by
   extension, teaching methods, and the writing of self-study
   materials. These persons will unite with the faculty of the
   Seminary to form a work and reflexion team. After the first
   weeks this team will plan workshops to be carried out in
   Guatemala and other countries. Following the three months
   in Guatemala, the participants will have one month in which
   to direct workshops and participate in consultations as they
   return to their own countries.

3. *The third stage* will take place in the local situation. The
   participants will make further analyses of the programs of
   their own institutions or associations and work with their
   colleagues toward the changes which may be indicated. It is
   understood that in the first stage these colleagues have
   agreed to back the project and that in the second stage the
   persons chosen have maintained contact with these colleagues.
   Then on their return from Guatemala with experiences
   acquired in the workshops, these leaders will be able to
   guide others effectively in study, evaluation, and innovation.

4. *The fourth stage* will take place the following year in
   Guatemala. The first group will return for one month to
   share their experiences and look for solutions to their
   problems and plan new developments for themselves, their
   institutions, and the theological education by extension

movement. The second half of this period in Guatemala will coincide with the initiation of the second group of candidates. Thus the first group will participate in the orientation of the second group and share their experiences and inspiration and problems with them. After this month in Guatemala the first group will again have one month for directing workshops and participating in consultations in their own countries and elsewhere.

B. *Calendar*

1. From July 1973 to February 1974—*the first stage* of the first group in their local situation.

2. March through May 1974—*the second stage* carried out in Guatemala.

3. June 1974—workshops and consultations in various countries directed by the first group and ALISTE personnel.

4. From July 1974 to February 1975—*the third stage* of the first group and *the first stage* of the second group in their local situations.

5. February 15 to March 15, 1975—*the fourth stage* of the first group in Guatemala.

6. March through May 1975—*the second stage* of the second group in Guatemala.

7. June 1975—workshops and consultations in various countries directed by the first and second groups.

8. From July 1975 to February 1976—*the third stage* of the second group in their local situations.

9. February 15 to March 15, 1976—*the fourth stage* of the second group in Guatemala.

10. On the basis of needs and resources it will be decided whether to form a third group from July 1975 to June 1976.

C. *Personnel*

1. The Central Committee of ALISTE will approve the plans, obtain funds, promote the project, and put it into practice.

2. The National and Regional Coordinators of ALISTE will participate in the search for candidates and in the organization of workshops and consultations.

3. The International Coordinator of ALISTE will direct the project.

4. The staff of the Presbyterian Seminary of Guatemala will be in charge of the study program and practical experience in Guatemala.

5. The Latin American Biblical Seminary of Costa Rica will offer, beginning in 1974, specialization in theological education by extension which will cover two years and lead to a *Licenciatura* in Theology. The two projects will be coordinated as far as possible.

III. CANDIDATES

The success of the ALISTE project depends a great deal on the candidates selected. No matter how excellent the program is, it will not have much effect if it does not interest the right people. As is explained in the objectives of the project, our hope is to find people who will be able not only to receive training but also to become the leaders of the extension movement in their countries and regions. Following are some guidelines for the selection of candidates and suggestions for finding them.

A. *Who Should Participate in This Project?*

1. It is understood that the candidates will be evangelical Christians with a living experience of Jesus Christ.

2. They should have a basic education and a biblical-theological foundation.

3. It is expected that these persons have maintained their identification with the local churches and with the reality of their socio-cultural context.

4. They should have had pastoral and teaching experience, and they should manifest a profound concern for the mission of the church.

5. They should be mature leaders, respected by their colleagues, sensitive to the needs of others, and gifted in leading and motivating others.

6. The people who participate in this program should have an understanding of what is theological education, a willingness to learn different methods and structures, and a desire to explore new possibilities and innovate for the good of the work of Jesus Christ.

7. Finally, the candidates should be Latin Americans by birth. A person of other nationality will be considered only if it is a very special case.

B. *How Can We Find These Candidates?*

1. ALISTE will launch a search for capable persons through its bulletin and through its national and regional coordinators.

2. We shall correspond with extension organizations, associations of theological institutions, and the theological institutions directly.

3. It is hoped that other individuals and organizations will help through personal contact and by letter.

4. The extension workshops and consultations that are held will also reveal the persons who can best benefit from the project.

C. *What Procedure Should Be Followed?*

1. An institution, person, or church which is interested in this project should begin by analyzing its own situation. It is important to have not only a capable person but also the backing of an organization that will work with the candidate. Both the individual and the organization should make contact with ALISTE and participate in the project from beginning to end.

2. The Candidate should request information about the project and fill in an application form that will be provided. There will be scholarship help according to the needs of each candidate and according to the resources of the organization recommending him. These scholarships may cover the candidate's travel plus expenses and support during the second and fourth stages of the project.

3. The first stage of the program is a study of the situation of the institution and the churches where the candidate lives. If possible, a person assigned by ALISTE will visit the candidate and participate in this study. The final decision with regard to the other stages of the project (and the scholarship) will depend upon the results of this investigation.

D. *What Countries Can Participate?*

The program will be carried out in Spanish, and it is planned for the Spanish-speaking countries. At first, however, we shall

emphasize Central America, Gran Colombia, and Mexico. The extension movement needs at least two trained persons for Mexico, one
for each country of Central America and Panama, one for Venezuela,
one for Ecuador, etc. We plan to limit the number of participants to ten each year in order to work as closely as possible
with them and to be able to utilize them in the training of
others.

14

Centers for Studies in Theological Education and Ministry

INTRODUCTION

The following proposal is at this stage merely an invitation to share some ideas about the future development of theological education in the Third World. It is still very preliminary and not well integrated. It comes out of the extension movement and tries to catch at a number of threads that seem to be within easy reach for anyone who sees the challenge to weave them into a significant program. This proposal may help to bring into focus the possibilities for future development of theological education; perhaps others will take up the challenge in several different ways.

The extension movement has in many places initiated a process of reflection and innovation that is becoming increasingly far-reaching. For some it was originally just a change in structure, but this change required a new teaching methodology. A new kind of student has entered into theological studies in large numbers, which in turn calls for a new kind of teacher. As never before (since the dawn of seminaries and Bible institutes) it has become possible to relate theological institutions to the churches, to integrate study and ministry, to "do theology" in the context of the life and mission of the church. The demand for new materials for theological study has led numbers of theological educators to consider seriously for the first time not only what should be studied, but also how it can be learned most effectively. Fundamental questions are being raised about objectives, basic curriculum design, and evaluation. Even the most hallowed concepts of "the call" and ordination are being called into question, and the situation of the ministry is in some places already changing due to the effects of extension programs. Large numbers of churchmen and theological educators in many different places are now becoming involved in these developments, participating in workshops, reading articles about various aspects of theological education, and introducing new practices and new perspectives in their own programs.

The time may be ripe for individuals, institutions, churches, and/or associations to take the initiative for this process of development in theological education in their own regions, to make full use and critical evaluation of what is being said and tried elsewhere, and to contribute to local programs and to this world-wide movement through study and experimentation. One way to do this would be to establish centers for studies in theological education and ministry.

I. SPECIFIC REASONS FOR THE PROPOSAL

A. As the extension movement spreads around the world, it is evident that some are simply transplanting a prescribed program without sufficient analysis of their own situation and needs, the nature of leadership development in their own culture, the processes of innovation, the formation of curriculum, etc. The new patterns of theological training would be far more effective if they grew out of investigations and experimentation by local people rather than being imported and promoted by visiting "experts" and expatriates.

B. Extension programs are capable of reaching much larger numbers of local leaders and candidates for the ministry. Although the training process may take much longer for the average student, some institutions are rapidly reaching a whole new generation with basic ministerial training. It is now possible and necessary to look beyond that task to other dimensions of theological education, such as continuing education of pastors, theological indigenization, renewal of the churches for mission, etc.

C. As extension programs take over an increasing load of the basic ministerial training, residence seminaries should look for new purposes and functions. Rather than consider themselves obsolete or left behind, they may well discover more creative and effective avenues of service. They have tremendous resources at their disposal; they must decide how best to invest them.

D. Some residence institutions have added extension departments; others want to adopt and adapt insights from the extension movement; still others are critical, defensive, or

indifferent. One option open to them is to get involved
with the movement so as to make significant contributions to
its future development.

E. Residential institutions have some special values that should
not be lost. These values should be identified and analyzed
and put to their best use, just as the dangers of this
approach should be identified and analyzed and avoided.

F. It has been stated that residential institutions are best
equipped for specialized, long term studies in theology. If
our outstanding theologians were relieved of the multiple,
time consuming tasks of residential pastoral training, perhaps they could really do this job effectively and still
contribute to basic pastoral training through the preparation of primary materials, instruction materials, and
personnel (for extension programs).

G. Large numbers of persons who take advanced theological
studies do so in preparation for teaching in seminaries and
Bible institutes. In the past they have concentrated almost
entirely on cognitive formation, on theology *per se*. They
should also be developing their competence as theological
educators.

H. As noted above there is an increasing flow of information
about new developments in theological education around the
world. It would be valuable, perhaps urgently necessary, to
get hold of that information and evaluate it locally, to
relate it to local developments, and to initiate a process
of reflection and experimentation in each situation.

I. There is a critical universal need for national leadership
in the development of theological education. Due to well
known factors this is the last major field of expatriate
dominance, and the extension movement has suffered greatly
from that dominance. Nationals must take the leadership not
only for theological formation but also for the development
of new patterns of theological education.

J. As nationals are trained for leadership in theological education, they need a vehicle for investigation and innovation.
This vehicle must be flexible and realistic in order to
function effectively within the limitations of their own
situations and to respond dynamically to the rich cultural
diversity of very different contexts.

K. The old system of values and the hegemony of hierarchial
accreditation are gradually breaking down, and the concepts
of contextualization are gaining acceptance. But this

thrusts upon us the urgent task of establishing new criteria and local values for theological education.

L. Today more than ever we need to discover tools for evaluation in order to maintain and increase the effectiveness of our theological training programs in service to Christ and His church in mission to the peoples of the earth.

II. THE CENTRAL CONCEPTS OF THE PROPOSAL

In recent years there has been a fundamental change in the concept of the teacher. Instead of being the source of information he is becoming the facilitator for learning, preparing the environment, providing and explaining materials, motivating and guiding the student. In a similar way this proposal recommends the formation of a new kind of theological program. Rather than being the source of theological knowledge and instruction, these centers would be facilitators of theological education, mobilizing and providing resources, organizing and participating in training projects, setting up and carrying out research projects, experimenting with and evaluating new media and techniques, etc. If these centers were free from the all-encompassing demands of a basic year-round program of ministerial training, they could be free to invest their resources in planning, research, and administration for many different programs.

These centers for studies in theological education and ministry would make use of the insights of open and non-formal education, leaving much of the task of leadership formation to others, especially to the participants themselves. Rather than pretend to inform and "form" candidates for special ministries, they would leave the basic responsibility for leadership selection and maturation to the churches and the individuals themselves (where it should lie). Then advanced theological study would be part of a process of self-development; it would not be confined to or identified with an institution; it would to a much greater extent depend upon the motivation of the student and respond to his felt needs in the process of his ministry.

The centers could develop program modules for specific goals through specially designed experiences and materials. These units would be administered by the centers themselves or by others. They would only be a part of and fit into the whole scheme of theological education of a given denomination. The bulk of basic ministerial training would be left in the hands of extension and other programs. Instead of trying to do the whole job of theological education the centers would help the latter do their job through the training of personnel, the preparation of self-study materials, etc.

The centers would attempt to initiate research and evaluation in theological education, leadership development, and the ministry. In spite of the huge investment that goes into theological education and the support of the ministry and in spite of the tremendous influence exercised by our patterns of theological training and ministry, very little research has been done in this area. At a time of rapid changes in theological education evaluation is urgent. In order to be effective, these studies must be made not by specialists outside the churches or even for the churches, but by leaders of the churches themselves. The centers for studies in theological education and ministry would help these leaders do research and introduce changes, providing evaluative tools, information and models, special study materials, and training experiences.

III. POSSIBLE TASKS FOR THE CENTERS

A. Publish a bulletin with articles, news, and bibliography related to theological education and ministry.

B. Look for and publicize new experiments, concepts, and materials for theological education and the practice of the ministry.

C. Develop materials and procedures for self-study and evaluation by theological institutions and churches.

D. Make surveys and investigate different aspects of theological education, the ministry, the mission of the church, etc.

E. Maintain current files of bulletins, reports, papers, syllabi, course materials, etc. from institutions in the area and elsewhere.

F. Explore ways to relate theological education to local church leadership development processes (discipleship, Sunday School, church officer training, etc.).

G. Plan and direct (or help others to do so) workshops on different aspects of theological education and the ministry.

H. Sponsor (or participate in) consultations at different levels (from the local church level to international) and on various topics (curriculum design, educational technology, the nature of the ministry, leadership needs of the churches).

I. Set up training projects for leaders of theological education programs.

J. Hold seminars and/or retreats for pastors, lay leaders, others.

K. Develop internship programs for personnel for different kinds
    of theological education.

L. Encourage others to write, share and criticize concepts of
    the ministry, theological education, theology.

M. Explore and interpret concepts and developments in other
    educational fields for possible application in theological
    education.

N. Provide stimulation and recognition for church leaders and
    theological educators; build a fellowship and teamwork among
    them.

O. Foment the reading of theological, current, and local
    literature through book-reading or reduced-rate book-selling.

IV. HOW TO OPERATE A CENTER

All of the foregoing material may give the impression that we
are proposing the establishment of more institutions with more
specialized personnel and increased budgets. On the contrary,
all of the tasks listed above can be carried out with no fulltime personnel, a very minimal expense budget, and no new
buildings or equipment. One person can to some extent carry
out half of these tasks in his spare time; a traditional or
extension seminary could set up a task force among its own
faculty members, or an institution could give over its entire
resources to these concerns. (In every capital of Latin America
there are numerous educated pastors who are not occupied in the
ministry and who might be challenged to take on this kind of a
task in their free time).

A center could operate at different levels: denominational
and interdenominational, regional, national, and international.
In Latin America, for example, the associations of theological
schools carry out some of the proposed functions (at high cost);
the Lutherans, Baptists, Nazarenes (and perhaps others) have set
up continental committees to coordinate theological education
along denominational lines: the Latin American Biblical Seminary
in Costa Rica has established a specialization in extension
theological education and has held a consultation on alternative
forms of theological education; the small faculty of the Presbyterian Seminary of Guatemala publishes the Extension Seminary
Bulletin, is directing the ALISTE project for training extension
specialists, participates frequently in workshops and consultations, has produced extension courses which have been translated
into several languages, and prepares papers and workshop materials for general use. Many seminaries and Bible institutes have
periodic activities for pastors and publications for promotion

purposes. Ecclesiastical assemblies, organizations, and agencies offer sounding boards for new concepts and studies related to theological education. But surprising as it may seem, none of these agencies has taken the initiative to set down systematically a strategy for future development in theological education.

The base for a center for studies in theological education and ministry may be any one of a number of places, as noted already. The resources may be very limited or very large. The starting point may be simply a mimeographed, quarterly bulletin or a multi-faceted program. In each case, the center should be flexible and build on its own experience, evident local needs, and developing interest.

From the beginning the organizer of each center should be fore-warned of the tendency to institutionalize and thus stultify new programs. This centripetal force should be counteracted by the central concept of this proposal, which is to help others to do the basic tasks of theological education. Rather than concentrate on increasing resources and programs and personnel at the center, the center should stimulate others to experiment and if possible spin off its own projects to other institutions. Only in this way will the center be free to explore new areas and respond to new development.

CONCLUSIONS

As noted at the beginning, this proposal comes out of the extension movement. This movement has brought upon us new problems and new possibilities; it has broken some of the barriers of tradition and opened the door to change in theological education. We should now open the door wider, take advantage of the momentum for change, and explore the many possibilities for development in the future. We should set up some vehicle to permit us to study the implications of the changes that have already been initiated and the changes that are now possible. We should be both responsible for this process and responsive to it.

The proposal is also an attempt to bridge the gap between residential theological education and the extension movement. If the traditional institutions are given a fair chance to study the facts as well as the propaganda of extension and to examine critically their own program, they will probably be more ready to place their resources at the disposal of the extension movement. The possible benefits for both branches of theological education are great. And this may bring us to a new synthesis, a new unity of purpose in what may in the future be called "Open Theological Education."

One of the most commented problems of theological education
in the Third World has been its dependence upon and imitation
of the U.S. and Europe. The present proposal should help Third
World churches to break that pattern, take the initiative for
the formation of their own program, and jump into the lead for
future development in theological education around the world.
Although the U.S. and European churches continue to have far
greater resources for experimentation and research, the Third
World churches are less weighted down by institutional inertia,
and they are under greater pressure to take new options (for
ideological, economic, and other reasons). This is evident by
the rapid spread of extension in the Third World in comparison
to the U.S. and Europe, where the need for extension is just
as great, though for different reasons. One outstanding Latin
American leader has already proposed the formation of a center
for studies in theological education that would not only serve
this region but also relate to Africa and other continents.

Educational specialists have pointed out that in the Third
World there is not only a strong tendency to imitate the U.S.
and European patterns but also an uncritical belief in education
as the panacea of development. They point out that large per-
centages of limited national budgets are being invested to expand
the traditional schooling systems in a tremendous effort to
"catch up." The unfortunate results of this tendency are that
these countries are chasing after an illusory goal, schooling
more people who will largely be frustrated, not usefully
employed, and perpetuating a social system which is elitist and
counter-developmental. The parallels in theological education
are all too evident. Third World churches want to emulate or
at least equal seminary education in the U.S. and Europe; they
strive to raise the academic level of their institutions and
they produce graduates who are ill-equipped for their actual
needs and unable to live on the salaries available in their
churches. To try to sell these churches new patterns of theological education (such as extension) is not often effective.
They must carry out their own research, make their own experiments, and come to their own conclusions. The proposed centers
for studies in theological education and ministry could facilitate that process.

It is noteworthy, also, that both the ecumenical and conservative branches of world Christianity are right now making heavy
investments in advanced centers of theological education in the
Third World. Unfortunately these advanced centers follow to a
great extent the traditional patterns, adding one more tier above
the present hierarchy of elitist training and concentrating
further the limited resources for theological education for the
benefit of a much smaller circle of content specialists who are
thus pushed further from the basic reality and needs of the

churches. The present proposal offers an alternative approach to advanced centers which would focus on the problems and possibilities of theological education itself, facilitate future development of programs at all levels, and perhaps even reverse the trend toward elitism and contribute to a renewal of the ministry of the whole church.

APPENDIXES

A. Extension Seminary Quarterly Bulletin: List of Articles

LIST OF ARTICLES

The *Extension Seminary* Quarterly Bulletin is edited and published at the *Seminario Evangélico Presbiteriano de Guatemala*, Apartado 3, San Felipe Ren., Guatemala, C.A. From 1970 to 1972 the editor was James H. Emery, from 1972 to 1977 F. Ross Kinsler, and from 1977 Nelly Castillo de Jacobs. Interested persons should send news of extension developments, related articles, addresses of new subscribers, and voluntary contributions to the above address. The bulletin is normally circulated by surface mail due to rising costs of postage. What follows is a list of all the articles published to date, some of which are included in this book.

1970--1. "New Name: Extension Seminary"
"Curriculum: Making the Menu"
"Definitions: What is Extension?"

2. "Definitions: What is Extension?" F. Ross Kinsler
"The Split-Rail Fence: An Analogy for the Education of Professionals," Ted Ward

3. "Definitions: What Extension Is Not"
"Some Questions about Classroom Teaching," Gennet M. Emery
"The CLATT Intertext Project"
"What Are Intertexts"
"African View of Extension"

1971--1. "Methodology of Theological Education by Extension,"
          F. Ross Kinsler

      2. "Bases for Extension, Number 1: Independent Study,"
          James H. Emery
          "Available Materials for Extension Programs"

      3. "The Idea Bank: Training for the Ministry?" Lawrence
          O. Richards
          "Comments from Here and There"

      4. "Extension Education and Programming," James H. Emery
          "The Growth of Extension Theological Education in
          Brazil," Richard Sturz
          "An Evaluation of Two Programming Workshops," Peter
          Savage

1972--1. "Latin America Faces New Day in Theological Education,"
          Rubén Lores

      2. "Training Nomads," Robb McLaughlin

      3. "The Spanish Intertext Project," F. Ross Kinsler

      4. "Modifications of the Extension Method for Areas of
          Limited Education Opportunity," George Patterson
          "Training God's Men in Rural Colombia," Charles Derr

1973--1. "The Case for Voluntary Clergy," Roland Allen
          "Development of Professors and Materials for Theologi-
          cal Education in Latin America," F. Ross Kinsler

      2. "The Extension Model in Theological Education: What
          It Is and What It Can Do," Ralph D. Winter
          "The Tent Maker Movement and Theological Education,"
          H. Boone Porter
          "Baptist Extension Program in Guatemala," J. Enrique
          Díaz
          "The Medellín Consultation," F. Ross Kinsler

      3. "Extension: An Alternative Model for Theological
          Education," F. Ross Kinsler

      4. "Combining Extension with Residence," John E. Huegel
          "First Impressions: Co-Extension," Raymond S. Rosales

1974--1. "The ALISTE Project for Training Extension Specialists"
          "Some Questions About the ALISTE Project," F. Ross
          Kinsler

2. "Village Ministries and T.E.E. in India: A Case of
       Unfulfilled Potential?" James A. Bergquist
       "A First Evaluation of the ALISTE Project," F. Ross
       Kinsler

3. "Let's Multiply Churches through Extension Education
       Chains," George Patterson
       "TEE in Asia--A Statement of Description and Intent"

4. "Open Theological Education," F. Ross Kinsler

1975--1. "Centers for Studies in Theological Education and
       Ministry," F. Ross Kinsler

2. "National Study Consultation on Theological Training
       of the Whole Church and New Patterns of Training,"
       Yeotmal, India
       "Extension Programs in India"
       "Workshops in Brazil," F. Ross Kinsler

3. "Consultation on Theological Education," Churches and
       Institutions of Southern Africa, Johannesburg,
       South Africa
       "Extension Programs in Southern Africa"
       "Production of Elementary Theological Texts: Anglican
       Extension Seminary," The SEAN Team, Tucumán,
       Argentina

4. "Concordia, Hong Kong: A Case Study in Transition
       toward a Non-Traditional Theological Training Pro-
       gram," Manfred Berndt

1976--1. "Guatemala Center for Studies in Theological Education
       and Ministry"
       "Botswana Theological Training Programme," Richard W.
       Sales

2. "The Challenge of the Extension Movement," F. Ross
       Kinsler

3. "A Working Definition of Theological Education by
       Extension," F. Ross Kinsler

4. "The Preparation of Leadership for the Pastoral Minis-
       try: An Historical Resumé," James H. Emery

1977--1. "Brazil's Internship Program for Preparing Extension
       Writers," Lois McKinney
       "Network: Forming Indigenous Ministry in Alaska,"
       David Keller

2. "TEE in its Teens," Wayne C. Weld.
   "Balewiyata Theological Institute of East Java," S.
   Wismoady Wahono

3. "Case Study Methodology," Kenneth Mulholland and Rubén
   Lores
   "PRODIADIS: Continent-Wide Extension Program for
   Latin America," Rubén Lores

4. "Theological Education by Extension: Service or
   Subversion?" F. Ross Kinsler

B. Guatemala Center for Studies in Theological Education and Ministry: Occasional Papers

OCCASIONAL PAPERS

The Guatemala Center for Studies in Theological Education and Ministry was officially organized by the *Seminario Evangélico Presbiteriano de Guatemala* in July, 1975 as an attempt to coordinate and project more effectively some of the endeavors in which the staff had already been engaged for some time. It was also intended to encourage colleagues in other places to pursue and coordinate their concerns for theological education and ministry through correspondence, publications, meetings of various kinds, workshops, and research, as outlined in Chapter 14 of this book. A network of such centers is taking shape in Latin America, and a wider network of innovative theological educators and church leaders is developing around the world. Following is a list of occasional papers now available (in English and in Spanish) from the Guatemala Center, Apartado 3, San Felipe Ren., Guatemala, C.A. Numbers 2, 3, 6, 8, and 9 are included in this book.

No. 1   *Self-Study Workshop on Theological Education*, 34 pp., $2.00.

No. 2   *Dialogue on Alternatives in Theological Education-- India*, 17 pp., $1.00.

No. 3   *Dialogue on Alternatives in Theological Education-- Southern Africa*, 14 pp., $1.00.

No. 4   *The Preparation of Leadership for the Pastoral Ministry:
        An Historical Resumé*, 11 pp., $1.00.

No. 5   *Non-Formal Education and the Seminaries*, 11 pp., $1.00.

No. 6   *Dialogue on Alternatives in Theological Education--U.S.A.*
        15 pp., $1.00.

No. 7   *Seminar on Theological Education: Analysis of the
        Components of Ministerial Training Programs*, 116 pp.,
        $5.00.

No. 8   *Materials for Workshops on Theological Education by
        Extension*, 62 pp., $3.00.

No. 9   *Dialogue on Alternatives in Theological Education--Latin
        America*, 33 pp., $2.00.